beyond
on life after death

FRED M. FROHOCK

 UNIVERSITY PRESS OF KANSAS

Published by the

University Press of Kansas

(Lawrence, Kansas 66045),

which was organized by the

Kansas Board of Regents

and is operated and funded

by Emporia State University,

Fort Hays State University,

Kansas State University,

Pittsburg State University,

the University of Kansas, and

Wichita State University

Library of Congress
Cataloging-in-Publication Data
Frohock, Fred M.
Beyond : on life after death / Fred M. Frohock.
    p. cm.
Includes bibliographical references and index.
ISBN 978-0-7006-1701-2 (cloth : alk. paper)
1. Future life. 2. Eternity. 3. Infinite. I. Title.
BL535.F76 2010
129—dc22

2009043736

British Library Cataloguing in Publication Data is available.

Printed in the United States of America

10 9 8 7 6 5 4 3 2 1

The paper used in this publication is recycled and
contains 30 percent postconsumer waste. It is acid free
and meets the minimum requirements of the American
National Standard for Permanence of Paper for Printed
Library Materials Z39.48-1992.

Our supreme insights must—and should!—
sound like follies, in certain cases like crimes,
when they come impermissibly to the ears of those
who are not predisposed and predestined for them.
—Nietzsche, Beyond Good and Evil

. . . and I look for the resurrection of the dead, and
the life of the world to come. Amen.
—The Nicene Creed

I love you in a place where there's no space or time
I love you for in my life you are a friend of mine
And when my life is over
Remember when we were together
We were alone and I was singing this song for you
—Leon Russell, "A Song for You," 1970

contents

preface

Since we may be the only sentient creatures who know that death is the natural and inevitable conclusion of life, it is understandable that we are preoccupied with its meanings and outcomes, in particular whether there is a coda that follows the last act. Survival after death in a renewed life is one of the more absorbing conjectures in human experience. Is there a life after death? What are the signs and possible proofs for such a conjecture? Or is death the final event in human life? Answers to these questions annotate texts throughout history in philosophy, religion, the social and natural sciences (both ancient and modern), and, of course, ordinary thinking. Now, at this moment in history, innovative explorations are revising the conjectures and discovering new indications of an existence after death, with studies of reincarnation and a renewed interest in the near-death experience (NDE) as it occurs and is defined in the cultures of the world (including versions of the experience that predate the more clinical NDEs that seem to be an outcome of current resuscitation techniques in medicine).

I suppose I am saying that the time may be just right for everyone to join an inquiry that has roots in the distant past and that is now leavened with fresh theories and new findings. One of my colleagues once told me that entering a discussion with ancient origins is like joining a parade. You move off the sidewalk, get in line, and start walking with the awareness that a lot of people extending to antiquity are part of the procession. The walking metaphor in this case represents a contribution to the complementary areas of theory and fact, meaning any concepts and any data that help expand our growing understandings of the parameters and possibilities of life after death. Everyone seems to have an opinion on the subject of an afterlife. It's time to dust off these holdings, which range from pure skepticism and disbelief to fervent beliefs in the truth of life after death, and get them all in the parade.

It is clearly time for me to get in the procession. Like most people in today's world, I have more years to reflect upon than to anticipate. Also, one cannot reach senior levels of life without losing friends and family along the way. The fact is that indefinable but very real thresholds of life render the prospect of death with a certain cachet, something that makes one thoughtful, even presenting a kind of moderate urgency that exceeds the intellectual attractions that make studies of the possibilities for an existence after death so interesting. I am also drawn again and again to anomalous areas of experience, especially when rival explanations all fit the experience at issue (as with the near-death experience) and no decisive test can authoritatively adjudicate, rank order, or demarcate true from false explanations without resorting to background consideratons. In short, the research findings have my attention for both personal and professional reasons. This book is my entry ticket into the procession. The contribution here is not the production of new facts (investigators are already doing that) but rather proposals for the best ways to think about the possibilities of an afterlife. These proposals try to identify the effective rules of evidence, inference, and argument to negotiate the issues and to display the competitive and complementary roles of narrative and scientific approaches in these areas of inquiry.

This holistic approach seems to me the only intelligible path to perhaps the most compelling topic in human experience. The subject does, after all, entertain the possibility that life after death may be at the epicenter of human consciousness, possibly shaped by the advent of the bicameral brain and accelerated in the theories of dualisms (a mind or soul in a body) that both haunt and nourish us; in particular by suggesting that there may be some central indestructible core in each of us that is distinct from our physical selves and capable of living on after the death of the body. From one point of view we may be evolving into creatures who have eternal life, or at least a life span that continues after death. I shouldn't have to explain how intriguing that possibility is for anyone up close and personal with the prospect of death.

I am grateful to a number of people who have helped me in the intellectual journeys leading to this book. My fall 2008 course at the University of Miami, "God, Science, and Politics," was an excellent staging ground for trying out some of these ideas in their more mature stages. My colleagues at UM have been more than gracious in supporting, or at least tolerating, what can only be regarded as an idiosyncratic research project. The topic, after all, is not the usual academic fare, and it isn't often that one finds a closet mystic on a secular campus talking on the subject of life after death. I am grateful for the comments I received and contrite (to a degree) about being so aggressive occasionally in seeking out critiques. One of my former students, Everita Silina, who now teaches at the New School in New York City and occasionally offers courses at NYU, found the references for the early research. Cyril Gosh, another of my former students who also lectures at the New School, compiled the bibliography and provided data to complete the notes. A special thanks also to Gavan Duffy for his comments on Chapter 6 and the uses of abductive logic. Erik Jacobson, then a University of Miami undergraduate, did excellent research for me on a number of topics and occasionally helped edit parts of the text, especially in the literatures addressed in Chapter 5. My wife, Val, helped in all the right critical ways in the final editing of the work. Also a special thanks to Eric Schramm, the copy editor, especially for ensuring continuity in the dinner party scenes. I am grateful for the assistance that these individuals provided. But my most expansive thanks goes to my editor, Michael Briggs, who proposed the topic to me, handled it all just right when I wanted to abandon the project at midpoint in the research and writing, and displayed heroic patience while I tried to control material that was in many ways outside my abilities to manage it. Thanks, Mike. Without you this book would not exist.

Fred Frohock

beyond

introduction

In the film *Michael Clayton*, Arthur Edens (Tom Wilkinson), a brilliant trial lawyer, is undergoing a complex epiphany triggered, according to his associates, by the fact that he has stopped taking his medication for manic depression. The legal profession to which he belongs sees his rants and erratic actions as a return of his illness. The problem is that Edens believes that he is experiencing reality, not hallucinations. The issue is legendary. On what grounds can we say that an experience is illusory, or real? Do medications like psychotropic drugs mask reality or control for delusions, prohibit access to alternative realities, or calibrate the real in experience? On what conditions can we label beliefs about the supernatural true and false? Perhaps the best inquiries into reality are crafted on the edges of sanity?

In one scene Edens tries to explain himself to a young woman with whom he has fallen in love. He tells her, in an intense phone conversation, what is now real to him: "Isn't it what we wait for? To meet someone . . . and they're, they're like a lens and suddenly you're looking through them and everything changes and nothing can ever be the same again." These are uneasy and even scary possibilities in Western secular life—that reality may be segmented—in part because they summon unconventional connections among radically different themes and scenarios. At their extremes they suggest rearrangements of settled matters. If they intersect with powerful interests, the results can be violent (in the film Edens is killed).

If we can bracket the corruption and violence at the center of *Michael Clayton* and concentrate on the tensions between the secular and the spiritual in the film, I regard this book as an effort to negotiate exactly those contrasting forms of thought and expression that may not easily fold into a single tool kit of concepts—in particular the profane and the sacred, the efficient and the lyrical, scientific and narrative routes to truth, fact and fiction, the natural and the supernatural. The simple assertion driving this work is that it may take different types of expression to illuminate and track the mysteries of human experience at its deeper levels. Jerome Bruner has written extensively about the importance of narratives in rendering experience intelligible. In most of this work he distinguishes between narrative and paradigmatic modes of thinking. Narrative approaches organize experience into sequential details, while paradigmatic thinking employs abstract categories of thought in logical orderings to make sense of experience. Each approach is vital, and presumably both are needed to construct the worlds we negotiate. But they represent different types of truth. In an interview while rehearsing *King Lear*, Ian McKellen was asked to respond to a provocative observation. "That's what you actors do, isn't it—you trick the audience into believing that the character is real." McKellen demurred. "We don't trick the audience," he replied. "We reveal the truth of the character."

Many might dissent from this depiction of acting, from the perspectives of both the interior expressions of Method acting and the surface performances of the classical school, but few would disagree with the proposition that a different species of truth is at stake in each of Bruner's categories of thinking. Narratives seem to be a welcome heuristic in two conditions: one is when we do not have adequate information, and the other is when we speak of things that exceed the parameters of conventional experience. In the first instance we seek shortcuts, like "satisficing" instead of maximizing rules, and other handy maxims (instructions, for example, to look for the good instead of the best), but also mythic, stock, and practical stories that coalesce available information into dramatic forms that help us to go on with our inquiries. In the second case, narratives are favored forms of oblique knowing in which a dimension of experiences, hypothetical or real, is depicted in allegory or parable, generally stories that refer indirectly to alternative realities. The drama of narrative in this second case can present revealed truth, often layered in the charming way that metaphor works: talking about A when one is really talking about B. In the famous Allegory of the Cave in Plato's *Republic*, individuals are imprisoned inside a cave, chained and unable to move, seeing only shadows cast on a blank wall from people and objects passing in front of a fire behind them. These shadows, they think, are reality. But when dragged up into the sunlight above the ground they realize that the reality of experience is outside the cave, in the objective world illuminated by the sun. The allegory indicates that sense impression is a source of error, that the abstract forms of things are the true locus of the real world. Talk in the allegory about a cave and the world above the cave is really talk about knowledge and the nature of reality in Plato's theory of forms. Narrative truth is often developed in this way, as a form of truth that states or crafts an understanding, not a scientific truth that has survived efforts at falsification. The allegory of the cave is a species of metaphorical thinking that not only presents a revealed truth but also demonstrates that narratives can depict the harder truths of logic in illustrative form. Different types of expressions can be brought together in powerful ways. To go back to Michael Clayton and Bruner's distinction, two entities that are distinct by nature (natural and supernatural, science and narrative) may in some circumstances be complementary, or folded into each other in one extraordinary dimension of experience.

I have become convinced of two things in my intellectual life (and not much else): that science in any of its incarnations produces a form of knowledge that is precise, powerful, but limited to certain sectors of experience, and that there are many forms of reliable knowledge outside the scientific community of investigatory rules. In the documentary chapters here I critically examine with fact and argument a variety of claims and putative experiences volunteered as indications, sometimes proof, of an afterlife. In the narrative chapters I explore claims about the supernatural as presentations in the context of fiction, a set of slices in the form of an incomplete and staccato novel. It's too easy in this instance to label the differences between documentary and narrative as a rendition of intellectual or theoretical organized experience versus lived, narrative experiences. The fiction is fiction, after all, not narratives that present actual experiences of actual individuals (as is the case in the field work I have presented in other books), and it is designed simply to provide insights into the supernatural that are elusive in the cold objective worlds of science. But there is also this. The fiction chapters may be more complex than they appear. They are stories told within a fictional dinner party (stories inside a narrative), enabling devices for a wide range of ideas, and the scenes contain their own logistics, meaning that they do not track the documentary chapters. Except for the opening fictional presentation of a past life (followed by the exegesis of work by Weiss and Stevenson on reincarnation), each type of discourse explores different themes. There is a point to this asymmetry. To present common ground, a sweet harmony gained by the comfortable development in succeeding stories and documentary chapters of the same themes, would be for me too precious, too singular, a *Rashomon*-effect amateurism.

In an important sense I am investing in the reader by providing an invitation, an opportunity, to *feel* the wider force of the supernatural in human experience, to experience it vicariously by reading the stories submitted by guests at a fictional dinner party. One part of this invitation requires the reader to subscribe to the modest parallel processing represented, say, in the omnibus structures found in the films *21 Grams* and *Babel*. The reason is self-evident. What follows is a set of takes on the supernatural and life after death negotiated with the use of distinct frames for experience, fact and fiction. These frames are interlocking devices not in terms of technique but through disparate themes that the reader must bring together for a coherent presentation.

I am suggesting that we should not make so much of the distinction between science and fiction that it leads us to accept an unbridgeable chasm between the two (nor take the easy way out by joining the two artificially, as in science fiction). A hard take on the distinction can blur some of the easy overlaps between these two ways of thinking. What was called the New Journalism of the 1960s in the United States witnessed some of our better novelists using the powers of fiction in writing about real-world events. Norman Mailer and Truman Capote were especially prominent and successful practitioners of this "new" art form. The results were sometimes sensational: Mailer's 1960 *Esquire* piece on JFK and the Democratic Party's run-up to that year's presidential election, "Superman Comes to the Supermarket"; his account of an antiwar protest march on the Pentagon in the article "The Steps of the Pentagon" (*Harper's*, 1968) and then in the book *Armies of the Night*; his book *The Executioner's Song* on convicted murderer Gary Gilmore and his fight for the legal right to be executed; and the superb articles and one book, *The Fight*, he wrote on the memorable boxing match between George Foreman and Muhammad Ali in Kinshasa, Zaire, in 1974. From Capote there was his rendition of the Clutter family murders in Kansas in the classic book *In Cold Blood*. Then there were the lighter touches provided, for example, by Tom Wolfe (before he wrote novels) in his three-part story on the Merry Pranksters (Ken Kesey and friends) in the *New York Herald Tribune's* magazine supplement, *New York*, and later the book *The Electric Kool-Aid Acid Test* (1968), and his send-up of Leonard Bernstein in a legendary article in the June 8, 1970, issue of *New York* magazine, "Radical Chic: That Party at Lenny's" and the book on the same theme (black rage and white guilt) with the more vivid title of *Radical Chic: Mau-Mauing the Flak Catch-ers*. All are products of fiction, its techniques, atmosphere, and attitudes, crafting and interpreting facts. This easy blend of fact and fiction has its predecessors and successors. In the trilogy U.S.A., John Dos Passos aligns documentary material with fictional texts. E. L. Doctorow's novel *Ragtime* and Don DeLillo's *Libra* present real-life characters and events in fictional garb. Mailer's more farcical *Oswald's Tale* weaves fact and fiction in imaginative scenarios.

Remember also that all science begins with a story about science; narratives are probably the most common way that human subjects understand their experiences and so are proper targets of the social sciences; and the best science provides developmental accounts of experiences, events unfolding in some fashion to weave a tapestry of independent and dependent variables in some corrigible pattern. Some scientific work relies almost entirely on narratives, as with Oliver Sacks's stories about neurologically damaged individuals. The clinical narratives and objective accounts of the pathologies and coping skills presented in Sacks's case studies are alien entries in data-driven science yet guide us to profound understandings of experience. Narratives, conceded, are not truth-functional in conventional ways. The acknowledged advantage of this indifference to truth is that a variety of truths can be housed and negotiated within narratives, some mutually contradictory but still intelligible in the more tolerant frame of a story. But there are also multiple versions of truth that both narratives and science might draw upon in different ways, from the personal truth of the memoir to the scaled and bounded truths crafted from those types of uncertain knowledge central to ethnographic studies, to the unions of evidence and conjecture in the open science of physics, on to the harder and uncompromising truths of experimental science. Finally, however, science must be true (in some sense) in terms of empirical information and formal logic, while narrative has no obligation to accord or be consonant with actual experience since it can present its own insights within a constructed experience. That is one important reason why science and narrative, even as complements, usually occupy parallel dimensions that only occasionally intersect in non-Euclidean conceptual space, though these intersections often present high intellectual payoffs.

In a book on abortion that I wrote twenty-five years ago, I presented the views of activists juxtaposed to the prominent arguments for and against abortion found in the legal, sociological, and philosophical literatures. The arrangement was simplicity itself. I would deploy the more formal pro-life and pro-choice arguments followed by, sometimes interspersed with, arguments for the contrasting views on abortion made vivid with the words of activists I retrieved in interviews, and so on. An intriguing pattern appeared. The activists were offering as their beliefs and a justification of their practices the arguments more formally rendered in the scholarly literature, but different enough on nuance and examples to benefit both forms of argument. It also speaks volumes that I concluded the book with an uncut and unedited interview with a young woman who had undergone an abortion. All these years later I regard that single personal story as the most powerful entry in the material I presented and discussed on the subject of abortion. I am trying something like this here except that fictional narratives, not the stories secured through field work, are the rough parallels to the more learned contributions. The suggested parallels of the present subject matter are not entirely symmetrical, the fields and claims on either side of the argumentative space not so neatly arranged, the polarization of the views not so cleanly projected. But the aim is the same: the use of disparate texts to enlighten a subject dense with acrimonious disputes over truth and validity, in these cases folding over into the scope and content of reality itself.

The use of narrative here does not imply, however, that empirical evidence is entirely missing in the domains of the supernatural. The legendary Liberal leader Jeremy Thorpe used to say that the British House of Lords offered proof that there really is life after death. Fortunately we do have two other distinct and intriguing bodies of evidence for life after death, though hardly proof in either case. One is the near-death experience, which often (though not always) occurs in clinical settings (not, of course, as a controlled experiment, that sorry and distorted movie *Flatliners* aside). The other is the work done on reincarnation, from the fascinating popular and commercial accounts like *The Search for Bridey Murphy* and (though offered as a serious work by Brian Weiss) *Many Lives, Many Masters*, to the respectable and impressive work done by Ian Stevenson on children who remember past lives. Both NDEs and Stevenson's research present visible material that requires (and has received) serious consideration by numerous scholars as data that suggest life after death. Whether or not one is sympathetic to this work, it is not the ruminations of New Age dreamers and fashionable mystics who invite beliefs grounded in (often misplaced) faith. These two areas of research are serious examinations of the possibility that we live on in some way after we die. My use of narrative does not bracket this type of work but suggests that other realms of experience, not presented with the evidentiary base of NDEs and certain reincarnation studies, are fugitive to a complete account crafted by scientific inquiry and yet are open to narrative renditions. Narratives also complement these data sets by helping to interpret them, say what they mean, determine whether they are genuine experiences on objective standards.

We live in an age of science developed in an age of mysticism. Maybe it has always been that way. Bishop Fulton J. Sheen used to say on his popular television show during the late 1950s that atheists have no invisible means of support. The line worked as a kind of vaudeville humor because an acceptance of metaphysical dimensions in the full scope of reality has marked human experience at all times in history. It's just that atheism is very much in fashion currently in the West at a time when religion is the dominant epistemic and political force in much of the rest of the world. If I accomplish one thing with this work, I hope it will be the recognition that both atheism and theism are unfounded. We simply cannot know with certainty whether God, or realms external to the normal parameters of human experience, exist or do not exist. But the very real possibility that higher forms of life and external realms exist has profound implications for meanings, opportunities, and constraints in human experience. As someone once said about the Middle East, it *needs* a peace process, even one with little chance of success. The possibility of transcendent realities, and a life after death, may be needed as enrichment for the uncertain and limited realms of human experience even as this possibility remains beyond our temporal grasp.

James Michener begins *Iberia* with an evocative declaration: "I have long believed that any man interested in either the mystic or the romantic aspects of life must sooner or later define his attitude concerning Spain." We might want to slide "man" into the more felicitous "person" and smooth out the hyperbole in the statement. But it is impossible to ignore Michener's reminder of the odd and powerful fascination that Spain has exercised for years over writers, artists, students, academics, priests, commercial tourists, and closet mystics posing as entrepreneurs. My own love affair with Spain might be explained as classic projection: the country parses the close parallels of material and mystical orientations to experience that have governed my life in almost every respect. Or, to reverse the connection, an understanding of life as a mystery resistant to linear modes of expression extends easily to the cultures of Spain. I also want to say that all of us must sooner or later define our attitude toward the supernatural.

This mystical orientation drives my enchantment with the nexus of the natural and supernatural. Those modern versions of the natural sciences that emptied human experience of all spiritual dimensions with powerful material explanations of the natural world are the feeding troughs for the atheists of the day. The explanations, and the natural laws they yield, make an impressive package that has been used to denigrate all religious or spiritual approaches to experience. But science in the twenty-first century is more nuanced than its beginnings. Quantum theory presents a counterintuitive reality that undermines the law-like and comfortable theories of Newtonian science, and string theory proffers alternative and invisible realities needed to complete theories of the visible natural world. An unanticipated connection appears between the realities we see and those invisible realms that are expressible only in mathematical terms. This far more complex account of the natural world invites conjectures about dimensions of the real that are inaccessible in complete form to human thought but yet can underwrite mystical and supernatural approaches to experience. It also helps explain why two of the leading scientific intellects of the twentieth century—Einstein and Gödel—were closet Platonists who accepted an external reality beyond human experiences.

This is the stuff that enriches my mystical temperament, and the fascination so many of us have with the meanings of life and death, and the possibility of a life beyond death. Like so many others I have had experiences that defy the limits of naturalism, mysterious experiences that I cannot explain in any of the terms of even adequate, much less good explanations. This puzzlement, odd as this may sound, also makes me lament the plight of materialists who seem not to have such experiences, and so somehow miss the obvious and compulsive importance of reflections on our spiritual natures and destinies. But this caveat: while we may speculate, think, believe propositions such as a life after death, we cannot know these things. Aristophanes was right when he said that "Whirl is king," but he missed the additional truth that uncertainty and doubt are at the epicenter of the human condition, and these are predicates that welcome movement and even moderate chaos. So, on the tired topic of my take on these matters, yes, I believe in each side of the dichotomies introduced in the opening paragraphs here: the profane and the sacred, linear and narrative expressions as routes to truth, and the natural and the supernatural. But I also subscribe to a theory of limits on what we can know about the truth of our best conjectures on the metaphysical dimension of human experience. The questions are everywhere, the answers provisional or permanently elusive, the conjectures important and unavoidable. The only good thing we can do within these limits is try to settle on how we can think rationally about what we cannot know in its entirety with any sense of certainty.

Suppose the starting path to the supernatural is as simple as these thoughts: how we see, and indicate the visible in doing so, is a complex process. At any level it invokes parts of the brain, including the visual cortex and the optic nerve. The story of Helen Keller, blind from the age of nineteen months, illustrates some of these complexities. Keller's teacher, Anne Sullivan, had the task of getting the young girl to "see" what are called ostensive definitions, meaning the ways in which words refer to objects in the world. In the narratives of their intertwined lives Keller knew language at first as a set of words made intelligible to her with the special tactile sensations of sign language. When Keller made the breakthrough, suddenly understanding that the signs for words referred to objects in the world, things she could touch, she "saw" reality, the objects indicated by the signs made on her skin by Sullivan. Later she began writing vivid depictions of that world even though her contact with it was absent of pure visual senses. This reality was visible for her through the mental senses and the referential powers of language. Maybe approaches to alternative planes of reality outside the visible worlds of materialism are issues of translation, of mastering a dimension of language that allows us to see the connections between the palpable and the mystical, the natural and the supernatural, the directly visible and the invisible, that so often elude us.

Unfortunately, this is a hard sell in the West today. In *Lives of the Psychics* I explored a variety of anomalous experiences on an explicit and unambiguous premise: the incompatible standing of explanations for events presented as supernatural, and an equally clear admission that I am attracted to this area of research precisely because of its anomalies. Put more exactly, rival explanatory models (materialist and metaphysical) can accommodate the same data set, thus presenting yet another real-life instance of how experience underdetermines theory. It didn't matter. Too often the nuances of the work, the tentative methodological forays, the uncertainties in its conclusions, were blithely ignored in favor of simple interpretive polarities: one had to buy into a kind of high school civics version of science or fall into a cabalist landscape of the secret and irrational, and an author who writes such a book has to be cast into the darkness of the latter category. Arthur Miller, after a series of critical and personal reviews of his play *After the Fall* (now we know what really happened to Marilyn Monroe, one critic opined), asked that in the future the critics review the play and not the playwright. To translate the Miller plea at far more modest levels: just take this book on its own terms as a guide and map across the cutting edges between the mysterious and the transparent that yield no polarities and very little about the author.

Listen: I am inviting you to join me in a journey through landscapes of death and the possibilities of an afterlife, a setting adorned with beliefs about what is real elaborated by those who have experienced epiphanies they cannot reduce to the naturalism that dominates Western cultures. It promises to be an intriguing exploration. But don't even think about having me killed if the discoveries are too unsettling.

a past life, no. 1

Think now of the supernatural elaborated within the frame of narrative fiction. Imagine a dinner party, one held on an evening in early summer. Let the skies be cloud — no, clear with summer lightning on the eastern horizon. No sound of thunder to mar the stillness of the evening, nothing but the words of the participants, the logos that Greek philosophers once believed was the center and expression of intelligence, nous.

Let's let the dinner hosts be a married couple, he a professor of philosophy and she a clinical psychologist. They are in their middle years (quaint phrase), their children grown and in colleges. I want them to be thoughtful people, though he with strong opinions argued with occasional cogency and she more deferential to the words and views of others. The guests are moderately distinguished in their own fields. One is a psychiatrist who has just been through an acrimonious divorce. He is the only guest at the dinner party who has not brought a companion. A second is an attorney who has been a criminal defense lawyer since leaving the Manhattan District Attorney's office and is looking for a position in personal injury law. Her husband is a professor of anthropology whose recent work has been in cultural linguistics. The two other guests, married to each other, also work in education. The husband teaches European history; the wife works as a grief counselor in a local high school.

Seven people in all. They are about to tell us tales of the supernatural. The dinner has been served and eaten, the Royal Doulton china rinsed and set inside the dishwasher for later cleaning. Coffee is being served. The cups and saucers scrape gently against each other as the guests drink the espresso the host prides himself on making. Brandy may be served, but no, let the wine be enough. The guests are drinking coffee to clear their heads of the wine, a Saint-Veran that flowed generously into their glasses and mouths. They are talking, their faces are moving, their words seem to have the cadences of music, the conversation exploding in quick and friendly laughter from time to time.

What are they saying to one another on this summer evening? The night is quiet *outside. From a point on the lawn sloping down to the trees at the back of the property a scene is visible, one composed of both deliberate and spontaneous movements behind the glass doors leading to the patio of the house. The white light from the indoor globes near the ceiling blends with the yellow glow of two standing lamps. Green napkins are folded and discarded on the table top. The dinner guests are arranged in languid poses, ready to play roles in the discussion that is evolving.*

Now one of the guests, or perhaps it is the host, is speaking to the entire group. He is dressed in a version of academic chic: khaki trousers, white shirt with a light grey sweater over it, no tie, soft brown shoes from Ecco. His face is thin and animated, his jaw line pronounced from a spare amount of flesh on his skeletal frame, gestures slow and controlled. Large eyes behind thick glasses. What is he saying?

The man is holding forth on Macbeth. "The key to the play is the choice made in the production of the ghost scene, whether Banquo's ghost, which Macbeth definitely sees at the banquet, is presented as a palpable visible figure, in which case Macbeth may indeed be seeing a spirit from the lands of the dead even as others at the dinner can't see this visitor. Or the specter is presented in the scene as a fantasy, invisible, not seen by the audience, in which case Macbeth may be hallucinating and — insane."

Everyone is silent.

It is the host who has been talking. He lifts the fingertips on both his hands to his forehead. "Actually, if you think about it, that binary set of production alternatives pretty much sums up human attitudes toward life after death. We are either crazy to believe in an afterlife, or the dead are actually here among us occupying a different but visible dimension of reality. But in both cases, as Macbeth saw, it can be a terrifying prospect."

Someone interrupts. "That's such a warlike reference. Shakespeare used ghosts in his plays to frighten his Elizabethan audiences. And to set up revenge in the dramas. Macbeth had Banquo murdered. Of course Macbeth was frightened by Banquo's ghost. Wouldn't anyone be if the guy you had killed comes back, and at a banquet, of all places?"

"And your point is?"

"That not all ghosts are terrifying."

The host is Frank Perry. He is dark and has a face with lines on it that settle into a relaxed mosaic when he is listening. He smiles now, his lips not letting his teeth show an expression that would be a grimace except for the amusement that friends swear they see somewhere behind his eyes. Ellen, his wife, is also amused at the conversational turn to ghosts.

"What do you suggest?" Frank asks his interlocutor.

"Why not Descartes? A benign presentation. The ghost is in us as mind or spirit, maybe to live on after the body dies." The man questioning Frank is the psychiatrist in the group. His name is David Johnson. He is stocky, thick with soft muscle, the body of a poorly conditioned wrestler with the energy of a manic coach of the sport. His blue shirt is pushed open at his waist; a button may be missing. "Gilbert Ryle's *The Concept of Mind* missed the point about the inner self and its capacities for renewal. It's not a ghost in a *machine*, but a mind in a human *body*. And by the way, how do your ghosts fit into reincarnation? Do you believe in that possibility for ghosts? Sorry—minds."

The host pauses before responding to the question.

"It's as likely as the opposite, that this life is all there is."

"Exactly," David replies. "So then what do you conclude? That the happier conclusion is to be endorsed? And which one is that?"

"No," Frank says. "Not that. Not just because it's happier, though that might be a reason to choose an alternative." He tries to look thoughtful, and does. "I think I am saying that the alternatives are equally plausible, which requires that the evidence for what are called supernatural events should be regarded with the same seriousness with which we weigh evidence for a material existence."

"Isn't that going backwards, from possible realities to evidence? Shouldn't it be evidence, then possible realities?" David leans forward in his chair, now an intellectual predator who has not had a successful day's kill in some time. He needs a victim, quickly.

"No. Not necessarily." Now Frank does grimace. "Data, raw data, are not evidence unless an ontology, some understanding of a reality, is in place. I mean, think of it. We do not see in some clean, direct sense. We bring to experience certain structural considerations—that the self is detached from the world, that events succeed one another in causal chains, that time is linear, irreversible—into which we fit and interpret observations." Frank leans back in his chair. He tries to shift the rhythm of the conversation by making a well-worn observation. "What gets me about this whole business is that so many people seem to believe in glamorous past lives. No one is a galley slave in a former life. Now how is that possible?"

"Not me." The grief counselor is talking. She is Lupe García. "I was a stable girl."

"Stable as in mentally secure, or stable as in shoveling horse manure?"

Everyone laughs at David's question, though only briefly. The group wants to hear Lupe tell her story.

Lupe shrugs. She is a bit intoxicated by the wine and the evening, and has this reliable, single gesture of surrender and bafflement that involves her torso and face. It is a kind of mime, a silent gesture that says she is a captive of the inexorable logic of the story that she is telling. "I cleaned up after animals, yes, and I also helped the village priest in his duties."

"There's a difference?" With this question David has gone too far and knows it. Several people say, "Shh." Ellen puts her hand on his arm.

"It was in Spain. A village near Córdoba." To the anthropologist in the group Lupe seems to assume the trace of an Andalucían accent, an inflection stressing vowels instead of consonants, though whether it is put there by the listener on hearing the geographical locus for the life story is impossible to say. She brushes her hair back with both of her hands. "I was born into a family of what we would call today 'modest means.' Basically, we were dirt poor by today's standards, though not so badly off for that time and place. My father owned one of those wagons, horse-drawn, which sold medicinal things to people in need." She has drawn out the last three words of this sentence, emphasizing each one as if pulling separate levers to conjure a practice false in all important respects. "We may have had gypsies in our family. Don't know. All of the details of life do not always survive time."

"Please, please, please forgive this interruption." Frank is speaking. "But how did you come to acquire this knowledge of your former life?"

"In hypnosis." Lupe sips her coffee. She has hair that is brown, streaked with blonde strands, and now she pulls it back sharply and attaches a clip that appears in her left hand. The effect is striking, intended. The hair now falls almost to her waist in a thin line in back. It is too long to be stylish, though everyone knows that she hardly cares. She is dressed in a simple maroon sweater, one strand of pearls, a beige skirt without complexities of design, flat and obviously comfortable shoes. Her skin is white, porcelain white, alabaster in a different cultural setting (or mode of discourse).

"I went to break my smoking habit. It worked. And I discovered a past life."

No one stirs.

"It's not easy to describe the texture of a life, the—what am I trying to say here—its emotional center. I remember the way the wind would blow my hair on cold sunny afternoons. The light, it would seem to strike the earth at a different angle. The grass, uncut and with thistles I swear three feet off the soil, the grass would bend like waves in the wind. This was in a field I would go to in the district." She pauses. Her eyes are what we label as distant, they have that opaque quality that signals an inward looking of some type, an inspection of a scene delineated in the mind. "The things with my family also. Sitting at the table in the kitchen while my mother served me a meal. Helping with the cooking when everyone ate in the evenings. The smells and sounds of that life."

She closes her eyes. Is this a gesture, a theatrical moment? No, she is remembering. Now she opens her eyes, the past summoned for description, for expression in language.

"The story, the narrative that reports the life, is simple enough. Like so many described lives, narrative lives, a single event was the decisive thing. My mother was—consumptive. Her cough at night echoed down the hall to my room and out my window to the village streets so quiet and still at those times. She became worse, of course, as she aged. Her movements narrowed, became clumsy. Slow. Her voice became quieter. She seemed to lose all of those vivid qualities that made her so attractive when she was young. Even the bony structure of her body seemed to contract as the illness progressed. Eventually she became permanently bedridden. We lived in the early nineteenth century, before Pasteur's germ theory of disease and without any idea that effective diagnosis, prevention, treatment was at some bright spot in the distant future. What we knew was what we saw. Nothing else.

"The priest in the Catholic Church was young. He wore a black coat when he came over to our house to tend to my mother's spiritual needs. His eyes were large, dark, set over prominent cheekbones. Oh, I know how this sounds, how dramatic. But this is the way it plays in my mind now. Today, who knows, this man might be an extra on a movie set. But back then he was a kind and devout member of the clergy.

"How does sexual attraction begin?" Lupe asks aloud. At these words the hostess, the clinical psychologist, shifts in her chair. Lupe's husband has not moved any part of his body since the story began.

Lupe shakes her head. "Summer it was, lovely hot afternoons. We would walk together. Simple as that at first. And talk of course. The sun just brilliant, a wind sometimes turning the leaves up on the olive trees, the foliage green and yellow across the field near the church and beyond." She pauses, her expression dreamy, her look now definitely inward, toward some interior landscape that she is still trying to communicate to us.

"We began by holding hands. Just like that, tactile sensations at the extremities." She laughs to herself, by herself, at this expression. "He told me that my hand felt like a small bird. Imagine that, if you can. His hand felt strong and bony in mine. I felt I could lose myself in those hands, so confident did I feel with him at my side holding just one part of my body. I know this sounds like an exaggeration. But you have to extend your imagination with me now. You have to transport yourself to that time and place."

She pauses again. "I had no experience with men then, nothing. They were mysterious, puzzling creatures, no more intelligible to me than the birds that flew in and out of the trees in the meadow where we walked. Now I found myself drawn to a man who cloaked his body in clerical robes, who draped a crucifix over his neck as sign of his allegiance to Jesus Christ.

"At first I saw him as a priest, nothing more, with all of the trappings of our religion attached to him like protective coloration. He wore the traditional vestments, of course. Black shirt and trousers, white clerical collar. A long dark coat during the winter months, which was when I met him. He would come to the house and bang on the front door, his breath white with frost when he exhaled. Big hands squeezed together in fists in front of his mouth. Sometimes he would be rocking up and down on his toes when I opened the door. Spontaneous gestures, not fixed in the routines of age.

"He would come in quickly, with bluster and high spirits. So unlike the missionaries from the central mesa who would come to our province to instruct in solemn rituals. I wondered then as I wonder now why so many clergy contrive good will when someone is dying. But it was always so good to see Miguel. He would remove the gray scarf he sometimes wore. Then he would kiss me briefly on the cheek before brushing past the rest of the family to go see my mother.

"I cannot forget those scenes in my mother's bedroom. They are the most vivid memories I have of anything in any life. Father Cortez—Miguel—would sit on the bed and hold my mother's hands. He would first say a prayer 'to relax them both,' as he put it. Then he would whisper to her, his mouth close to one of her ears, quiet words straight into her thoughts. Arrows into dreams to shift the equilibrium of her soul more strongly in the direction of faith, of God.

"Watching him began to change everything for me. I used to stand in the hall at the door to my mother's room. At the beginning of these vigils Miguel was a pure expression of religious convictions, exemplar of the Church. Then my perceptions slowly moved to something else. The contours of his body became male, his movements slower. More languid and flowing. At some point I could no longer see his bodily form as a simple physical presence. He was in some kind of soft focus sketched by the growing intensity of my feelings. His movements from one point in space to another were in a different matrix, calibrated on no physical axis I knew. The emotional coordinates from within my soul began to take over, to dominate everything. I could not go within ten feet of him without feeling physically aroused. My appetites dominated all reason, all spirit.

"At one point I broke down, unable to stop crying. Miguel thought it was concern over my mother's condition, and in a way it was. She was dying in obvious ways now, her skin like oversize clothing wrapped around her skeletal frame. It was horrible. But it was Miguel who was the source of my growing confusion and distress. It was then that we began to walk the stone streets holding hands. He consoled me, encouraged me with God's promise of grace and the gift of hope. We took lunch out to the adjoining field one day. Cold chicken, a kind of salad with black olives and cheeses, fresh and very thick bread made that morning. A local white wine that was clear, without color, when I held a glass up later against the mid-day sky. It must have been summer. The leaves were still on the trees like bright green strips of paper glinting in the sun. A dry topsoil collected on our shoes as we walked down the road to the open country. We were meeting to discuss my own soul and the fact that I had stopped going to confession."

CHAPTER ONE

life beyond life

DEATH AND AN AFTERLIFE

The inevitability and denial of death are household partners in human history. In his play *A Man for All Seasons*, Robert Bolt depicts an interrogation of Thomas More, on trial in sixteenth-century England for failing to sign either of the two loyalty oaths required by Henry VIII of all his subjects. The interrogator, Cromwell, reminds More that the penalty for his treason is not imprisonment but— "*Death*," More says before Cromwell can utter the word: " . . . comes to us all, my lords. Yes, even for Kings he comes." And so he does. More is beheaded in the Tower of London. But of course Cromwell and the other players in the spectacle, including the king, also die in the years following More's execution. The one true and unassailable fact in human experience may be the certainty of death as a culmination of sensory or material life. We *all* die at some point in our lives. Death is the one promise nature makes at birth that is always kept.

Yet, curiously enough, the occurrence of death often comes as a surprise—an accident, a homicide, fatalities in war, a sudden illness in the prime of life, even a prolonged fatal sickness can seem odd and even inexplicable to friends and family when it ends in the unwelcome death of a loved person. There is also the individual denial of death coupled with the predictable speculation on whether death will always be inevitable. William Paley, founder and longtime chief executive of CBS, reportedly asked friends as he entered the final stages of his life, "Why do I have to die?" The question is especially poignant in the age of scientific miracles. Will medical science at some point in the future banish death as the natural conclusion of life?

Attitudes toward death may be influenced by our puzzlement over what it means to die. Is death the end of individual existence or the beginning of a different life? These are thoughtful questions in any culture, and often enough they yield contradictory answers. Poets and philosophers range from hope to despair on these matters. Shakespeare was especially patchy on the prospects of an afterlife. Hamlet muses on death as "the bourne from which no traveler returns," for example, even though his dead father has just returned as a ghost to set the play in motion. A more straightforward and consistent approach to death is found in antiquity. There is evidence that primitive humans regarded death as a natural and conclusive end to a span of life that was hard and brief and that conjectures on a life after death followed an extension in the longevity of human life at some point in the distant past. But the conjectures have been vivid and significant for a long time, enriching literature, philosophy, and even medicine with the spate of recent reports from survivors of near death.

Beliefs in an afterlife sometimes are dramatically augmented by reports of individuals who have had mystical or near-death experiences. Plato, in Book 10 of *The Republic*, reports a story told by Socrates about Er, the son of Armenias, who dies in war and then, his body still quite fresh after twelve days, revives and describes his prolonged sojourn with death as a visit to another reality, "a marvelous place" of judgment, punishment, and reward that we are to enter when we die. (This is one of the first, and quite detailed, reports of a near-death experience.) In an earlier Platonic dialogue, Socrates parses such experiences with a story of the soul's migrations after death. Ernest Hemingway nearly died in 1918 from the explosion of a mortar shell while serving with the Red Cross in the First World War. He believed that his spirit had briefly left his body at that instant, was about to begin a journey, and then returned to his body. This near-death experience influenced all his later work.

Today at least some of the evidence for life after death has fortified these experiences and conjectures with clinical and scientific findings. In the by-now classic (and continuing) study of individuals who have almost died, the NDE (Near Death Experience) project at the University of Virginia has presented powerful narratives of afterlife experiences in the survivor's own words, and these words stretch over 500 cases and thirty-five years of reports and evaluations. Clinicians have been slow to explore such experiences with their patients, but support groups like the International Association of Near Death Studies have provided settings for individuals to share their experiences with other NDE survivors. The importance of NDE research is simply immeasurable. If true, the NDE redefines physical death as an entry into a life after the death of the body.

Dr. Sam Parnia, one of the world's leading experts on the scientific study of death, is engaged with colleagues at the Human Consciousness Project in a three-year exploration of the biology underlying NDEs. The study—known as AWARE (an abbreviation derived from AWAreness during REsuscitation)—enlists the cooperation of twenty-five major medical centers in Europe, Canada, and the United States in examining 1,500 survivors of cardiac arrest. In one central part of the research project clinicians place pictures in the rooms housing the stricken patients that are visible only from the ceiling. The test is to see whether individuals whose brain functions have ceased but who report later, when fully recovered, that they left their bodies during this critical time can describe these items. The aim of the experiment is to determine in a controlled environment whether these reported events are actual out-of-body experiences (OBEs) or hallucinations conjured by a dying brain. Parnia believes that the project addresses the objections of skeptics and perhaps delineates the legitimate differences between the mind and the brain. Such tests may provide glimpses into the intriguing possibilities that we can exist outside of our bodies, and, by implication, after our bodies die.

The problem is that even the best designed scientific experiments rely on assumptions that contain cultural expectations, in this case that what remains after death floats upward (instead of assuming a downward trajectory). Of course, that expectation is woven into the reports of NDE survivors that they do indeed float above their bodies. But since we have no understandings of the natural laws that govern the movements of astral selves, it might be interesting to go against type by placing some of the photos in a sealed room in the basement. Also, the tests often avoid polarities that NDEs might accept. Note in the Parnia study the conventional test assumption: If the astral self cannot read the photographs distributed in the room housing the patient, this counts as evidence that the experiences are hallucinations. But there may be a third possibility lodged between these two research-design extremes: that an NDE might transport individuals to a realm of being as real as ordinary life but without full visual contact with the conventional world left behind in death. This is a possibility not testable by science, but it does fold easily into the robust beliefs in an afterlife found in critical pre-test variables, many of which postulate a transcendent reality mainly disconnected to the ordinary reality of temporal life. This belief in an external realm might be comfortable with nonporous partitions that block visual access across the two worlds. That an astral self cannot read texts or see pictures inaccessible to the conventional viewing habits of living individuals would not—on the terms of this belief—count as a critical falsifying test.

DEATH: SURVIVAL OF THE BODY VS. THE MIND

Death, oddly enough, is presented in all cultures as both objective and subjective. In the most obvious sense death is the cessation of most and eventually all biological activity in a living creature. The body dies. It is too easy in spiritual discourses to miss the significance of that physical entity, the body, in identifying the person. In one of the more moving scenes in *Anil's Ghost*, Michael Ondaatje has one of the main characters in the novel, Gamini, flipping through autopsy reports on recently deceased individuals when he encounters a physical account that makes him rush from his office to the morgue downstairs. The headlong flight down the stairs triggers a powerful emotion in the reader because we know what Gamini will find. As he pulls back a sheet covering the body that has the number of the autopsy report he has just read, he looks down and sees his dead brother Sarath on the cot. The physical description of the body in the report was the sign that summoned his brother's identity.

Then, in another arresting passage in the novel, we are reminded in different and even starker terms of the role of the body in identifying the person. It is a scene that follows a suicide bombing: "At four P.M. on National Heroes Day, more than fifty people were killed instantly, including the President. The cutting action of the explosion shredded Katugala into pieces. The central question after the bombing concerned whether the President had been spirited away, and if so whether by the police and army forces or by terrorists. Because the President could not be found."

The physical self, the body, is the venue for identity, how we know one another in everyday life, a locus celebrated even within spiritual texts. Judeo-Christian Scriptures prophesy that the bodies of the dead will be resurrected on Judgment Day. The Egyptians of ancient times prepared the dead for a journey that began with the entombed and preserved body. The full preparation was costly and so was reserved for the wealthy, particularly pharaohs. (The poor were simply buried without accoutrements.) The pyramids of Giza and the enormous tombs in the Valley of the Kings were elaborate burial sites that included jewelry, food, clothing—all placed there to be used by the dead. In Abydos, during the first Egyptian dynasty of 5,000 years ago, the pharaoh's burial team included his flotilla of seventy-foot ships to take him to his destination in the next life, donkeys to carry his goods, and his entire retinue of servants, who were sacrificed to meet his needs after death as they had in life. The craft of mummification developed into a high and precise art form between the years of 1,550 and 945 B.C., driven by the simple conviction that the body must be maintained in order for the god Thoth to recognize the deceased and lead *akh*, the spirit or life force of the individual, to a physical place in an afterlife presided over by Osiris.

In Hindu eschatology there is an intimate relationship between the lived life and the fate of the individual in a succeeding life here on earth. Hinduism assumes continuing reincarnations (*samsara*), with the proviso that a person's current life is in some way the result of previous lives (*karma*). Release from the cycle, or liberation (*moksa*), is possible if the individual finds the right path to salvation in one of his/her incarnations. There is some thought that the flight to salvation, a union with divinity in the afterlife, is a reversal of the caste system in India, which evolved from marginal cross-caste mobility into a rigid arrangement that permits no escape from one's station. But this inverse linkage between the profane and the divine, promising a way out of the travails of life here on earth, also suggests a certain intimacy between the body and the spirit. The actions committed when incarnate determine the standing of the spiritual self in between the series of lives on earth and the possibility of a salvation that breaks the cycle. Or, the person made flesh is decisive in determining the standing of the same spiritual self in the afterlife.

The survival of a soul or spirit freed from the body is stressed by many religions in stories of death and an afterlife. In Islam, death is a passage that connects two lives, the one on earth and that which follows death. The part of us that survives death is the soul, not the body. The Qur'an discusses a critical event in the afterworld, the Day of Resurrection, or the Hour, when the soul of the deceased will enter a spiritual reality determined by how the individual has lived on earth. A prudent preparation on earth, doing good over a lifetime, will allow the individual to face God after death with confidence that Allah will discharge the soul toward paradise instead of hell. The story is a familiar one in many venues, including the medical in NDEs. The death of the body, a passage of the individual to another reality, a review and judgment by God or an expert witness or a friendly authority figure, a soul that can find eternal life in heaven or hell—this is also the view of death and "the life of the world to come" in Christianity after St. Paul.

There are, of course, substantial differences between Islam and Christianity. The Christian God, for example, is more willing to accept verbal contrition for sins than Allah, and the heavenly rewards bestowed on the elected souls are more sensuous in Islam than in Christianity. (The promises in Islam include the sexual use of young and attractive virgins in the next life. Christianity promises union with God, presumably a chaste coupling.) But the stories of death and spiritual rebirth are remarkably similar. In both Islam and Christianity death is regarded as a release of the soul from the body and a journey of the spiritual self to an eternal life of splendor or privation. The body of the person is left behind. Thomas More believed that he, meaning his identity as defined by his immortal soul, would be united with God for eternity in the afterlife. The pattern of spiritual release and journey also follows the structure of the near-death experience, though in the NDE the individual returns to life before reaching the light, or God.

An even more comprehensive program of spiritual survival after death is described in Buddhism. In this religion the form and content of human experience are structured by the thinking and perceptual powers of the human form. Our brains, for example, seem to be hardwired to organize experience in terms of partitions, to establish dualistic arrangements separating self and world, self and others, self and cosmos. But in Buddhism these dualisms are regarded as artificial, even false in a larger sense since reality is seamless, without distinctions or differences. The goal of Buddhism is to gain access to this undifferentiated reality through deep meditation, achieving a momentary fusion with a universe unmediated by the human intellect or senses, to see the world *as it is* in its pristine actuality. This fusion of self and reality is difficult even for those who are trained in Buddhism, but it occurs naturally at death. Buddhists believe that the self is merged with reality as it leaves the body, absorbed into a nature that annihilates the individual spirit even as temporal nature reclaims the dead body. Not to press the point, but the NDE also fits Buddhism as far as the experience goes: the NDE's distant light of love and fulfillment that the individual does not approach in the end may be the annihilating point in Buddhism.

DEATH AS A PASSAGE

The stories in Islam and Christianity that testify to the survival of the soul or spirit, as well as the salvation paths of Hinduism and perhaps even the transition and absorption stories of Buddhism that report the illusory individualism of the human spirit—all these, one would like to say, are more intelligible than the accounts of bodily resurrection. Almost all literary depictions of the afterlife focus on a spiritual survival of death. In *War and Peace* Tolstoy describes a dream that the dying Prince Andrey has one afternoon. "He dreamed that he was lying in the very room in which he was lying in reality, but he was not ill, but quite well." Many people are with him, and he is "talking and disputing with them about some trivial matter." Then, as the Prince is "uttering empty witticisms of some sort . . . these people began to disappear, and the one thing left was the closing of the door." But the Prince cannot move quickly to bolt the door, "his legs would not move," and then he experiences "an agonizing terror," which is the fear of death. It is death that is on the other side of the door. He struggles with the door, trying to keep it shut, but his efforts are in vain "and both leaves of the door are noiselessly opened. It comes in, and it is death. And Prince Andrey died.

"But at the instant in his dream when he died, Prince Andrey recollected that he was asleep; and at that exact instant when he was dying, he made an effort and waked up." Tolstoy has the prince utter the crucial insight. "'Yes, that was death. I died and I waked up. Yes, death is an awakening,' flashed with sudden light into his soul, and the veil that had until then hidden the unknown was lifted before his spiritual vision." He understands immediately, with "a strange lightness of being" that stays with him through his death, that the death of the body is merely an awakening and entrance into another life by the individual soul. From the moment of the dream Prince Andrey withdraws from his loved ones and begins slowly awakening (he believes) from life into another life that begins with death.

The death on an African safari of Harry Walden, the main character in Hemingway's short story "The Snows of Kilimanjaro," is presented in two scenes. In the first, an old friend, Compton, arrives in a plane to carry him to a hospital to treat his infected and gangrenous leg. Compton is wearing "slacks, a tweed jacket, and a brown felt hat," and the plane is the Puss Moth, a familiar vehicle that has room for only one passenger. The scene is classic Hemingway realism, concrete details set against metaphysics. The ordinary and familiar appearance of Compton competes with the early, more mysterious parts of the story: the opening description of the frozen carcass of a leopard close to the western summit of Kilimanjaro (the summit that the Masai called Ngàje Ngài, the House of God); the early images of death as a hyena moving across the open area near the camp every night and then slipping "lightly across the edge of it [death]"; a bird; two bicycle policemen; Harry musing that death sometimes came "in pairs, on bicycles, and moved absolutely silently on the pavements"; the appearance of a shapeless something crouching on Harry's chest so that he cannot breathe; and, outside the story, the very real probability that Compton is modeled after Denys Finch Hatton, who died in an explosion of his plane, the Gypsy Moth, a few years before Hemingway arrived in Africa. Compton, standing for Hatton (the lover of Karen Blixen, the real name of writer Isak Dinesen), may be a spirit returned from the dead as a guide for Harry (a common occurrence in NDEs). In the short story Compton passes on the tea after a brief private conversation with Harry's wife. Then, after explaining to her as they prepare to leave that she can't come along because the plane can take only one passenger, he takes off with Harry for a flight that includes a stop at Arusha to refuel. Hemingway describes the African plains as the two friends ascend, filled with zebra and wildebeest and then "mountains dark ahead."

> And then instead of going on to Arusha they turned left, he [Compton] evidently figured they had the gas, and looking down he [Harry] saw a pink sifting cloud, moving over the ground, and in the air, like the first snow in a blizzard, that comes from nowhere, and he knew the locusts were coming up from the South. Then they began to climb and they were going to the East it seemed, and then it darkened and they were in a storm, the rain so thick it seemed like flying through a waterfall, and then they were out and Compie turned his head and grinned and pointed out there, ahead, all he could see, as wide as all the world, great, high, and unbelievably white in the sun, was the square top of Kilimanjaro. And then he knew that there was where he was going.

The scene suggests an afterlife of brilliant transcendence. In the second death scene, the last scene in the story and the only one framed from the wife's point of view, "the hyena stopped whimpering in the night and started to make a strange, human, almost crying sound." Harry's wife doesn't awaken at first. She is dreaming of being at the house on Long Island the night before her daughter's debut. Then the hyena makes a noise so loud that she wakes up, "and for a moment she did not know where she was and she was very afraid." She takes the flashlight and discovers her husband's dead body in the tent, "his bulk under the mosquito bar but somehow he had gotten his leg out and it hung down alongside the cot." This scene indicates two things to the reader: that Harry died earlier in the story, in the scene preceding the arrival of Compton in the plane, when the figure of death crushing him suddenly released the pressure "while they lifted the cot, suddenly it was all right and the weight went from his chest," and in death the body is left behind.

Such scenes are striking representations of intuition, hope, awe, and common sense. They express by conjecture filtered through fiction our best and most glorious expectations about death, that it is not all there is, and some vital part of us, our identity, survives the demise of our bodies. We know that the human body is impermanent from observing how it changes during life, and it is an irrefutable fact that the body starts deteriorating immediately after death and disintegrates entirely. But we can also feel, if we conduct an honest and deep survey of our interior, psychic landscapes, that we seem to be a kind of self within and immersed in our bodies, and the particular selves we project, corrigible but somehow also an evolving and permanent spirit or identity that is not entirely accounted for by the best physiology or psychology. We don't feel like just bodies, in other words, or as the public selves we extend to others, but as something else, a private identity that locates us within the scheme of things, a self that may change but is continuous over our lifetimes. An identity that is real and not coterminous with the physical body, and which seems crafted by our genes and our circumstances to exist as our truest nature within our bodies. No such natural appeal accompanies the argument that we are little more than bodies in a physical universe, which simply is counterintuitive and unable to offer a complete explanation for the fact and inner space of consciousness, and of self awareness.

To the skeptical reader: try to imagine yourself as merely a body without a soul or spirit, a mental identity. Does the exercise ring true? Can you really entertain the possibility that you are a zombie, a person without an inner self, a body without a soul or spirit or mind? To most the thought is unintelligible, even malignant, for the direct reason that it is the mind, seen modestly just as the venue of thinking, which is speculating on the prospect that one does not have a mind. The opposite line of thought seems more persuasive. Each individual seems to be a kind of mental field of experiences configured in unique ways—the ordering of objects and persons, the complement of thoughts and perceptions. This depiction of individuals suggests an even more arresting image: that if death annihilates the individual, then each world that expresses an individual is lost with each death.

If there is a case for life after death, then, on both cost-benefit and intellectual considerations it is probably located in those accounts of survival that talk of the soul or spirit or psyche as liberated from the body, and not an afterlife for a physical self with the same needs for food, clothing, jewelry, and wealth in general that attend to the body's survival. If life after death is real, it is this sense of self that may have survival possibilities, a metaphysical self that death has released from the limitations of the body and that has always required its own special ministrations in ordinary secular life—meditation, private space, serenity. Of course such a self could also perish with death, transmuted into a form of antimatter. But the inquiry into an afterlife seems initially more intelligible when centered on the survival of a noncorporeal self rather than the transport of a body to an afterlife. It may be significant that the individual experiencing an NDE often sees his/her body left behind as the journey begins.

Complicating all inquiries into an afterlife is that evidence in these areas is often presented within a frame of events that are so intense that they consume the cool demeanor of objective science. The skeptic's take, the wait-and-see attitude that characterizes science, is occasionally overwhelmed by the sheer force of a story. William Wharton, a distinguished novelist, lost his daughter, her husband, and their two infant daughters in a fire that engulfed their car. It was triggered by the agricultural practice of field burning, which incinerated their car when it was caught in a twenty-three-car pileup on an Oregon highway in 1988. The horror of this tragedy was followed by what Wharton is convinced was an actual contact with his daughter and her family in a dream of their afterlife, and the inexplicable appearance of a bird that flew into their home and seemed to be a familiar member of the household.

Wharton's reported contact with the afterlife, of course, lends itself to the usual psychological vocabularies of mind-construction occasioned by grief. But it also invites the possibility that the experience was real, actual. Here is the critical and chronic issue. How can we craft a language that adjudicates the rival interpretation of experiences that are presented as vivid and powerful accounts of a reality outside conventional parameters, and especially in seeming to yield indications of an afterlife?

The ancient Greeks, home to the origins of Western philosophies of ethics and politics, believed in a soul that survives the body, which they thought perishes at death and need not be preserved. These beliefs, surprisingly enough, were developed in a culture dense with the pantheism of Ionian science, Plato's more austere theory of forms, Aristotelian transcendence, and the pantheon of gods rendered by Homer and presented as a stylized higher world of dysfunctional supreme beings who love and fight very much like humans do, except that they possess odd and scary powers. The best presentation of ancient Greek beliefs in a spiritual afterlife is occasioned by a famous trial, and the death resulting from the penalty phase of this trial. These two events led a thoughtful man, condemned to die, to speculate on the migration of the soul after the death of the body.

Socrates, who claimed that his wisdom was represented in his acknowledgment of his own ignorance, was found guilty in 199 B.C. by the Athenian Assembly of impiety toward the gods and corruption of the young. It may be one measure of Socrates' innocence in the thickets of political realities that, in response to a guilty verdict voted by the Assembly and a proposal of the death penalty by one of the prosecutors, Meletus, he suggested to the Assembly that his penalty be a fine of thirty minæ (less than $600 US today). It also may be a measure of the irritation that this suggestion provoked that the Assembly voted for the death penalty by a greater margin than the vote for his guilt. As we know now, and to the consternation of the Athenian authorities then, Socrates chose death over the exile usually selected in place of the penalty of death, and in doing so provided two thousand years of succeeding philosophy its first and lasting hero.

The death of Socrates also gives us one of the more dramatic and moving death scenes in literature, and some of the earliest conjectures and arguments on what follows death. It is an enchanting text interpreted in different ways throughout history, and has been regarded as one of the earliest inspirations for religious beliefs in an afterlife. In describing the migrations of a soul that is eternal and a body that is not, Socrates also presented an unusual treatment in Western thought at the time, though a dualism of soul and body was common enough even then in Eastern religious philosophies. In the Crito Socrates reviews the death penalty that the Athenian assembly has given him, and offers the classic defense of political obligation that restricts him from choosing exile instead of his own execution at the hands of the state. This is the text that political theorists study and love. But Socrates also reflects in the *Phaedo* on a life after death as he contemplates his own imminent demise. Surrounded by his closest friends and shortly to drink the hemlock that will end his life, Socrates underwrites the immortality of the human soul.

Some among his friends are skeptical at first. Simmias raises the classic and continuing objection to immortality, which is that the person depends on a human body that dies at death. Simmias frames the issue this way: Is the immortality of the soul and the mortality of the body like that between harmony and the lyre? The soul, like the harmony of the lyre, is invisible and divine, but once the lyre has been destroyed, the harmony vanishes since it requires that physical instrument to exist. Or, as elaborated, is it that when the instrument eventually perishes, the grammar of the music will live on? And if this is so, then human immortality is formal only, like axioms in logic, and fragile in having palpable existence only in and through a corporeal body of some sort. And when the harmony of the body is disrupted and eventually destroyed through the disorders brought by illness or injury, the ravages of age and debility, then does the soul lose its defining order and perish as well? In contemporary terms this proposition is expressed as a reliance of the self, the sentient person, on the brain. Like the harmony of the lyre the conscious self depends on the continued viability and existence of the brain. At death the brain dies, sometimes preceded by morbidities that ravage its chemistry and order. On the classical terms of dependence the self ceases to exist since it loses that substance needed for its existence.

But these kinds of observations depend on the simile or metaphor used. Think now of a wood-burning fire. When the wood is exhausted the fire normally dies. But now imagine a propane gas stove nearby that has just been turned on but not lit. A wind springs up and the fire leaps to the stove, or maybe someone takes a newspaper and lights it with the embers of the wood and carries it over to the stove. The fire revives with the transfer to the new conditions, a propane base of energy. In this simile the dependence of the fire on finite conditions does not mean that the fire cannot be rekindled and nourished in other conditions. If the soul is like the fire, the death of the body may not be the death of the soul, which might find renewed existence in a different venue.

Socrates reassures his friends with a different argument. He reminds them that, since knowledge is a type of recollection that indicates a previous life, we may conclude that the soul exists before the body and so is eternal. Or, the soul, the part of us that is divine, had a life before birth and will exist after death. In this way it is more substantial than the body even as it is invisible. Also, like all things, it cannot receive its opposite (as the odd repels the even). No, the immortality of the soul cannot admit death to its realm. Socrates tells us that in life, the soul is enthralled by the body, with each pleasure and pain like nails and rivets binding the soul to the body. But when the body dies, the nails and rivets are loosened. The soul escapes to another level of existence. When the individual dies "the genius of each individual, to whom he belonged in life, leads him to a certain place in which the dead are gathered together for judgment," the beginning of a journey that will contain purification rituals in a lake for crimes, the more serious deeds requiring a year or more in the boiling water and mud of Tartarus, and for others who have committed much evil a permanent residence in the worst parts of Hades (the next world).

When Socrates drank the poison his friends wept. One "broke out in a loud cry which made cowards of us all. Socrates alone retained his calmness: What is this strange outcry, he said. I sent away the women mainly in order that they might not offend in this way, for I have heard that a man should die in peace. Be quiet then, and have patience. When we heard that, we were ashamed and refrained our tears." Later, as the poison took effect, Socrates uncovered his face and uttered his last words: "Crito, I owe a cock to Asclepius; will you remember to pay the debt? The debt shall be paid, said Crito; is there anything else? There was no answer to this question; but in a minute or two a movement was heard, and the attendants uncovered him; his eyes were set, and Crito closed his eyes and mouth." Socrates had embarked on that mysterious and still largely uncharted journey that we must all take at one time or another as our life ends.

EARLY MYSTICISM

Socrates said that he was guided throughout his life by an oracle or daemon, a voice of sorts that spoke to him privately. He was a mystic, in other words, a man who also was ascetic and chaste in his orientation to experience. For Socrates the mastery of soul or *nous* over the body was the mark of the integrated and whole human person. Yet he was rational to the core, concerned his entire life with reasoned argument, and conducted lucid examinations of language as a way to get to truth. He offers reasons for immortality when the subject is discussed in the

Phædo, not intuitive insights or faith. He was engaged in the only species of inquiry that makes sense when examining the possibility of life after death, which is that we must select the proper frames for our inquiries, look at evidence, use proper rules of inference and argument, and reach conclusions on what is true rather than what is desirable.

I stress this because one of the more powerful incentives for believing in survival after death is that it consoles us by removing the prospect of annihilation, a critical matter since we are sentient creatures who usually wish to continue existing. A character in a Sartre short story, one of three prisoners who have been sentenced to die by firing squad in the morning, tries to imagine the world that will continue after he is executed. He cannot do so since he is the one seeing this world, which is paradoxical since he will not exist after his death to perceive anything. He cannot make sense of his own impending non-existence, which to him is inconceivable, a thought simultaneously so horrible and contradictory that he cannot get his mind around it. But his belief in his coming death is still very real and yet imponderable.

When belief in life after death is so desperately needed to make life and death bearable, even intelligible, one must be extremely careful to arrive at truth rather than just comforting beliefs. The stories of life after death present new beginnings, sometimes with a day of judgment for past sins, but also with a promise that death is the beginning of a life of redemption with marvelous rewards. Religion itself is compelling for many individuals in promising (as it often does) that we will have eternal life in a better world after we die. It resolves the most primordial of fears, death as the end of all conscious life, by offering immortality in heaven in its place. It also describes a release and salvation from the tribulations, the hard facts of ordinary life that all of us face at least from time to time and sometimes all the time. The lasting attraction of Socrates' conjectures is that they are arguments for the immortality of the soul, not wishes or hopes.

But do the arguments work? Are they successful? No, or at least it does not seem so to the modern mind. For one thing, Socrates examines language as if he were examining the world that language depicts, and quickly reaches extremely ambitious conclusions from just a few acknowledged facts. So, for example, he recognizes the mental powers that we all have, the capacity especially to think abstract thoughts, and surmises with all other philosophers of the time that intellect or mind (nous) is the essence of our natures, and these thinking powers are distinct from our bodies. Though persuasive arguments for a separation of mind and body will have to wait for Descartes' arguments almost two thousand years later, Socrates follows the commonsense belief that we are mental selves expressed as bodies, and these bodies provide sensory powers but do not tell the whole story. The whole story must include the fact (for Socrates) that we have or are souls, which are invisible entities that are not identical to our bodies and in fact predate and survive—on the arguments Socrates deploys—the life span of the physical self. Remember also that when Plato presents the tripartite ordering of the individual in the *Republic* it is the soul that is ordered into the famous hierarchy of intellect—spirit—appetite, and without a trace of either of the later versions of dualism, substance or property, explored in modern philosophy.

A note for the historians among us: René Descartes is the philosopher who developed the modern case for substance dualism, the thesis that the human animal consists of a soul or spirit in a body. The modern extension of this thesis as property dualism more modestly posits a mind or mental self within a body. The implications are the same, however, amounting to the conviction that the human self is a composite of an ineffable mental self and a body. The contemporary attempt to refute this proposition is Gilbert Ryle's influential book *The Concept of Mind.* Ryle argued against a Cartesian dualism that he called "the ghost in the machine," the thought that there is some homunculus within us that directs the body and is in some way independent of its physical venue. For believers in an afterlife Descartes' "ghosts" are the entities that move across the threshold of death to the other side of human existence.

But the best work today in neurology advises us that our brains are the needed venues for thinking powers, and the fact that we are thinking creatures is in itself not evidence for an independent soul. The main work today in artificial intelligence and neurological studies rejects the doctrines of dualism. Even scholars as different from one another as John Searle and Daniel Dennett abandon dualism in favor of a complete biological account of brain and body. But it is in the conceptual space between variants of Cartesian dualism and the presentations of a biologically intact human self that the explorations of life after death are typically conducted. The Darwinian revolution in biology has even presented a rough account of how natural selection produced the mental powers that we see exhibited in the human species. It is true that natural selection alone has a hard time explaining the survival values in Bach's music and our powers to comprehend particle physics, but when combined with the biological laws that govern organic development natural selection can produce the marvelous combinations that Stephen Jay Gould called "spandrels," the hybrids that emerge from the interactions of natural laws with the conditions of competitive advantage. We may be particularly nuanced hybrids. That we are thinking creatures is unassailable. It is what we make of that assignment in concluding things about the world that is contestable.

The more promising part of Socrates' arguments may be in the assertion that knowledge is a form of recollection, and our natural abilities to comprehend things suggests that learning is a form of remembering. The psychologists of today would balk at the vocabulary, but much work on the learning curves of infants suggests at least that the brain is hardwired to see a reality before we experience it, and then as infants mature and gain experience this reality is perceived differently according to cultural influence. The possibility that this innate ability is evidence for an existence before birth is generally dismissed. But pegging evidence for survival after death to life both before and after life may provide a more robust way to explore the possibility of life after death. If we have had previous lives, then at least a different and perhaps more extensive span of existence is part of human existence. What we really need is a theory and an evidentiary base that instructs us on the possibility (or not) of an existence beyond the scope of sensory experiences.

SCIENCE AND MYSTICISM

Whatever else it is, scientific inquiry, when organized successfully, is designed to falsify statements. Karl Popper's felicitous statement—that even the most venerable scientific principle or law is little more than a hypothesis that has so far resisted disproof—speaks to the provisional truths that guide science. This understanding is not skepticism but an acknowledgment that the critical testing of statements is definitive of science, with two implications. First, the kind of privileged or revealed truth in religion and other discourses is outside the parameters of scientific truth. Second, empirical statements are the main nourishment in science. If falsification is the definitive method of science, then the only licit statements are those that admit the possibility of critical testing for falsification purposes. Religious truth, by contrast, does not readily admit falsification. Such truths can be revised, and dismissed, as happened in the Reformation with Luther's reversal of the providential direction of action-to-intention. But they attend to unseen and inaccessible dimensions of experience. "God exists," for example, has been supported with a variety of logical proofs (with mixed success), but no observation statements are universally shared as a basis for falsifying or maintaining the truth of the statement.

The critical though narrow difference between science and religion is in the domains of inquiry marked off by the two practices. Science, in the popular sense of things, addresses empirical worlds and negotiates them with the languages of technology and mathematics. It does not address realities that cannot be presented in terms of falsifiable statements. The issue of life after death is — finally — not amenable to formal scientific proof. The full experience is not replicable through controlled experiments. The NDE, for example, is confined to single individuals isolated from others during the critical experience, and offers a non-physical existence whose true meaning, reasonably drawn from the full scope and conclusion of the experience, is always suddenly broken as the individual returns to the world of the living. What we have as data are reports that are to count as evidence, reports that are subject to the same parsing that therapists use in dreams reported by patients: it is the report of the dream that is the datum in treatment, not the dream itself, or whether the dream in fact occurred. The same logic holds for NDEs. We can never get beyond the report of the NDE anymore than we can get beyond the report of the dream in therapy. The evidence is always secondary, indirectly connected to experience by the subject.

No version of science is in direct opposition to conjectures about an afterlife. It is a truism that the skepticism drawn out of science, even the best science, is often limited in retrospect as mythical events and venerable stories turn out to be real events and true stories as new evidence is uncovered (literally, in some cases) by more sophisticated exploration. Put succinctly, in science the unlikely and strange can turn out to be quite true. Also, since even the most sophisticated science inadequately explains the full scope of reality and the laws that govern it, the hypothesis that life extends beyond death is at least a coherent proposition that can be explored. Ruling it out of court without critical examination might be too much like the clerics of the seventeenth century refusing to inspect evidence for the then-radical Copernican thesis. The telescope was in the room, its special powers known to all. At least, as Galileo is said to have pleaded with the Church authorities, just look at the evidence. In at least one dramatic account no one stepped up to peer through the instrument. The source of the Church's resistance to the new astronomy was intriguing. The controlling belief was that sacred texts provide all relevant knowledge about reality, and the new instrument was a contrivance that presented a world created by the man-made artifact. Better to rely on the texts issued by God to humanity than on the instruments created by humanity to reveal God's creations. This stance was also coupled to the kind of consideration that we know now compromises science and knowledge in general: fear that the new view of the cosmos would weaken the allegiance of the people to the Church, with a resulting instability in the social order.

Here's an interesting slant on that famous dispute that allows critical inquiry while protecting the standing of sacred texts. Eighteen years before Galileo abjured his opinion on the Copernican system, a Carmelite friar, Paolo Antonio Foscarini, attempted to reconcile the heliocentric view with Holy Scripture by distinguishing the truth of a text from its interpretation. He affirmed that all of Scripture is true, but we still have to determine what the text teaches or intends, what the text means. Galileo himself, in staged debates, dinner party conversations, and various published works, consistently subscribed to the truth of Scripture in the years before his trial. It is God's word, he said, and true everywhere. But, relying on Foscarini's distinction, he proposed that we can be mistaken about what it means, in this case on the issue of the geocentric or heliocentric view. Cardinal Bellarmine, accepting the contested view that Scripture makes claims about the workings of the natural world, acknowledged the interpretive powers of natural science with a concession: if Galileo could demonstrate his theory, provide a conclusive scientific proof of the Copernican system, then the Church would accept a nonliteral interpretation of the passages in the Bible that bear on the issue.

If history teaches us anything, it is that science in any of its guises cannot address metaphysical issues in ways that lead to closure, and so cannot rule out the possibility of life after death. Science is finally a continuation of the ancient effort to uncover the structure and deeper codes of nature, though now with observation and mathematics and technology. The model of science suggested by these rudimentary assumptions and observations is tiered, with the conceptual space between the tiers presenting welcome continuities and often puzzling but enticing discontinuities. At one level statements in science are transparent, ordered, serene, and closely linked to evidence. Replication of experiments is routine. Knowledge is cumulative. But at another level a rich assortment of (typically) under-examined assumptions, like dark matter in the universe, drives a more conjectural version of science. Of course it is more comfortable to stay at the explicit level. Unfortunately for the risk-averse among us the explicit tier of science relies crucially on what is not examined, the indirect and often metaphorical languages that inform a practice famous for its luminosity. Or, science, like religion, has its own protective belt shielding certain privileged matters from critical scrutiny (though not with the explicit label of the "sacred"). A gaze at these less inspected areas of science on occasion rearranges concepts to yield a deeper look at the nature of reality than can possibly be found and explored with the thinner direct and explicit methods of conventional science.

Science is also a practice closer to demystified intuition than we like to think. One of the greatest natural scientists in history, Isaac Newton, spent considerable time exploring alchemy and the occult. The brilliant twentieth-century physicist Richard Feynman was said to have mystified his colleagues by intuitively seeing solutions long before the findings could be established through experiments or mathematical proofs. The young genius in the film *Good Will Hunting* conveyed what great scientists in the real world sometimes acknowledge when he said that he didn't know how he came up with his solutions to complex mathematical and scientific problems. He just saw them. In a science that has discovered, in its more lucid and linear moments, a fabric of space and time and matter that in no important way represents the ordinary, earth-bound realities we mainly occupy, and that reveals alternative realities and sub-atomic worlds that seem to violate the most esteemed notions of causality and sequencing of events—it is inane in this intellectual context to regard the possibility of life after death as entirely outlandish and not worth pursuing. And the deep certainty of atheists that all of reality is material with no spiritual presence, and certainly no God, is a species of arrogance utterly unsupportable by deep and sophisticated understandings of true science.

Let the following informal observations be a framework for our inquiries into alternative realities, including a death process that might lead to an afterlife, and also serve as a mantra or guide that will take us through some deep and disturbing possibilities. Start with this. We are strange and almost indefinable creatures, maybe with infinities within our grasp and inside our heads. To say that life after death is impossible in the grand world of the universe, a universe that we barely comprehend but seem able to touch with chronically open thoughts and feelings, cannot be uttered by a person who truly understands the limits that science identifies, the humility these limits require, and the limited hubris that our minds deserve. The model of bounded knowledge implied in this humility invites conjectures and imaginative speculations on the possibility of life after death exactly because we do not know enough to rule the possibility in or out. It would require a person of unimaginable intellectual powers, one who had mastered all realistic possibilities and dimensions, to rule definitively on the possibility of life after death. But God is not an available and uncontestable resource in our efforts to understand these matters and settle the question. So we must be pragmatic to our cores, holding that all human knowledge is contingent, tentative in the best sense, and utterly capable of being dismissed as new discoveries occur. Life after death, in short, is in play as a topic of legitimate inquiry given our intellectual limitations and the mysteries of human consciousness.

This book is an invitation to summon sacred texts, mystical experiences, and theories of materialism with the interpretive powers of the current worlds of neurology, clinical data, critical studies of narratives, and decision theory. I want us all to be Cardinal Bellarmine. If the evidence is there for external realities, for life after death, even (or especially) if secured with contemporary science, or if the case for an afterlife cannot be secured on a preponderance of evidence and argument, then let's be prepared to revise our most cherished secular and/or religious understandings of the full dimensions of human experience. After all, we may be wrong about what it all means as we decipher the truths stated in the ancient and current texts that explain human life. And if the discursive languages that are sometimes needed to explore these worlds, those driven by simile, metaphor, and narrative, are offensive or spoken to those deaf to nonlinear discourses, at least we can ask the direct question: How can we explore the full range of reality if we make an arbitrary stop at what we know and perceive at any moment in history? The existence of an external reality assumed by both Gödel and Einstein is actually the starting assumption in both scientific realism and religious approaches to experience. The issue is how we can most effectively gain access to this dimension and present it in intelligible ways.

In the film *Blade Runner*, Rick Deckard (Harrison Ford) has to track down and terminate four replicants who have hijacked a ship in space and returned to earth seeking their maker. One of their goals is to extend their lives beyond the terminal points built into their programs. Toward the end of the film Deckard is trying to explain in the voiceover why the last replicant, Roy Batty (Rutger Hauer), had not killed him when he had the chance. He suggests that maybe at the end of his own life Batty had loved life, all life, so much that he just wanted to end the killings. Then Deckard says that the replicants were asking the same questions that we all ask: where did we come from, who are we, where are we going? As he died Batty had said, "I have seen things you people wouldn't believe." Then he slowly described vivid events in the far reaches of the universe, spectacular scenes that no human would ever see, the memories of which now, he said, would all disappear: "All of those moments will be lost, like tears in rain." Then he murmured, "Time to die," lowered his head, and died.

These are questions that are real and compelling. Are the private moments of each person's experiences erased at death? Or is there a secure existence after death for these moments, and the conscious carriers of the memories they provide?

But the answers to these questions may not satisfy those looking for hard truths. *Solaris*, a film directed by Steven Soderbergh (and a reprise of a true masterpiece on the same themes with the same title, the 1972 Russian film directed by Andrei Tarkovsky, both films based on the novel by the Polish science fiction writer Stanislaw Lem), presents some of the dilemmas and possibilities of life after death. The style of the film in both versions is consciously ambiguous. In Soderbergh's version the cutting from scene to scene, and sometimes even within scenes, compromises two of the most important verities in human experience, time and space. The story rendered centers on a psychiatrist, Chris Kelvin (George Clooney), who falls in love with and marries a complex and fragile woman named Rheya. We see Chris and Rheya falling in love, playful and serious over poetry, in particular Dylan Thomas's "Death Has No Dominion." But the marriage is as gloomy and ambiguous as the film's atmosphere. One day Chris discovers that Rheya has had an abortion without telling him. His rage, which fills their small apartment with the negative energy he imagines a child would have redirected as a positive life force in their marriage, goes over the top when Rheya pleads with him not to leave her. "I can't make it without you," she cries. "Then you won't make it!" he shouts at her as he departs. Later in the afternoon he returns and discovers her dead body. She has killed herself by overdosing on drugs.

The film cuts back and forth along the dimensions of the two dominant stories: Chris's loss of his wife and the odd happenings on a space ship, *Prometheus*, that is slowly orbiting and surveying a distant and mysterious planet, Solaris. Chris is summoned to view a video transmission from Giberian (Ulrich Tukur), the senior member of the space crew in the film who also happens to be one of his best friends. Giberian's face fills the screen as he tries to describe conditions on Solaris. But Giberian cannot describe what is happening, and he suggests that Chris should come to the ship to see for himself and help save the crew and its mission. Chris does so and discovers that Giberian has by then committed suicide and the crew is in complete disarray. The later cryptic revelation by Giberian, who appears to Chris during the night but cannot even explain his own suicide ("I thought it was a good idea at the time. Now I think I may have been mistaken."), maps the tense and intimate connections between some form of an afterlife and the secular life that these scientists and physicians are trying to live. Giberian, a visitor from the dead, tells Chris, "There are no answers, only choices."

On *Prometheus* replicas of the dead appear, including those of his dead wife. The ship finally takes Chris to his death in a slow gravity-driven crash on Solaris. In the final scene of the film Rheya appears again with Chris in their old apartment. As they hold each other Chris asks if they are alive or dead. She replies that they don't have to ask that question anymore. She also tells him that "everything is forgiven, everything." Their life trajectory appears to be an arc set permanently on the outside of human sensibilities, always observing, never experiencing. The suggestion of reincarnation in this final scene does, however, fit the classic texts. Chris and Rheya seem to have entered a dimension of reality where many of the natural laws that govern earth have been suspended and the mistakes of the past life are forgiven, but without explanations.

The critical and easy response might be the reply Jake makes to Lady Brett at the end of Hemingway's *The Sun Also Rises*. "'Yes,' I said. 'Isn't it pretty to think so?'" The more deliberative response from a perspective of intellectual modesty might be, "We need to know more about all of this if we are to negotiate our way through *any* of the evidence for life after death."

a past life, no. 2

The previous Saturday afternoon Lupe had been out shopping for hours looking for a matching blouse and skirt to wear at a wedding the next month. After a failed search through all her favorite stores she had returned to her apartment frustrated and hoping for some rest before her son came home from junior high. She collapsed on the sofa and began a chant to help herself relax. The television set, its volume very low, sounded like small animals grunting and growling in the corner. She quickly reached that state between awareness and sleep that always brought her sadness, especially when the late afternoon sun is almost at the horizon and descending with that peculiar orange color behind the city buildings across the street. She felt her whole body relax, every part slowing down. She thought that her soul might be sinking down into the sofa, but then — easily, comfortably — she slowly ascended and left her body.

She was frightened at first. The sensations were crisp and welcome. But she felt lost, not connected to anything physical. She floated near an airliner, a commercial plane that looked like a metal pellet in the sky, and when she got closer she could see two passengers inside eating meals, a flight attendant in a blue coat leaning over one of their trays to open a napkin. She sent a small quick prayer, memorized from her recent entrance into the practices of Santería, asking Oshun for protection and guidance. At some point she thought there might be a presence, a male figure, with her. She asked the spirit to identify himself. At that moment she was back in her apartment as someone very gently reached over and touched both of her closed eyelids. His hands were very cold and smooth, like scales. They made her shudder as he brushed slowly over her skin. She could still feel them on her as she came back into her body.

At that moment of return Lupe knew what had joined her. The images in her head were so vivid, of dancing, drums, flashing lightning, thunder, movement everywhere, red streaks of sun rays in the sky. The muscular male beauty of a single figure shaking to the drums. Shangó. He had entered her landscape, her spiritual self, her mind, to watch, to observe, to monitor. She could still smell him, feel him, the movements of flesh in thoughts during holy mass. The one who makes you touch yourself in the confessional. The tiger. The double ax. The goat's appetite in a loving heart. These Lupe knew as the lusts of Shangó, the orisha who fears the dead. According to legend Shangó was once so angry that he hanged himself in the forest from a cedar tree and entered the land of iku, the dead, which scarred him forever.

Now she is bracketing that experience, everything, all memories except for the story of reincarnation that she is relating at the dinner party to a group of friends.

"Shared stories," she continues. "That is what I remember from the start of that day. In one long soliloquy I told Miguel the story of my life. Poverty and reduced opportunities would be my theme today. Then it was piety and fugitive love. I believed in the Church, in the Trinity and transubstantiation, in the forgiveness of sins and the resurrection of the soul in the life hereafter. Christ descended into hell for our sins and then ascended into heaven — I believed all of that then. It simply had nothing to do with how I felt.

"You may wonder how a peasant girl tells a village priest that she loves him. I asked him what someone should do who is in love with a man who does not know of her feelings and cannot respond to her. He looked at me for a long and thoughtful time and said, 'Cannot respond.' Then he reached over and put his hand on the side of my face. That is how it all began. A hand touching my cheek and neck, and then a man bending over to put his mouth on mine.

"Love. I told my daughter just last week that there is no high like love, nothing that can match romantic love even when the cultural context provides no label for this phenomenon." Lupe leans back and seems to stifle a laugh. "I did not tell my daughter about cultural context. And I certainly did not know about historical limits back then. I only knew, experienced that sweet fusion of physical and emotional that can steal your identity, remake you into something else. Substance into air, bread into flesh, darkness into light.

"Our lovemaking was tentative at first." Lupe pauses. She still feels lightheaded from the wine but some memories are private even to the inebriated. She remembers but cannot describe to the others the sessions that followed their first knowledge of each other's bodies. The times when she would lean back against the blanket and put her hands behind her head, inviting her lover's deliberate advances and he would knead and stroke her body, relentlessly probing tips and crevices until she entered a deep lassitude that would be broken only with sharp spasms of pleasure.

"Our concentration on the particulars was complete. We washed away every abstract thought, every principle of conduct, in those sessions. Human love is physical, remember, not at all like the sentiments of divine love. We were trading off loves, abandoning the love of Christ for couplings that became so intense . . ."

Lupe looks up and smiles directly into the camera, as if there were a camera, with a look of affectionate dismay at the company of friends who are utterly silent and unmoving.

"You tell a hell of a story," David tells her.

"Not through yet." Lupe sips from her coffee. "Ugh. Cold."

Frank starts to get up but stops when Lupe waves him back to his seat. She is not about to break this spell she has cast.

"The descent into time that revealed this past life was quite an experience. It was like sliding underwater with your eyes open. The landscape changes, but so do one's perceptions. Light is refracted in different ways, everything seems to be on the other side of a clear fluid. Then, when I fell in love, or saw myself in the other life fall in love, my lover's face became doubly blurred, like Plato's depiction of poetry as twice removed from reality. I remember my lover's eyes as radiant, however, in the luminous way that eyes are filmed in some movie scenes today." Lupe laughs briefly. "Cinematic eyes.

"The knowing is the hardest part to describe. I was that girl living in the early nineteenth century, and I am the woman you see now. No—she was not like the picture all of you have conjured here in your thoughts. Admit it—a thin, graceful creature, something along the lines of Audrey Hepburn. I was strong, with the muscular legs of a dancer. My skin and hair were dark. My eyes were striking, black, I think, and perhaps cunning. I saw that physical form in mirrors. That form was my expression then, as this form—the physical individual you see here, at this dining room table—is my expression now. Yes—souls must be the locus of identity for this observation to work. But I accepted the existence of souls in both lives, and must now believe in the existence of my soul in order to tell you this story of multiple lives for the same individual.

"The story of love I am relating to you could have no happy ending. Miguel and I were anomalies, sexual outlaws of the worst sort. It was also impossible to keep that kind of secret in a small village. Our absences began to be noted. When we were together it did not matter. Nothing mattered. We were sealed off from everything, everyone. But it became increasingly difficult to find a place where we could be together. The countryside was exciting—there is nothing to compare with lovemaking away from shelter—but dangerous. Spectators are possibilities. We honestly did not know if we were being observed or not. I did not care during the moments we had. Miguel—I don't know. Sometimes I think he was excited at the possibility that we were in the vision of another. But when we returned, and especially when we were apart, the risks grew in our thoughts and became almost unbearable.

"Once we went to Córdoba together. It was only a three-hour ride in one of our horse-drawn carts. We left before dawn. We saw the farm workers waiting at the sides of the roads to be picked up in wagons that would take them to the fields for the day's work. They held their lunches in white cloth bags. Skins filled with water, some with wine, were attached to their bodies with leather belts. The sun at first deepened the grays and blacks with first light filtered across the rocky landscape, making the waiting figures shadows if you looked east. And then the morning light was illuminating the land and the people with a brightness I have never seen since.

"We had a meal together in a small bodega set off the street in an Arabic courtyard. The floor was covered with blue and white tiles. Vines and plants were everywhere. It was cool inside, the air a moist contrast to the desert heat of the city at mid-day. Miguel wore a floppy white hat and a faded light blue coat to conceal his clerical identity. He looked like a friendly scarecrow. I remember that the bodega had many arches—over the doorways, the windows, the partitions separating the dining areas. There was no breeze, nothing, the air was absolutely still. The only sounds were the quiet movements of cutlery on glass plates as the few other patrons ate lunch and the voices of the waiters as they described the day's options in muted voices. A man, I would guess the dueño of the restaurant, sat against the far wall reading a book and glancing at the customers from time to time. Soon after we ordered, a large dog, obviously with ownership privileges in the bodega, came over and lay down under our table at our feet. Miguel smiled and rubbed the dog's neck and ears.

"We talked about possible futures. Miguel could leave the Church and find a job somewhere. We could live together, eventually marry. But we knew even as we talked that these scenarios were impossible. They were only stories that we were telling to one another to avoid the reality of our lives, our fate. This was nineteenth-century Spain, remember, not a modern liberal democracy with a market economy. We were fixed in status, without any important freedom of movement. Miguel was a priest in the Catholic Church. I was obligated to my mother and family. Such were the controlling facts in our lives, the subtext in our conversation. Only gypsies and outlaws could travel with impunity. We were both, in a way, but also we were neither in spite of our actions and the vague travels required by my father's business.

"I do not remember the conclusion of our conversation, nor the end of our lunch. I recall my life episodically from this point on, with gaps, stretches of time missing in that last long day. We returned to the streets of Córdoba, I know that, walking together again. We came upon the orange trees surrounding the mosque in the city. I know that we went inside the mosque, but first to the courtyard where the pools and fountains are located, and then to the tower that overlooks the surrounding plains and the streets of the city. We climbed to the top of the tower, arm and arm where possible on the long circular wooden stairway to the highest platform. I remember seeing the tiled roofs of the houses below collected in a kind of mosaic arranged like an elevated floor. When we came down and entered the mosque, a woman was standing at the entrance. She had a shawl over her hair and a single red flower on her blouse. A long and stiff linen cloth with ornate lining was draped from ceiling to floor along one of the walls.

"Inside we walked slowly among the columns and arches, looking in silence at the red and white stripes painted on the stone. A kind of mist obscured the far end of the mosque. Some individuals were praying quietly against the walls. In the middle of this structure we saw the Christian chapel with spires stretching up to the highest parts of the ceiling, a slice of Christianity in the midst of an Islamic shrine. Reaching for a transcendent God in a Muslim tent. I remember the ornamental altars in the cathedral, the smell of incense, the bells, the icons, the detailed architecture signaling the return of Christianity to southern Spain. It was a story my parents had been telling and re-telling since I was a child. Then, not stressed much in the stories, the lateral space of the mosque itself, its flat expansiveness across the sacred earth. And the suggestion presented by the mosque itself that some Islamic practices were still in place in parts of Andalucía.

"Outside we walked back across the courtyard. A vendor had somehow gained entrance to the grounds. He wanted Miguel to buy some cured animal skins. We had no money since paying the bill at the bodega, not even for the beggars outside the entrance in the street. One was a boy, blind in one eye. I gave him my scarf."

Lupe leans back in her chair and shuts her eyes briefly. "The rest of the story, of our lives, is not pleasant. I do not enjoy telling this part of it." She sits up and looks at Frank Perry. "A crowd was waiting for us when we returned to our village. Miguel had put on his clerical vestments during the trip back home. But it made no difference. We had been found out as lovers. Someone had seen us, reported us to Miguel's superiors in the Church with those graphic descriptions only the morally offended can draw up. I know—several in the crowd shouted these descriptions at us. To them, and also to us, we were worse than adulterers. We had been unfaithful to God, and indifferent to the vows Miguel had taken. We did not try to flee. It would have been pointless.

"The explosion of violence is silent in my memory. The only sensations I recall are those of sight and touch. I do not even recall fear, though I know we both must have been terrified. I am an observer now, watching two young people come to a tragic end. I was pulled by my hair down the street to a pit at the edge of the village. My clothes were torn, there was blood coming from my mouth and eyes. I was thrown down into this pit next to Miguel. Then the objects—stones, chunks of mud, limbs from trees, bricks—began hitting us. Jarring sensations rather than pain, the heavier objects progressively crushing our skin and bones. The pressure, then the darkness and the last sounds of breathing. Then—nothing."

Lupe looks around. "Then—here I am. Here and now in a different life."

Silence is required after such a story, and silence has followed Lupe's performance. The clinical psychologist, the hostess, is the first to speak. "Quite a tale. I feel breathless."

More silence follows.

Frank Perry is the next to speak. "More coffee for anyone?"

"I could use some cognac." It is David's request.

"Done." Frank gets up and goes into the kitchen where he keeps his liquors. He returns with several cognac glasses that he proceeds to fill. "For anyone in need," he announces.

Now the group is silent again. The only sounds are the shifting movements of bodies, soft rustling of clothes, glasses gently scraping across the table top, as individuals take the offered cognac into their hands. These may be sounds like those heard in the Córdoba bodega where the two young lovers shared a last meal.

"You did not descend to hell." Mark Hiller, Lupe's husband, has made the observation. He is staring at her.

"No," Lupe answers. "Or if I did it was brief as historical time goes. And I have no memory of it. I was there, living in that village, and then I am here in this life."

"It cannot be hell if it's limited in time."

"True," Lupe responds.

Frank groans. Lupe looks at him smiling. "What?" She pats his arm.

"I am in a state of unrequited questioning."

"Then ask," Lupe says. "Ask. Ask."

"What is the you that has survived across two lives? Maybe more, if the account is true. And what is the mechanism that makes it all possible?"

"Frank. I am the one that has survived. Who has survived. That same sense of self that you feel across sleep and waking moments. The self that moves from one point to another on the earth, that survives modestly over time. Where is the mystery? Not here. Elsewhere."

Silence again.

"I do not believe it," Frank says.

"The obligatory response. But we cannot believe or disbelieve, Frank. We cannot know enough for that. It's not in the cards for us to know."

The conversation continues, deepens, raises and disentangles the expected issues. But nothing conclusive occurs. No transformations, revelations, conversions. The members of the dinner party use words, talk, arrange arguments and evidence. Verbal meanings stretched across language.

Each member of the conversation game is trying in different ways to map the thoughts, actions, lives of Lupe's story so that the line she has drawn through past, present, future will connect all the parts in the told experience. It is a puzzling exercise, since to accept any part of Lupe's story as true requires that most of the other parts be accepted as well. But then large sections of conventional material reality, attested to by the canons of contemporary science, would have to be abandoned. No one wants to accept any of the alternatives that seem to be offered by the discourses at hand.

"I am getting into major distress here." The speaker is Paul Lorca, the anthropology professor.

"It's my fault. My story." Lupe raises a glass in a mock toast.

"Blame Lupe. Lupe." Paul seems to be trying out her name in a Gregorian undertone.

Lupe does not seem to be listening. She is a part of what dinner party hosts call a thoughtful silence.

past lives and reincarnations

RETURNING FROM THE DEAD

Death, curiously enough, is often presented in art as a woman. Throughout the film *All That Jazz*, Jessica Lange portrays death as Angelique (the Angel of Death), a lovely blonde woman dressed in white chiffon and bantering with the main character, Joe Gideon (Roy Scheider), as he slides toward death after a heart attack. Near the end of Giuseppe di Lampedusa's novel *The Leopard*, the deathbed room of the Prince of Salina, Don Fabrizio, is filled with family and friends. Almost everyone is weeping; even his nephew, Tancredi, is overcome. Then, at the back of the room a young woman appears and starts making her way through the group to his bed. She is

slim, in brown traveling dress and wide bustle, with a straw hat trimmed by a speckled veil which could not hide the sly charm of her face. She slid a little suede-gloved hand between one elbow and another of the weeping kneelers, apologized, drew closer. It was she, the creature ever yearned for, coming to fetch him; strange that one so young should yield to him; the time for the train's departure must be very close. When she was face to face with him she raised her veil, and there, modest but ready to be possessed, she looked lovelier than she ever had when glimpsed in stellar space.

But these images and stories tell us little about the time after death. We do not see the prince again in *The Leopard* after he dies, and in Roy Scheider's last scene in *All That Jazz* he is being zipped up in a transparent body bag. Are there journeys that we can enter after death that will take us around to another beginning? Are there powers that can overcome death with an extension into another life on earth?

Summoning powers from another world to perform magic and overcome the strictures of natural laws is one of the most common spectacles in human history. Of all the tricks attempted, the most fantastic has been turning death into life. Resurrection stories are among the more dramatic renditions of this event, an extraordinary exhibition of supernatural powers, a reversal of time and natural laws at the most fundamental levels, a redefinition of a whole life. The story of Lazarus of Bethany, for example, has become a legend in virtually all languages and cultures. The historical Lazarus was the brother of Martha of Bethany and Mary Magdalen, a disciple of Jesus Christ and, on later accounts, one of Christ's most esteemed apostles and close intellectual confidants. In the biblical story Lazarus becomes ill, probably in the late fall or early winter of the year preceding the crucifixion of Christ, and is cared for by his sisters. They notify Jesus that their brother, a man he loves, is sick. He tells them that the illness is not grave, certainly not fatal, and remains another two days outside Judea. But Lazarus dies during those days. Christ relays to his disciples the news that Lazarus is dead and suggests to them that they all return to Judea. They warn him of the increased hostility from the Jews and the risks he will incur if he goes back. But he does go to Jerusalem, only fifteen furlongs (less than two miles) from Bethany. Martha goes to meet him in her grief and tells him that had he been present Lazarus would not have died. He tells her that her brother will awaken from his sleep. By this time Lazarus has been entombed for four days.

When taken to the tomb where Lazarus lies, a cave with a stone in front of it, Jesus instructs those with him to take away the stone. Martha warns him that her brother will "stinketh" since he has been dead for four days. But Jesus reminds her of the powers of belief and faith, he prays briefly, and then he says in a loud voice, "Lazarus, come forth." Lazarus does come forth, his feet and hands bound, his face covered with a cloth. Jesus tells those witnessing the event to free him from his bindings and let him go, which they do. The miracle is witnessed by any number of people, some of whom are convinced by the event and convert to the mission of Christ. Others report the event to the Pharisees and to the high priests; both of these groups begin to talk about putting Jesus to death. The resurrection of Lazarus is generally conceded to be the event that eventually leads to the arrest and crucifixion of Christ.

Little is known with certainty about the historical Lazarus, either before or after the miracle, and of course there is much dispute over whether the resurrection occurred at all. On some accounts Lazarus fled the area after the crucifixion, traveling to Cyprus where he became a bishop in the church and lived another thirty years. The resurrection narrative, however, has been the imaginative source for a variety of interpretations and retellings. Thom Gunn, for example, has written a poem, "Lazarus Not Raised," in which Lazarus is a reluctant participant, not much interested in returning to life. In *Crime and Punishment* Dostoevsky has Raskolnikov visit a casual friend, Sonia, after he has killed both an old woman and a young relative of hers who unluckily comes upon the scene at the moment of the first murder. He asks Sonia to find and read to him the parable of Lazarus. She does so reluctantly and with barely controlled emotion. Raskolnikov seems to use this passage in the Bible to bid Sonia farewell as he continues on the journey to turn himself in for the murders. Dostoevsky also reprises the story of Lazarus in "The Grand Inquisitor" section of *The Brothers Karamazov*. Again, the catalytic event in the persecution of Christ is his intervention in death, once more bringing someone back from the dead, in this case a dead child of seven whose cortege passes him in the street. This event is witnessed by a religious authority, the cardinal, and on his signal the guards arrest Christ. In both cases, the biblical parable of Lazarus and the story imagined by Dostoevsky, there is never any doubt about the validity of the resurrection. It is just that the religious authorities in both worlds cannot countenance a wild card messiah who has supernatural powers of the highest order. The Grand Inquisitor enters the jail cell and explains to the Christ figure in front of him that he knows he is the real thing, the Second Coming, but the Church neither needs nor can tolerate his return. The established Church cannot accommodate the real messiah. Throughout the entire discourse by the Grand Inquisitor Christ is silent. It is a delicious story that tracks the boundaries and hostilities between the conventional and the supernatural in religious discourses.

Shakespeare was cautious about assigning magical powers to humans, probably represented in the skepticism voiced by Hotspur in *Henry IV*. In a famous exchange, when Glendower declares that he can call spirits from the "vasty deep," Hotspur replies, "Why, so can I, or so can any man; But will they come when you do call for them?" There are witches, ghosts, fairies, even Puck as a singular presence hovering (leaping, really) between the human and the extra-human world of fairies and other magical creatures in *A Midsummer Night's Dream*. But only a limited number of supernatural powers are given to humans throughout Shakespeare's oeuvre: precognition (the soothsayer in *Julius Caesar*), psychokinesis, of which there are only a few instances (Prospero conjuring a storm in *The Tempest*), and ambiguous events in the possible realms of the supernatural, such as the uncertainty over whether Paulina actually brings the statue of Hermione to life in the last scene of *The Winter's Tale* (or is the statue just the live Hermione in disguised still life and so proof that she never really died—my favored interpretation), and, yes, a doctor becoming a kind of indirect shaman in *Pericles* when he attends to a dead woman who returns to life. The doctor, Cerimon, instructs two gentlemen to open a chest thrown upon the shore from a ship. They comment on the odor from the chest—"it smells most sweetly in my sense," "a delicate odour"—and realize when they read the note in it from King Pericles describing the dead woman within the chest as the deceased queen that the container is a coffin. But the body looks fresh. Cerimon instructs the servants to build a fire so that "yet the fire of life kindle again." The fire and cloths, the music "rough and woeful," do the trick. The queen moves: "nature awakes; a warmth breathes out of her," her eyelids stir, she revives and begins to talk: "Where am I? Where's my lord? What world is this?"

The purist will note that the doctor technically does not perform a resurrection miracle since the queen seems to accomplish a revival all on her own with only minimal assistance. But the questions she asks upon awakening are the expected ones in a resurrection, especially "Where am I?" and "What world is this?" All these puzzles and miraculous happenings are artifacts of the definitive standing of death, its irrevocable powers to settle things once and for all. It is a threshold event of the highest order, the profound division between life and the absence of life, at least as it is known and lived within human cultures. James Baldwin once remarked that the United States is a country that knows very little about sex and death. The first item is probably more open and understood now than when he wrote (or perhaps not), though the mysteries of the second are still very much in place and undoubtedly shared as mysterious in all other countries. That is what makes a return from the dead, a life that follows death, so stunning and unsettling and intriguing and contestable.

PAST-LIFE REGRESSION THERAPY

One of the more compelling narratives in reincarnation literatures that yet exhibits the main problems of reincarnation claims is Brian Weiss's *Many Lives, Many Masters*. Weiss is a practicing psychiatrist in Miami, Florida, with all the bona fides of a professional: a graduate of Columbia University and Yale Medical School, and chairman emeritus of psychiatry at the Mount Sinai Medical Center in Miami Beach. His scholarly publications are robust and impressive, and include important early papers in biological psychiatry and substance abuse. He is, in short, a person of considerable gravitas, a respected professional as far removed from New Age speculations as one could find. The story he tells about reincarnation is, by any standards, spectacular, credible, and very moving.

It begins when a twenty-seven-year-old woman, Catherine, comes to his office "seeking help for her anxiety, panic attacks, and phobias." Weiss at first used conventional therapeutic methods on his patient. After eighteen months of intensive psychotherapy, in his words, "nothing seemed to work." Then he tried hypnosis. This worked, but in unexpected ways. In the induced hypnotic trances Catherine retrieved memories of past lives she seemed to have led, and reported on them in some considerable detail. She also was able to channel spirits who provided information on life and death and the nature of an existence across life spans and after death. All this was entirely new and amazing for Weiss. As he relates in his book, "Nothing in my background had prepared me for this." On a more mundane level the past-life regression therapy worked for Catherine and, in a few months, she was able to resume her life free of her symptoms (whose causes, according to Weiss, were in the memories of her past lives).

The hypnotism therapy was preceded and occasioned by an unexpected event. Catherine at the time was in a six-year affair with a married physician, and one day, in spite of her fear of flying, she accompanied him to a medical conference in Chicago. While there they went to an Egyptian exhibit at an art museum. During the guide's description of artifacts Catherine began correcting him. It turned out that she was right even though she had no training or education in Egyptology. It was this inexplicable display of knowledge that led her to agree to a hypnotic session with Weiss that was aimed at retrieving the childhood memories that might be complicit in her anxieties and phobias. She had been reluctant to try hypnotism, but apparently was now also interested in understanding the source of the mysterious knowledge she had displayed in Chicago.

The first regression that Weiss led Catherine through was routine for his profession, and both illuminating and difficult for his patient. As he took her back in time while she was hypnotized a painful experience from the age of three surfaced. She was in her bed one night when her father came into the dark bedroom reeking of alcohol. He began touching her sexually. When she resisted he put his hand over her mouth, impeding her breathing. Reliving this terrifying experience in the hypnotic state Weiss had induced was itself traumatic. She began to sob. Weiss told her to remember all that she had told him. This post-hypnotic suggestion is a routine way of unearthing and dispelling pathological causes, in this case what Weiss thought was the source of the panic attacks she had been having. Catherine woke up and left his office still shaking from the exposed memory. But Weiss was certain that the difficulties of facing the early experience would be more than compensated by the healing that would shortly ensue.

In the session the next week, however, Catherine reported that her "symptoms remained, as severe as ever." Weiss was more than a little perplexed. The point to psychotherapy is to retrieve traumatic experiences that have been repressed, and in revealing them to the conscious self mute their effects. He had helped his patient confront a distressing experience she had as a small child, the likely and even obvious source of her current troubles, and the therapy seemed to have had no beneficial effects. In the words that Weiss used to describe the situation, "Her nightmares were as terrifying as ever." So, like any good psychiatrist, he decided to regress her to an earlier age in the next session of hypnosis. Perhaps there was a traumatic experience before the age of three that was the source of her current troubles.

It was at this second session, while deep in a hypnotic state, that Catherine began talking about, and seemingly from, a previous life. At first her voice slowed and fell to a whisper as she moved back in time, to the age of two. No significant memories appeared. So Weiss instructed her to "go back to the time from which your symptoms arise." It was at this point that Catherine suddenly began describing a scene that could not have been located in an infant's life. In her words, quoted by Weiss from his notes, she saw "a big white building with pillars, open in front." Weiss was confused, not sure what was happening. He asked Catherine what year it was and what her name was. "Aronda," she answered, and she was an eighteen-year-old woman approaching a marketplace. The year, she reported, "is 1863 B.C." Weiss listened to the descriptions Catherine was providing and then asked her to go several years ahead and tell him what she saw. Catherine described herself at twenty-five "wearing a long, coarse brown dress and sandals. I have a child whose name is Cleastra." Weiss was stunned. Catherine's descriptions were vivid, lucid, definite. He simply did not know what to make of them.

In the succeeding months the stories that Catherine related when hypnotized and regressed to a past that preceded her present life were rich with details of happy and sad events, fulfillment and tragedy, and always engrossing in the ways that life stories are when related by a skilled storyteller. Catherine had led many lives before according to her accounts. Several times she described her own death at the end of these lives, by drowning, fire, old age. These events were often stressful experiences followed by a lull, a complete state of relaxation as her body died. Soon she was describing the experiences between lives, a state of being in which higher forms of life began dictating information about the nature of existence. Weiss appeared in Catherine's lives from time to time. Often he was a teacher. "You are old with gray hair. You're wearing a white dress [toga] with gold trim. . . . Your name is Diogenes. You teach us symbols, triangles. You are very wise, but I don't understand. The year is 1568 B.C." Weiss notes in his book that this date is roughly 1,200 years before the famous philosopher Diogenes appears in history, but he is correct in observing that the name was quite common in Greek culture.

CATHERINE'S REVELATIONS

What can we make of such narratives?

The one assumption we might reasonably make as a professional gesture before a critical examination of the work is that Weiss is telling his own story of Catherine in good faith and with integrity. What makes the book a good read is the perspective of the author, a trained professional, a scientist by education and temperament, with a detached gaze at what we assume must have been a riveting and shocking experience for him. The combination of voices is irresistible—Weiss as the dispassionate therapist trying to make sense out of a presentation from a patient utterly at odds with his own take on life and understanding of professional limits, Catherine's voluble and more intense voice rendering an account of serial lives she had presumably led and that were distributed over generous spans of historical time. The key to the credibility issue for the entire rendition is that the stories Catherine told Weiss are presented as memories of some sort. She claims that she did not make them up, was regarded by Weiss as incapable of conjuring such stories out of whole cloth, and so in some still problematic sense, not clearly understood by Catherine or perhaps anyone else, what she described originated in the subconscious state of mind (or brain), or, more contestable, as a derivative of her experiences in the past.

One key finding in Weiss's account is that no pathology, no psychosis, was at issue in these renderings. Catherine came to his office with the anxiety, panic attacks, and phobias that brought her into treatment. But he found no deeper problems, no evidence of schizophrenia or any serious mental disorders in his patient. No auditory or visual hallucinations, no delusions or multiple personalities, no signs of sociopathic or antisocial tendencies. She did not take drugs or hallucinogenic substances and used only minimal amounts of alcohol. She was not an actress. In Weiss's precise language, "There was only one Catherine, and her conscious mind was totally aware of this." The story of reincarnation evolved from a contact between a good and competent psychiatrist and a mentally stable young woman. Further, the telling of her past lives was effective therapy for Catherine. She was freed dramatically from the problems occasioning her decision to undergo therapy. Discovering and relating her past lives were the escape routes from her problems to a full and complete cure.

Weiss believes that the stories Catherine related to him are true. His beliefs predictably follow both evidence and the persuasive force of a good narrative. They have also and understandably transformed his life. The critical evidence, which is fascinating in its standing and acceptance by Weiss, came in a surprising turn in one of the therapy sessions. As a professional therapist Weiss had worked with the traditional stricture that the psychiatrist must be a tabula rasa, a blank slate upon which the patient could write his/her own story. One practical requirement for following that rule is that the physician must tell the patient nothing about his/her own personal life. One entirely private matter for Weiss and his wife was the death of their infant son twenty-three days after he was born. He had an extremely rare heart defect at birth, an incorrect and fatal routing of the pulmonary veins. They entered the heart on the wrong side, "as if the heart were turned around, backward." It was the death of his son that convinced Weiss to go into psychiatry instead of internal medicine, simply because he was angry that modern medicine had been unable to save the tiny baby that was his son. Another private matter was the sudden and unexpected death of Weiss's father from a massive heart attack at the age of sixty-one. His father's Hebrew name was Avrom. Weiss and his wife named their daughter, born four months after his father's death, after him. Her name is Amy.

Catherine began describing a scene in which she was a servant. In the course of the session she reported pain in her chest, difficulties in breathing, and later her own quiet death. Then she entered a different life where people were dying from the waters that they bathed in and drank. In that land, barren and dry, she also died, this time floating above her body after her death. Then something dramatic happened in the session. Catherine began speaking in the husky voice that indicated a "between-lives" existence. What she said in that provisional state of being stunned Weiss. She described the presence of his father and son, telling Weiss that his father says that his name is Avrom, that "his death was due to his heart," and that Weiss's daughter was named after him. Then she said that his son had also died from a heart problem, that the heart "was backward, like a chicken's." And that his death was a great sacrifice to show him, Weiss, that "medicine could only go so far, that its scope is very limited." Then she stopped speaking. Weiss was stunned by these revelations. More than anything else they convinced him that Catherine's experience was genuine and her stories authentic.

I cite these passages from the book because they are critical to establishing for Weiss, and for the reader, the authenticity of Catherine's stories. Weiss maintains that it was impossible for Catherine to have known in any way these private facts about his life. As he put it, "There was no place even to look it up." After these revelations Weiss took the session in a different direction. He asked Catherine who was there, who was telling her these things. "The Masters," she replied. "The Master Spirits tell me. They tell me I have lived eighty-six times in a physical state." The information, in short, was both compelling and introduced another dimension to the therapy sessions. Catherine could channel higher forms of life that had access to privileged information about the nature of existence. The story itself was now a source of its own authenticity in providing insights into the possibilities of an existence beyond temporal life.

Though Weiss's report of Catherine tends to elicit awe and respect from his readers, it is possible to raise questions about both the evidence for her past lives and the account she provides of advanced beings who describe a higher and more expansive reality. Small breaks in perspective leave one uneasy. For example, Catherine cites, presumably from the knowledge base of her past lives, the dates of her experiences. In one of her sessions, for example, she says that the year is 1568 B.C. But of course no one living at that time could have known the year B.C. (before Christ) since the birth of Christ was still in the future. Yes, Catherine could be a bifurcated self in the session, both living in the past and reporting from the present. But unless she has entered that past life, absorbed completely by it apart from her present life, and is living and thinking and speaking as each of the particular women in the past (which is the way she presents herself in the sessions), she could not have known exactly how she was living a particular life and who she was in that past life. In other words, if she is truly located at a time so distant in the past, then she could not have known that she was living in a time *before* Christ. One would have expected her to provide a different dating system than one that originates much later in history.

Then there is the delicate issue of access to information about Weiss's life. Catherine was a laboratory technician in the hospital where Weiss was chief of psychiatry. She was having an affair with a married physician, "a successful physician, strong and aggressive." Eleven years before the critical therapy session in which Catherine related the private information that Weiss maintains she could not have obtained, the son with the defective and fatal heart condition was born. Weiss's father died two years before that. These events, which Weiss regarded as confidential, were in some sense public events. Medical records on his son would have to be part of a medical history filed away in cabinets (not, at the time, in computers). The death of anyone's father must be recorded in a death certificate. In principle, medical records (though not death certificates or notices) are private and confidential. But anyone who worked in a hospital in the years before the stricter Health Information Privacy statutes and rules (HIPAA) were in place knows how porous that system was prior to 2003 (and most concede that information still leaks even with the best efforts to ensure privacy). Doctors, nurses, respiratory and physical therapists, pharmaceutical representatives, medical students, social workers—the list of individuals parading through even the best hospitals and medical centers would surprise the most jaded observers. The question is open, not closed: could Catherine have gained access to the information that clinched Weiss's belief in her credibility? Could she, as a laboratory technician employed by the hospital, or through the physician with whom she was having an affair, have secured confidential information on Weiss's father, daughter, and son?

Even if the possibility is remote, it is still a possibility. It is simply not clear what Weiss means when he says that "there was no place even to look it up." Of course medical records can be looked up, copied. There is no easy way to pursue this possibility of access and fraud, nor should there be. But it is imperative to look carefully at the evidence for claims that, when accepted as true, rearrange the basic configurations of reality. The narrative Weiss presents to us does exactly that. If it is true, then we are occupants in a life that is sequential in the extreme, permitting us to live and live again across vast stretches of time while absorbing lessons that might take us to higher realms of existence. In 1917 two young girls in England, ten and sixteen years old, presented to the world a proof—in the form of photographs—of fairies. The Cottingley fairies (as they came to be called) were accepted as genuine by notable individuals, including Arthur Conan Doyle (creator of the most famous fictional detective, for God's sake, of all time). Yet the photographs were rigged, taken of cutouts stuck on hatpins by overly imaginative girls. It goes without saying that there is no room for the type of spectacle represented by the Cottingley fairies in an examination of life after death. Every skeptical possibility must be pursued, no matter how offensive to the believer or (in this case especially) the author.

Now, having said all that, the chances of this kind of fraud are exceedingly remote in this instance. But it is also important to note that there is no hard evidence for Weiss's account other than Weiss. It is a wonderful and credible narrative presented by an individual with solid credentials. It is a narrative, however, and though drawn from a seemingly impeccable source, it must be taken on faith. Confirming evidence is wholly within the story, and largely internal to the doctor-patient relationship.

PAST LIVES

Ian Stevenson's work presents a different kind of evidence for reincarnation. Actually, he presents three types of supportive evidence. One consists of testimony from children who say they have led a previous life. A second is a range of inexplicable phenomena regarded by Stevenson and his team of researchers as explainable only on the assumption that the individual has led a previous life. The principal version of this evidence is a child speaking a language that s/he has not heard before but was spoken by the individual the child claims to have been in a former life. Still another type of evidence is the correspondence between birthmarks on the bodies of the children who recall a former life and injuries to the deceased individuals they claim to have been.

In one case a ten-year-old boy named Nirmal died in 1950 of smallpox in the town of Kosi Kalan in India. The next year, in August 1951 in the town of Chhatta, India, a boy named Prakash was born. At the age of four and a half Prakash started saying that his name was Nirmal, and that he belonged in Kosi Kalan with his real family. When taken (at his constant insistence) to Kosi Kalan he had vivid memories of a childhood there, recalling the names of Nirmal's relatives and friends and other details of that life. He began running away from his Chhatta parents to return to Kosi Kalan, with his Chhatta father beating him each time he was returned and commanding him to forget about Kosi Kalan. Stevenson could find no evidence that the two families had ever met before the initial contact of Prakash's first visit.

In another case, Victor Vincent, a full-blooded Tlingit who lived in Angloon, a city in Alaska, and died there in the spring of 1946, told his niece (with whom he was especially close) about a year before his death that he was coming back as her next son. He also said that the boy would have scars corresponding to two operations that he, Victor, had had and that he showed her: one on his back and the other on the right side of the base of his nose. Eighteen months after Victor's death his niece gave birth to a boy, Corliss Chotkin, named after her husband, the boy's father.

Let Stevenson's words describe the phenomenon: "At birth this boy had two marks on his body of exactly the same shape and location as the scars pointed to by Victor Vincent in his prediction of his rebirth." Corliss Chotkin also seemed to have many of the same memories as Vincent. For example, at the age of thirteen months Corliss said to his mother, "Don't you know me? I'm Kahkody." Kahkody was the tribal name of Victor Vincent, and the child uttered the two sentences with a letter-perfect Tlingit accent, as Vincent himself would have. A series of recognitions occurred as the boy aged—at two, on seeing the grown son of Victor Vincent, saying, "There is William, my son." Then, also at the age of two, Corliss recognized many of Vincent's relatives and friends, including a stepdaughter of Vincent whom Corliss called correctly by her name, Susie. At the age of three Corliss recognized the widow of Victor Vincent, saying at a crowded gathering, "There's the old lady. There's Rose." The "old lady" designation and the name "Rose" were exactly the language that Vincent had used in referring to and addressing his wife. The list of recognitions goes on, with impressive effects. Stevenson offered these two cases, Prakash and Corliss Chotkin, among his many case studies as contributing to a proof of reincarnation.

In general, these indications of a life before and after death are crafted on three different types of evidence. One is the often vibrant descriptions of the near-death experience (NDE) recounted by those who have "died" and then returned to ordinary life. The NDE is a first-person narrative that presents an experience the subject claims to have had while near death. Its special prominence and importance derive from the fact that it is a direct account of a life that is presumably to begin immediately after dying provided by the one who has briefly experienced that life. It depends (as all first-person accounts do) on memory occasionally supported with harder evidence (such as confirmed reports from the momentarily deceased individual of what the doctors and nurses are doing while s/he is unconscious or clinically dead). A second consists of the reports of observers near or at the scene of a death experience. This evidence is in the form of third-person renditions that complement (or contradict) the first-person accounts provided by a subject of the experience. This type of evidence is crucial in establishing the conditions that validate the death experience with clinical or informal testing of the body of the individual experiencing a form of death. It tells us, in short, whether the subject's vital signs suggest an altered physical state correlating with and warranting the first-person account. It is also helpful in providing information on the attitudes and, in general, states of mind of those about to die and the relevant details of the death.

The third type of evidence is more nearly physical. Here I would count as illustrative the evidence gathered by Stevenson on a continuity of wounds from the body of an individual who has died to birthmarks on a living individual claiming to be the deceased individual in a former life. This latter type of evidence is at once the most and least reliable evidence that we have for that type of survival of death known as reincarnation. It is most reliable in being physical and so escaping the notorious fallibility of memory and eyewitness accounts (a fallibility limited in the controlled settings of, say, emergency rooms and other clinical units in hospitals). It is least reliable in its enigmatic status. What does evidence like continuity of physical marks across different lives tell us about life after death? If reliable it suggests that the afterlife experience is yet another physical life, in all important respects like the one we are living in our own present states, and not at all the spiritual existence indicated in all forms of the NDE. The first question is obvious: How do we explain the differences between reincarnation and near-death experiences? But physical evidence for reincarnation also shares the mystery found in all evidence that we take as valid indicators for life after death. Even if the evidence is compelling, what is the mechanism that explains the phenomenon of survival? What laws or principles explain the events, or at least make them intelligible in human terms? Also, *why* would we have a life after death, and how does this possibility affect our understanding of the universe in which we live and the meaning of our lives in the temporal world?

The first thing to note is that Stevenson had a list of nearly six hundred cases worldwide suggestive of reincarnation, a third of which he and his assistants personally investigated. Roughly 250 are considered strong cases. The second is that Stevenson and his team were sensitive to methodological standards and took pains to ensure that controls were in place in their investigations. The unlearned languages, for example, were taped and examined to ensure that they were not gibberish and did in fact indicate at least a practical mastery (at a child's level) of the language in question. Interviews were repeated for verification, a written record was kept and published, and demarcations between the certain and the uncertain in data collection were codified and published. The weaknesses in cases are identified in Stevenson's work. Even the most skeptical critics concede that Stevenson was a researcher of integrity (though several have asserted that biases he did not recognize influenced and sometimes compromised his work).

Again, as with Dr. Weiss, the principal investigator was not a New Age guru driven by intuitions but an acknowledged professional engaged in research that is respectable by any standards. Stevenson attended St. Andrews University in Scotland, graduated with a bachelor of science degree from McGill University in Canada, and earned the M.D., C.M. degree (Doctor of Medicine and Master of Surgery) that McGill awards to all graduates of its medical school. For most of his medical career he was at the University of Virginia in Charlottesville. He joined the UVA faculty in 1957 as professor and chair of the Department of Psychiatry. In 1967 he resigned from the department and founded the university's Division of Personality Studies, assuming the posts of both director and the Carlson Professor of Psychiatric Medicine, which he held until 2001. In 2002 he became Research Professor of Psychiatry at UVA. Board certified in both psychiatry and neurology, he devoted most of his professional life to the study of evidence for reincarnation. Stevenson's research interests were primarily children who claim to remember previous lives, but he also did research on near-death experiences, apparitions (deathbed visions), mind-brain problems, and survival of the human personality after death.

Stevenson's most compelling cases of reincarnation in children are generally drawn from cultures dense with beliefs in reincarnation. One aspect of this fact is that the individuals themselves are not surprised by the findings. But the effects of culture cut even deeper. One should not be shocked that events are expressed in the verbal and even symbolic apparatus of the cultures in which they occur. How could it be otherwise? Culturally influenced beliefs also can affect the logic or pattern of the reincarnations Stevenson identifies. For example, if a culture does not contain beliefs in a provisional place individuals occupy between lives, a gap between a former life and a reincarnated life, there are fewer intervals reported by those claiming previous lives (such as the in-between world described by Catherine in Weiss's regression therapies).

Cultural influences are not deal breakers, however. Of course there will be a greater number of reports on reincarnation in cultures that accept such experiences; conversely, phenomena widely regarded in a culture as deviant or false can be expected to be under-reported, even repressed. Perhaps also the memories of these experiences and the dissonances they create are manifested as some kind of pathology—schizophrenia, for instance. Or sent to the overflowing Western trash bin of "unexplained" phenomena. On balance, cultural influences do not invalidate past-lives memories when they do occur and are reported, even as the frequency of reports on these phenomena are augmented or diminished by cultural settings. Put more directly, if reincarnation does in fact occur, the fact that it tracks and is influenced by cultural patterns in its manifestations is neither an undermining nor (especially) a falsifying phenomenon. Suppose, for example, that certain postmodern paintings are created predominantly by males in culture x, and by females in culture y. This cultural variation might speak to gender bias in each of the cultures (perhaps females are excluded from art instructions in x, males excluded in y), but the reality of the postmodern paintings is not called into question by the fact of cultural variations in their manifestations. At least the skeptical take on reincarnation has to wait on the particular explanations for the variations to see if the variations matter in settling the authenticity of the events.

What is it that makes a case a strong case for reincarnation? First, since Stevenson's research relied on testimony by the family and friends of the child claiming a past life, consistency of story lines and convergence of evidence in the testimonies are indicators of a strong case. What Stevenson sought is what every researcher seeks: a good narrative with an unbroken and plausible report of events. Second, a strong case would indicate little incentive for fraud among those presenting the evidence. Stevenson generally believed that the standards for genuine reports, for truth telling, were usually met. He reported that few if any families benefited financially from their reincarnation claims and more than a few found the publicity surrounding the reports of their experiences "vexing." Third, a strong case would have eliminated the possibility of what Stevenson calls "cryptomnesia," by which he means those instances of a child "remembering" information about a previous life that the child acquired from a person or source in this life with the information.

Stevenson did not present cryptomnesia as fraud since the information may have become available innocently in casual conversations, and the child claiming a past life may simply forget the source of the information and actually believe that it came from a previous life. But, though Stevenson regarded cryptomnesia in general as more likely than fraud, he minimizes its importance, for several reasons. One, a young child unable to read in the rustic setting of, say, village life in India, would have to acquire the relevant information from a person, not a newspaper, magazine, radio, or television. But, unless there is fraud, the information acquired in a conversational setting would be scant when compared to that possessed by the children describing former lives in Stevenson's research. Two, one of the most powerful types of evidence in reincarnation cases is the recognition of places and people from the former life. The children cited by Stevenson could pick out the family members and sites (houses, schools, rooms, streets) filling out the former life. Since recognition is one of the deeper and more complex of human experiences, and definitely relies on forms of tacit knowledge, it is unlikely that it could be established from verbal accounts or even from photographs. A strong case would rule out transmitted information from others, but Stevenson was certain that this experience could not account for the reported identifications of persons and sites in the claimed former life. It is telling that Stevenson did not dismiss cryptomnesia, and in fact conceded that it could explain away some of his cases. But, though he did not find an ideal model for cryptomnesia, when he looked at actual cases of the phenomenon he asserted that they did not resemble the rebirth cases he had accepted as genuine.

Finally, and as a compendium of criteria, most of the strong cases in the Stevenson inventory would have been investigated by him or his team personally, "soon after the main events of the case occurred," and be rich in detail and/or presenting very plausible accounts from many witnesses. Also, the evidence would be arrayed along multiple variables, such as vivid and accurate memories, the child's command of a language not spoken or read in his/her home but associated with the deceased person supposedly reincarnated, identification of key events and persons in the former life, and/or physical evidence of continuities across lives. Conversely, a weak case along these dimensions would be one that is investigated and presented by others, explored only after some time has passed, is weak on detail with testimony from few witnesses, and rests on evidence along a small number of variables, as indicated by, say, weak or uncertain memories or unreliable or no identifications of past life markers (persons, sites, events). Also, a weak case usually contains no physical evidence.

Stevenson's evidence for reincarnation is both stunning and often inexplicable. The example of Victor Vincent and Corliss Chotkin is illustrative. The recognition reports are impressive. But the physical evidence is even more dramatic. Again: Corliss Chotkin was born with birthmarks that seemed identical to scars on the body of Victor Vincent. One mark at the base of Corliss's nose was reddish, though slowly over the years it lost much of its pigmentation while still maintaining its depression. The other mark was on Corliss's back, "about eight inches below the shoulder line and two inches to the right of the midline. It was heavily pigmented and raised. It extended about one inch in length and a quarter inch in width." One salient characteristic of the birthmark was that it had several small round marks outside the main line, "lined up like the stitch wounds of surgical operations." The two birthmarks were located in the precise spots corresponding to the areas on Vincent's body where he had two surgical scars from operations, and the contours of the birthmarks corresponded to the physical features of the scars.

Stevenson devoted almost his entire professional life to securing evidence for reincarnation. The corpus of work is by any standards impressive, extensive, and carefully obtained and presented. Any study of reincarnation must begin with Stevenson's research findings. But the work also raises questions, some about methods, others about the implications of the evidence for establishing exactly its main subject: the reality of reincarnation as a human experience.

The first set of issues on methods is easy to state but difficult to adjudicate. These are what might be called the low-level challenges that can be made of almost any work in cultural anthropology. Stevenson worked almost exclusively in cultures remote from his own, primarily in the countries of India, Ceylon, Brazil, parts of Alaska (the Tlingit Indians), and Lebanon. He professed fluency in English, French, and German but not in any of the indigenous languages spoken by his research subjects, such as Arabic or Hindi, or any other South Asian vernacular language, nor in Tlingit or Portuguese. Though many of his subjects also spoke English as a secondary or tertiary language, he had to rely in many cases on translators. It is yet another indication of Stevenson's integrity that he addressed the problems of "undesirable influences by interpreters . . . in some of the cases in India, Ceylon, and Lebanon." But it is the research distances that are important here, not the unfortunate instances of interpreter creativity.

The bulk of Stevenson's research data consists of testimonials, reports of children claiming privileged knowledge, uncanny recognitions. In no cases, of course, did Stevenson have direct access to the experiences described. His evidence is secondary evidence filtered through his own interpretive apparatus. For example, he used behavioral and personality theory developed in the West to assess the validity of witnesses and subjects. This is cultural anthropology from the outside in, without the prolonged experiences of participant observation studies, noted most vividly in the depictions of anthropologists living in a culture, absorbing its language and practices, seeing it from the inside out. Stevenson was a visitor in the cultures he studied, and his studies are oriented to a narrow slice of these cultures, essentially a set of discrete cases. This is not to say that his methods are fatally flawed, but the meanings of the terms and events at issue are naturally indigenous. A situated understanding of even the key experience, "reincarnation," is elusive in any approach crafted at such a distance from ordinary life. Or, put bluntly, what Stevenson means by reincarnation and what his subjects meant by it might not be identical. The same may be true of any of the terms used in the interview reports, including identification of other persons, memory retrieval in general, self-reference ("I am such-and such"), and so on.

Then there are plausibility issues, which of course are exacerbated by the problem of research distance. Many of the children who claimed to have been reincarnated from a former life were amazingly precocious. Let's revisit Corliss Chotkin, for example: "Don't you know me? I'm Kahkody." This sentence is reported to have been uttered by Corliss (in flawless Tlingit) at the age of thirteen months—an age when most children are not yet speaking in full sentences. Here is the problem. Stevenson tells us that even the best child subjects lose their memories of a former life as they move into late childhood: "About the age of nine, Corliss began to make fewer statements about a previous life." By the time Stevenson saw and interviewed him he was fifteen years old and "remembered nothing of the previous life." This is truly research at a distance. The research material consists of testimony by others of the utterances of a very young subject, and the subject cannot, when more mature and mentally competent to do so, verify the testimony. It is a melancholy polarity. Direct evidence, that provided by the subject, occurs at such an early age that its proof is secondary, meaning it consists of testimony provided by witnesses who know the subject. Nothing later can confirm the memories except follow-up interviews of the same witnesses. This is hearsay evidence in all respects, and it is difficult to see how it can be avoided in studies of the sort that Stevenson undertook.

There is also the issue of what the evidence signifies even if and when it is valid. Stevenson was conscientious about entertaining alternative hypotheses to explain his data. The possibilities of fraud and cryptomnesia, for example, are discussed with care in the cases. This is standard in good critical research. But there is a different set of alternative explanations in this type of research, and their nature makes it exceedingly difficult to sort out the primary explanatory variables. In the simplest sense an adequate explanation of the events Stevenson examines ought to be able to identify causal variables that establish a law-like relationship between evidence and reincarnation. A causal relationship is generally construed as a set of antecedent variables in a sufficient relationship with dependent variables. In this way we explain a variety of physical events by discovering the law-like relationships between the two sets of variables. For example, a hemorrhage of a certain level of severity in macular degeneration causes a loss of sight, in the sense that whenever the severity level is reached there is loss of eyesight. The hemorrhage event is what we mean by a sufficient condition. It yields a law-like connection between antecedent and dependent variables. Necessary conditions are not needed and in fact confuse matters in causal chains. A necessary condition says a certain outcome never occurs without the condition. It is something that must be present for the dependent event to occur. But to say that loss of sight always requires the bleeding of macular degeneration is obviously false since eyesight loss can be occasioned by any number of conditions.

Now, any causal relationship is developed on two other matters. One is *ceteris paribus* clauses. Usually a rich assortment of side conditions, represented in the phrase "all other things being equal," must be in place for causality to occur. For HIV to become AIDS, for example, a standard array of genes in the afflicted person must be in place. The importance of the array is demonstrated by the extremely rare person with HIV who never becomes ill with AIDS due to a rare (nonstandard) gene that offers protection. The second item is contiguity. A correlation cannot suffice for causality (Hume aside) because it might be just a constant conjunction (Hume's language) with no actual connection between the antecedent and dependent variables. Sunspots, for example, can be in a perfect pattern of coordination with business cycles and no economist will ever assert causality between the two sets of events. The reason is that there is no forcing mechanism in evidence, no explanation for how sunspots can have any contiguous relationship to business cycles. Causal relationships have to contain an account of contiguity between independent and dependent events.

Stevenson's work, like all work in reincarnation, does not identify the *ceteris paribus* conditions or the mechanisms of contiguity in the data. Suppose all the evidence is valid (although it is not). Even as valid evidence it cannot serve as evidence for reincarnation unless we have at the very least an explanation for reincarnation that can identify the evidence needed to support the experience. Look, for example, at the correlation between birthmarks on the living person and scars on the deceased person. What does that tell us? That physical properties are transferred between bodies across successive lives? But even if the event is true it cannot establish that the same person has been reincarnated in the later life. Identical twins have exactly the same DNA. Biologically they are the same person. But no identical twin would acquiesce in having his life taken because his physical clone still exists. Physical identity is not equivalent to personal identity. The physical evidence Stevenson adduces is consistent with the possibility that there are, or may be, two distinct persons in the experience, not one moving over from one life to another. The verbal testimony on patterns of recognition falls into the same trap. Why should recognition of persons and sites from a different life be evidence for reincarnation? We need a mechanism of contiguity, a theory of why and how such evidence counts as evidence for reincarnation. Yes, Stevenson was, or might have been, retrieving inexplicable patterns of information. But until they become intelligible in terms of a theoretical pattern that establishes a contiguity *that makes for reincarnation*, we may be doing something like gathering evidence for business cycles from sunspot data.

The problem in establishing the right covering law is that the explanatory models relevant to the experience cannot be easily rank ordered in importance. Stevenson recognizes a form of this problem when he addresses the possibility that extrasensory perception plus personification may account for some of the cases. It works this way. The information disclosed by the child claiming to be the reincarnation of a deceased person may have been acquired by ESP on the part of the child. Now one may want to say that ESP is an unproven event. But so too is reincarnation. The point is that we have entered a world where conjecture, and sometimes just speculation, rule. Almost anything goes. Stevenson is very effective in dismissing ESP as an alternative explanation. He argues that "extrasensory perception alone does not adequately account for the organization of the information available to the subject in a pattern characteristic of the deceased personality." Of course this argument presupposes that there is a pattern of organizing information characteristic of a personality *and* characteristic at a very early age.

There is also more than ESP as an alternative explanatory model. Among the models in vogue among students of *psi* (the in-house term for all psychic abilities) are precognition (knowledge before the fact) and psychokinesis (mental powers to affect physical or exogenous mental items). The latter is a stretch in this case since it is hard to conceive of a child's mental powers reordering the minds of a significant number of adults as a way of shamming a reincarnation experience. Precognition is also a marginally acceptable explanation, though possible in a narrow sense as a form of mind reading that would allow the child to anticipate events and thoughts in building a reincarnation case. The low probabilities with both these putative powers as alternative explanations for the reincarnation cases are as much in the typical way they are manifested as anything else. When people are attributed with these powers they seem to exhibit them in robust and broad form. The thought that a child would use either of these powers only in the narrow sense of pretending to be reincarnated, and in no other way, challenges the imagination even in a methodological world where license trumps order.

But then there is the possibility that possession is the true explanation fitting the evidence. Here there are real problems in sorting out the possible explanatory models (possession vs. reincarnation). Stevenson cites the well-known Thompson-Gifford case, in which Thompson, an engraver, became obsessed with the need to paint certain scenes (in Stevenson's words) "which arose vividly in his mind." Though possessing no known skills and never having shown any interest in painting, Thompson succumbed to these impulses and painted a number of scenes from hallucinations that he was having. The scenes uncannily resembled sites visited or painted by Robert Swain Gifford, a painter whom Thompson knew slightly and who had died (a fact not known by Thompson) six months before Thompson's eerie experiences. One explanation proffered by observers is that Thompson had somehow come under the influences of the discarnate personality of Gifford. In fact, Thompson himself later wrote that "during the time I was sketching I remember having the impression that I was Mr. Gifford himself."

The possibility of this kind of possession is itself inexplicable, based on current theories of the natural world. It seems to suggest that a dead person can somehow enter and direct the desires and actions of a live person. But suppose that the experience is genuine. Can it be folded into the reincarnation experience? Stevenson thinks not. Here is why. It is reasonable to think (if we accept the reality of possession) that the experience is graded. The cases suggest that. In two other cases described by Stevenson graded levels of possession are in evidence. In one the personality of a girl, Mary Rolf, who had died when another young female, Lurancy Vennum, was one year old, seemed to displace entirely Vennum's personality for a period of several months. But during this time of possession Rolf never claimed to be Vennum. It was just that she was occupying Vennum's body temporarily (let this way of expressing the phenomenon go unchallenged for now). After the occupation the Rolf personality returned to, one supposes, its rightful place. Another case was more of a full possession. Jasbir, a three-and-one-half-year-old boy in India, died in 1958. But before the boy could be interred the body stirred and returned to life. The return was marked by a change in identity. The "reborn" child claimed to be Sobba Ram, the son of Shankar of Vehedi, and he wanted to return to his home in that village. Observers reported that the behavior of the child was remarkably different, including his insistence on eating food only if it had been prepared in the Brahmin tradition of his "real" caste. All the details reported by those witnessing the case indicated that the child's body had been taken over by Sobba Ram, who had died in May 1954 in a chariot accident. This possession was permanent, though the newly identified child gradually assimilated into his new physical identity in the family and village life in which Jasbir was born.

If these are cases of possession, are they distinguishable from reincarnation? On the surface, yes. The standard form of reincarnation is one in which an individual is reborn to begin another life, and some of the evidence for the rebirth consists of memories of the former life. Possession is more intrusive. Here one individual forcibly (no informed consent is given) dominates within, or expels another individual from, the physical and mental terrain of the body initially housing the second individual. It is a scary experience in ways that reincarnation never is. (What happens to the initial individual when the possession is permanent? Is his/her identity extinguished? Can another body be found for this individual?) Possession, unlike reincarnation, is a form of displacement, with all the strange possibilities that any dislodgment of personal identity suggests. But in a deeper sense the main feature of reincarnation is fulfilled. An individual who has died is made incarnate, is (metaphorically, at least) reborn. It just happens that the rebirth, the reembodiment, is at the expense of another person. Furthermore, if we allow for the reality of possession, we can never be entirely sure that it is not the paradigmatic form of reincarnation. How can we be sure that all reincarnation experiences (e.g., memories of a past life) do not originate with a very early displacement of another identity? At least permanent possession at the beginnings of life would be indistinguishable from reincarnation.

Two comments. First, one supposes that to some this is a distinction without a difference. Put in strident terms, who cares whether reincarnation is a benign rebirth or a zero-sum displacement? The point is that an individual life is continuous across death and birth. But of course to the displaced individual the possession experience is important and decisive. The nature of the experience is also at stake. Is reincarnation a form of beneficent continuity, a rebirth that defeats death? Or is it another instance of nature red in tooth and claw, a form of natural selection in which some lose and others win in a competition with unbearably high stakes—the conquest, or not, of death with renewed life? Second, the ambiguity between possession and reincarnation is yet another indication of theoretical impoverishment. We simply do not have adequate definitions or explanations for the reincarnation experience that allow the basic demarcations needed for determining its validity. Until we do, until we can say with reasonable precision what the experience is, and how it is possible, the data being gathered to support it cannot really be labeled as *evidence* for reincarnation.

As expected, Stevenson had many good and some not-so-good things to say about the differences between reincarnation and possession. The not-so-good things, interestingly enough, evince the Western biases that are most troubling about the entire work. For example, Stevenson asserted that the reincarnation cases present no motive for a discarnate personality to possess the seemingly reborn person (as there are, he avers, motives in standard possession cases). But this surely exceeds boundaries. To ascribe motives to discarnate entities is just a plain extension of Western psychology, not just to non-Western cultures but to a spiritual world and its occupants about which we know almost nothing. Then there are the good things Stevenson says in critiquing the putative assimilation of possession and reincarnation. There is first "the patchiness of the information apparently remembered by the (possessed) child." The cases present a counterintuitive outcome: the possessive personality, while strong enough to alter the identification of the dominated person, still cannot remember nearly as much about the former life as the original reincarnated personality. Stevenson's observation is persuasive. Second, in a fascinating passage, Stevenson returns to the correlations between wounds and birthmarks across lives. He speculates that we may yet discover an ideal case in which "the birthmark may account for the story of a previous life invented to fit the birthmark." He believes that the "rebirth story may come from the birthmark, but the birthmark cannot arise from the story because it represents some antenatal influence on the developing fetus." Or, since a birthmark has its inception before delivery, then the apparent memories of the past life associated with the birthmark would rule out possession as an explanation for at least those marked cases of reincarnation. Of course theories of maternal psychokinesis (the pregnant woman's thoughts affecting and perhaps carving the telling birthmarks) call this explanation into question. But then this alternative explanation works only if the mother has knowledge of the child's previous life.

It is clear what is going on here. Stevenson accumulated a great deal of information on assumed cases of reincarnation without the explanatory mechanisms that can transform the information into evidence. So much of the brief for reincarnation seems to turn on individuals knowing things that the individuals could not know unless reincarnated from previous lives. But this is a more subtle and complex claim than generally recognized. Causal precedence, the relationships between physical marks and individual identity, the possible symbiotic connections between biology and narrative, the invention of a life to fit the inscription of a physical mark, even the reconfiguration of human life to accommodate reincarnation—this is the rich and promising stuff yet to be broken down, filled in, tracked for effects, and reordered as explanations for reincarnation experiences. Until we know more, a lot more, about how reincarnation is possible, about how it occurs if it occurs, no closure is likely that will settle the quite reasonable reservations of the skeptics.

The point is that survival after death in a renewed life on earth is one of the more absorbing conjectures in human experience. Many good and thoughtful people have moved from conjecture to belief in such a life after death. This is the belief I am trying to comprehend. How can I examine this belief from the provisionally skeptical state of mind that is most effective in determining whether something is true or false? Can anyone study from an impartial perspective the most profound issue in human history? How can we answer a question objectively when the answer opens a door on the ultimate subjective issues, who and what we are? This does not lead to the same caveat that one cannot just believe in something because it is better (more desirable) than its alternatives. The invitation is more demanding, and severe. Choose one of two polar alternatives on the best evidence available: death as a passage to another life, or death as the conclusion of life in any form. If our inquiry is to be credible we have to face the undesirable consequences of either alternative. But the intriguing observation is that it seems impossible on rational grounds to reach certainty on either of the two alternatives.

OTHER LIVES: A MOST DESIRABLE THING

In two of the more exhilarating scenes in the film Titanic, Rose (Kate Winslet) is held aloft by Jack (Leonardo DiCaprio) on the bow of that immense vessel as it plows through the ocean and says, "I'm flying." "I'm king of the world!" Jack cries out in another scene as Rose joins him in the pure joy of soaring above the vast waters and even (or so it seems) the very ship that carries them aloft. Audiences respond to these scenes, even those who can't stand the film, because they represent transcendence in a minor key, our capacity to levitate above the mundane in human experiences, to fly even as we know we are earthbound creatures wedded to locales in the cartography of the human soul. These two capacities, the welcome acceptance of place in familiar and comfortable surroundings, and the need to leave, to move beyond the ordinary to the strange and distant, seem to define the widest ranges of human inclinations. They are also reflected in attitudes toward the natural end to all human life, death as a return to the inert properties of the earth, our natural location in the dust and soil of our planet, or death as a release to an existence beyond the earth, a flight above the boundaries of ordinary sensory life to something new and wonderful. These are thoughts that track through almost all of recorded human existence. They also express the standard polar extremes in attempts to explain life and death in human experience.

Art cashes in on death and an afterlife in a variety of ways. In *Death Takes a Holiday* (remade more recently as *Meet Joe Black*), Death, as a kind of very odd anthropologist, visits the human community to try to see his own profession from a human perspective. In the original version of the film Death stops working (no one dies) while he tries to understand why so many plead for more time before dying—a year, a week, a day, an hour, even one minute more of life, please. Death wonders: what is so precious about life? Why the desire to live, to avoid death, to hold on to life even when measured in minutes and hours? *Meet Joe Black* presents a more sanguine view about life and death, though still working the edges of practical knowledge. In this film Death stays on the job during his sojourn (people still die while he explores life). One of its characters, a Jamaican woman who is dying, likens life to a holiday in the islands, filled with a need to have experiences and a record of the trip. When she admits to Death that she has enough pictures in her head and wants to die, he gently takes her over to the other side. In this film, like many an anthropologist, Death gets too close to his subjects. He falls in love, both with a young woman and life itself. When he thinks that he might take the woman back with him he reveals enough of himself to see the horror in her face before retreating to his human disguise. One might conclude that anthropologists cannot easily take individuals away from their native culture, but especially that death is a repulsive prospect for those who are alive, even for a woman in love with the figure of Death and with an invitation to live with him in an afterlife.

The natural repugnance of death coupled with the need to get it right in life, to have enough pictures in the head, to feel that one's life has been fulfilled before its inevitable conclusion, may inspire the belief that death is itself not the end of life. A fresh start, a second chance, another opportunity to complete oneself, is part of the classic American dream. Nowhere is this maxim of forgiveness and hope more generously expressed than in the possibility of reincarnation—a renewed existence, another set of whole life chances to get things right. What could be sweeter than the prospect of starting over from the very beginning? To have a new set of choices in a renewed human life on earth after death must be regarded as a golden opportunity. The risks, however, are real. In Nietzsche's eternal return the individual faces a continuous repeat of the past life, the self caught in a *Groundhog Day* nightmare. Without memory of a past life, after all, the same good and bad choices could be made again and again through each successive reincarnation. If the conditions of life are unchanged, if *everything* is reincarnated in totality, even Bill Murray would demand a rewrite. The alien character in the film *K-Pax* ends the movie with the admonition to choose wisely, because all choices will be repeated for eternity. This, on any interpretation, is a scary panorama in conditions of imperfect information about past lives. Again, what we need is an identification and account of the critical variables in these experiences that make sense of reincarnation if the stories of such phenomena are to be regarded as true, or even minimally sensible.

the migratory self, no. 1

Now I want you, the reader, to come back with me to the imaginary dinner party. Remember that the discussion of reincarnation in the last chapter has revolved around the nature of the self, and the issues of whether our identities are lodged in our bodies, in particular configurations of the brain, or whether we have an identity that is in some way independent of our bodies. Can we consider the possibility that we are spirits, able to occupy with full sensory powers an undead strip of reality between life and death? Do some people migrate to different forms of life, occupying other bodies than their own? Can we stretch our own physical boundaries to exceed the normal parameters of the self, being both in and out of our bodies? The stories told by the guests in this time frame of the dinner party try to address these issues.

"Science will save us." The sentence has been uttered by Janet Dorsey, the attorney.

"Save us from what?" David asks.

"From aberrations. Distortions. Myths. Superstitions. You name it."

"Can one have faith in science?" David smiles.

Frank stands and stretches. "Science, science. Just remember, please, it's a human construct with human limitations. I do not see how it can arbitrate among metaphysical matters, supernatural events. Or the kind of story that Lupe has told. Even though I do not believe the story."

"Why not?" David asks.

"My faith in empiricism forbids it."

"Bullshit," David responds.

"What is this, Thrasymachus? A new way of argument, by abuse?" Frank raises a cognac toast to David.

The group is more relaxed and irreverent now. They have spent the last forty-five minutes discussing Lupe García's story. Most of those present at this dinner party do not believe in the reincarnation that is the foundation of her narrative, though like all members of all good audiences they have been deeply moved by the presentation. The story appeals to them even as they resist its powers.

"Another story?" The question is from Paul Lorca, the professor of anthropology.

"Do you have one?" Frank asks. "Yes. By all means."

"I am not a performer. So my, what, offering will not—cannot—top Lupe's splendid narrative. To start with, all of the events occur in this life. What a downer, as we used to say. The story is about something that actually happened to me."

"And mine did not?" Lupe raises her eyebrows in a poor attempt at a Groucho Marx gesture.

"Let's suspend all judgments and listen to Paul." Frank slides back into his seat and nods to Paul.

"Like Lupe I ask for extended sympathy. Imagine now what I will try to describe from memory." Paul pulls away from his shirt the St. Christopher medallion he always wears on a chain around his neck and rubs his fingers across the metal surface. He does this unconsciously and frequently, now unaware of the effect he is having on the others with this casual embrace of his Roman Catholicism.

"Let me begin with a scene. Just draw it up in your mind from what I say." He pulls briefly at his beard. "Think—first see a hawk on the lowest limb of a tree only ten feet in front of a boy. All right? Now I am standing in a circle of pine needles, the only clearing I could find within the thicket of trees and mangroves, and I can see both the hawk and the boy. The boy is seated in a kind of lotus position, legs spread to his side with his body resting on his heels. Like a young imitation of the Buddha, except that he appears exceptionally relaxed, but not really serene, and is dressed in jeans and flannel shirt. His head is bowed down on his chest, eyes closed. The hawk's head and eyes are jerking in these sudden uneven movements—like this," and Paul imitates the hawk to the sound of bravos from his audience, though he looks in truth as if he is having a mild seizure. "The hawk, at bottom—it looks ready to fly at the slightest provocation."

Paul's movements suddenly cease. His hand drops down from his beard. He leans back in his chair.

"The boy was from a Cuban family some of whose members practiced Santería. He lived just off S.W. 8th street in Miami, 'Little Havana,' it's called. Very interesting section of Miami. I used to go there for Cuban food even when I was growing up in Key West. The boy's father ran a local bodega further west on the Tamiami Trail. At the time I was a part-time instructor trying to complete my dissertation. I was teaching one course each year in the junior college while living with my brother and his family. The boy in this story was the nephew of one of my colleagues in the junior college.

"The ceremony in the woods on Plantation Key, I must confess this, was no more than an exercise in futility from my point of view. The boy had come to believe that he could assume the body of a hawk. Yes—this is true. He actually believed that and shared these beliefs with me. Family lore had set him up. The traditional stories told by his father and other adults in Santería always included possessions of humans by orishas—spiritual figures with the usual powers. The boy had accepted these stories as literal truths, and had expanded on them from discussions he had begun with members of the local Seminole tribe. He had come to believe in reversals of identity between humans and animals—that a human could inhabit the body of a bear or wolf or bird or some other animal for a brief period of time. The human body would be the resting place for the animal soul until the human returned.

"Look—my puzzlement over this case was not simple. In fact it was very complicated. Arranged, you might say, in sectors in my head. I could not understand how the boy, who was one of the honor students in the local high school, could believe such nonsense. Until that time I had associated intelligence with secular affinities, not spiritual beliefs. Nor could I comprehend the density of the boy's father in allowing his son to confuse allegory with facts. It was also hard to understand how the santeros in Santería and Seminole elders could communicate this kind of lore as events and possibilities in the real world. I was obviously in a judgmental mood."

"So unlike you," David observes.

Paul ignores the comment, as does everyone else. He continues with the story.

"But my deepest puzzlement was reserved for what I had just witnessed. I had accompanied the boy on this excursion to the Keys partly out of concern, partly out of curiosity, but mainly because the boy had invited me. I was fond of him and had accepted the invitation in order to keep the bonds between us strong and also as a favor to his uncle. It was a mark of the affection among the three of us that my skepticism was acknowledged by the boy as a condition for my cooperation. They knew I was a big-time doubter.

"Now—at one moment in the woods on Plantation Key—I had to question my skepticism a bit. The boy had told me that he was going to call the hawk into his presence. He had knelt on the ground and closed his eyes. Shortly afterward I had heard the sound of wings flapping overhead and had looked up to see shades of brown and gold against the slants of sunlight through the tree limbs, one sharp eye in the plumage watching me as it descended to the lower tree limb.

"The boy continued his meditation. The hawk jerked about and then fell still on the limb. I could see the bird's breast rising and falling rapidly as it breathed the air under the trees. The center of the bird's chest was beating in small, fast movements.

"Then—I recall this so vividly—the air seemed to change its texture suddenly. I could feel something, but it was not clear to me what had happened. The boy and the hawk had seemed to look at each other for one brief coordinated instant, though I could not be sure even of that since they had now resumed their separate stances. But I was certain that during the instant of visual contact there was no sound of any sort—no movement of leaves in the wind, no insect or animal sounds, nothing but a sudden and brief stillness.

"Now—for the record—I do not believe in transference or the migration of the soul, and I reminded myself of exactly this belief on that day in the Keys. But I still just stood there, in the clearing of pine needles, watching the boy and the hawk. The air was cool but I could feel my body's heat under my shirt and trousers. I kept very still so as not to disturb whatever mood had been conjured by the boy.

"Now a second change seemed to occur. All connections within the scene shifted. My attention seemed to drift for some reason. The scene appeared two-dimensional. I was looking at a collage, a collection of prints representing trees, a boy, a hawk. At that precise moment the hawk turned slowly and looked at me. Then the bird rose gracefully against the still life and flew away from the scene, its body turning and finding the path to the sky, wings moving through the air with the sound of feathers brushing against drums.

"I turned to look at the boy. He remained in the Buddhist position, unmoving, eyes closed. His face was still bowed toward the ground. In profile he appeared to be praying. I could see that the boy's left eye was partially open, the iris darting about sharply as if following movements in a dream.

"I remember sitting down heavily on the pine needles and leaning back against one of the trees. Talk about shock. The hawk was gone, I was left with thoughts of the earth framed from above, over the woods, perhaps the Seminole nation territory and even the junior college in Miami where I taught anthropology. But I could not imagine what the hawk saw, how its lofty reality appeared, only that it was moving swiftly in a domain that humans could not possess or even see with any detail. Nor did I know what was happening.

"Two hours passed. I smoked three small cigars in silence. The smell of the smoke was a connection to something mundane, an anchor for thoughts that flowed over the events I had observed. The boy seemed safe in his prayerful stance. I did not have the nerve to intervene, to walk over and touch the boy's shoulder and see the expression on his face when he turned around.

"In mid-afternoon the hawk returned. It settled gracefully down on its former perch. I tried to study the bird. It shifted its neck as if freeing a muscle strained by too much use. More time passed. I felt alert, but this time could sense nothing happening.

"Then the boy suddenly raised his head and stood up. The hawk jerked back and flew up abruptly at almost a vertical angle. It moved away very fast.

"I quickly turned back to the boy. 'What happened?' I asked him.

"The boy would not meet my eyes. 'A dream,' he told me after a long silence. 'I dreamed that I was flying.' I remember his words. 'I cannot describe it.'

"I did not know how to respond. We remained silent as we walked out of the woods to the car. Nothing was said during the drive back to Miami.

"Did the hawk dream, I kept wondering to myself. The question of course was pure theater, probably a memory trace from the computer HAL's question to the programmer guru in 2010 just before it timed the ignition for the escape back to earth and its own destruction, 'Will I dream?' I had no methodology to examine what I had observed, no inquiry that could impartially address the events. To accept anything seemed out of the question. A denial was equally impossible since I was not even sure what it was I would be denying.

"The boy never brought up the events for discussion. I was grateful.

In time the events receded in memory. I resumed my empirical life, eventually going on to my doctorate in anthropology and then the ranks of the largely secular academic world."

"Do you believe now that the events were real?" Lupe asks immediately.

"Believe," David scoffs. "Why all this importance on belief? The events are real. Or they are not. What we believe has no bearing on this issue."

"I'm just curious. Paul?"

"Lupe, I do not know. My skeptical nature is still in place. I simply report the experience to you, the facts — or the surface of the facts, since they may be different at some deeper level — that enter and identify the experience. What to make of the experience — I simply do not know."

CHAPTER THREE

transitions: from life to near death

DEATH AS A PROCESS

Death has been viewed historically as a definitive threshold event demarcating two states of exclusive being. Like being pregnant or not ("you can't be a little bit pregnant"), a person in premodern times was generally regarded as either alive or dead. In a dramatic scene in the movie *Déjà Vu*, an ATF agent, Doug Carlin (Denzel Washington), flashes a pen laser light onto a screen showing a woman moving and talking in her home shortly before she was brutally murdered. She inexplicably turns to the light, which on the natural laws of time and space—the scene on the screen depicts a past event and the light is from the present, the future from her perspective—she cannot see. Carlin asks the technicians in the room whether she is alive. No one can answer the question since she has died in conventional time and is being viewed in an actual past on a time-warped screen in extraordinary time. Carlin picks up a small electronic device and says that it is alive, then he throws it against the wall where it breaks apart. Now, he says, it is dead. Is she alive, or is she dead, in these terms?

It is a good movie scene and a good real-life question, but the dichotomy does not work today in biological terms. Medical technology now provides clinical standing for the undead, for transitional states of being between life and death. In a slide remarkable for its importance, Western medicine has shifted its goals away from a restoration of the patient's health to the prevention of the patient's death. In traditional medicine the patient was restored to some modicum of health or allowed to die. In contemporary medicine death is an enemy to be fought at almost all costs, even when health cannot be restored. (In my field work in intensive care medicine I often heard residents proclaim, "Nobody dies on my shift, nobody.") One well-known consequence of this change in goals is the survival of patients who occupy the newly crafted transitional state between life and death. They are in an odd kind of limbo, alive but without the powers that mark the human condition of life. These states of morbidity, which are basically *flat* near-death experiences, have occasioned some thoughtful inquiries into death, including whether individuals have a right to die, to secure that natural state of being that inevitably, in one way or another, follows the end of life in any of its forms. It is also somewhat striking that the state of being undead is a well-known part of Haitian culture as an induced condition among individuals popularly known as zombies. All these phenomena are testimony to the growing recognition that death is not an event but a process.

Two recent legal cases in the United States help frame the medical issues in accidental occurrences of a transitional state between life and death. In the only pure right-to-die case that has reached the U.S. Supreme Court on its merits (I am excluding the more complex physician-assisted suicide cases), *Cruzan v. Director, Missouri Department of Health* (1990), the Court reviewed the plight of Nancy Beth Cruzan. In the Court's summary of the particulars, "Cruzan lost control of her car while driving down Elm Road in Jasper County, Missouri, on the evening of January 11, 1983. The car overturned and Cruzan was discovered lying face down in a ditch without detectable respiratory or cardiac function. Paramedics restored her breathing and heartbeat at the accident site."

In the weeks that followed the accident Cruzan's condition deteriorated. After a coma that lasted three weeks she slipped into what the courts in this country call a permanent vegetative state. In this state the person has reflexes but no significant cognitive functions. As all hope for Cruzan's recovery receded, her parents asked the hospital to withdraw artificial nutrition and hydration so that their daughter could die. The hospital sought court approval for this action. A state trial court authorized this action on the grounds that a person has the right to refuse or have treatment withdrawn, and that Nancy Cruzan had expressed in a serious conversation with a housemate friend that she would not wish to be kept alive in the conditions which in fact described her current state.

But the Supreme Court of Missouri reversed this decision. The court accepted the common law doctrine that an individual can decline medical treatment if s/he is competent and the refusal harms no one (other than the individual), but found Cruzan's statement to her friend "unreliable." The case made its way to the U.S Supreme Court, which found that Missouri had every right to adopt a "clear and convincing" standard to assess an individual's desire to withdraw life-maintaining measures. The judgment of the Supreme Court of Missouri was thus affirmed. Nutrition and hydration were eventually withdrawn from Nancy Cruzan in December 1990, on a pragmatic basis (the legal system did not intervene in the action). She died later that month, but not before pro-life activists entered the hospital for a sit-in vigil replete with efforts to offer Cruzan a drink of water (when she had not had a "drink" of anything for over six years).

The Terri Schiavo affair was a haunting refrain of Cruzan, with the exceptions that Schiavo's parents wanted their daughter's life maintained independent of its quality or the wishes to the contrary she might have once expressed. The resulting cause célèbre was also denser with political issues and major players, including a state governor and legislature, the U.S. Congress and president of the United States, operatives in the Republican Party trying to make political capital out of a tragedy, and a variety of courts, including a district court and the Eleventh Circuit Court of Appeals. There was also a husband fighting Terri's parents to let his wife die with some modicum of dignity and pro-life activists who continued to act in blissful ignorance of informed consent and privacy rights, nutrition and hydration for brain-dead patients, and even life and death. The measured evaluations in Cruzan seem eminently judicious by comparison. If we can look past the emotional noise of this more recent affair, the earlier case offers more thoughtfully crafted arguments.

One such argument is the dissent written by Justice Brennan (and joined by Justices Marshall and Blackmun) in the Cruzan case. After recognizing that "medical technology has effectively created a twilight zone of suspended animation where death commences while life, in some form, continues," he objected to the "markedly asymmetrical evidentiary burden" of requiring no proof that "the incompetent patient would wish to continue treatment." The objection suggests a question that has yet to be answered by opponents of a right to die: Why presume that patients in Cruzan's or Schiavo's condition would want to be maintained just on the absence of "clear and compelling evidence" that they would prefer death?

Neither Cruzan nor Schiavo reached the longevity of Sunny von Bülow, a beautiful, shy heiress who remained in a coma for almost twenty-eight years after her slide into what turned out to be a state of permanent unconsciousness. Von Bülow's ordeal, which ended with her death in a nursing home on December 6, 2008, was marked by a sensational trial that spawned a best-selling book and popular movie. Neither offered privileged knowledge of the tragedy. At the end of the film based on Alan Dershowitz's book recounting the events in the case, *Reversal of Fortune*, Sunny (Glenn Close) says to the audience in a voiceover that the source of her coma is not for them to know, with the intimation that she and her husband, Claus, are the only ones who know that truth. But while Claus may have known, Sunny likely did not. For reasons that will remain obscure, a young woman of abundant wealth and comfort slipped into that unaware state of the undead, that unconscious existence where (to turn Brennan's observation in a different direction) life has all but ended and death has not yet been joined.

We might ask the obvious question: what do these transitional states tell us about death and those forms of life in that twilight zone between a full life and a complete death?

INDUCED PERSISTENT VEGETATIVE STATES: ZOMBIES

In these sad and contentious cases a young woman at the center of the dispute is in what the medical profession calls a permanent vegetative state (PVS), a term that describes over 13,000 individuals in the United States. In medical practice this state is distinguished from a minimally conscious state (MCS). Individuals who are minimally conscious are, in important though minimal ways, sentient. They can respond (somewhat) to stimuli, interact modestly with others, and, in general, are recognized as bearers of a right to life with all the protections afforded by that right. The PVS individual lacks all possibility of sentience. The difference between an MCS, where some awareness does exist, and a PVS, in which no awareness exists, is not an easy call to make in diagnosis. For one thing, extended time is required to be even reasonably confident that one or the other state is in place, and time is a scarce commodity when proper therapy is at issue and political and legal groups join in battle. For another, there are two tests for the conditions. One is behavioral. Does the individual respond to stimuli, or interact with other persons, even minimally? The other is brain imaging. Do MRI scans of the brain, in measuring, for example, concentrations of glucose and oxygen in central sites of the brain, indicate a possible state of consciousness?

Both tests are flawed to some degree. Behavioral activity can be misleading in the extreme, as when the apparent tracking eye movements in both Cruzan and Schiavo, the seemingly (and fleeting) alert glances by both women, turned out to be low-level reflexes; autopsies of their badly damaged brains displayed no visual cortex of any significance, meaning that they were both blind. Brain imaging depends on neurological correlates between the physiological states of the brain and consciousness, except that we have no such reliable correlates. The only certain diagnosis of MCS or PVS is autopsy, which, of all things, is both morally and physically postmortem. But while the tests may be uncertain and difficult paths to certainty, the differences between the two states are profound. The MCS individual is a badly damaged human person. The PVS state is occupied by the undead, individuals who do not respond to stimuli or interact with others, and are regarded as in that state between life and death cited by Justice Brennan in the Cruzan case.

Both mythology and pharmacology contain alternative narratives of an existence between life and death that is said to be *induced* for questionable practical intentions. In some cultures the undead are regarded as creatures that exist in human communities and are believed to be dead individuals who have been reanimated, though without free will or many of the routine cognitive functions of living persons. Sometimes these undead are regarded as mutations of existing persons who have succumbed to the spells or chemical brews of a shaman. These spells or chemicals are thought to destroy the thinking powers of individuals while still allowing them to function as mindless near-corpses with ambulatory powers and the ability to carry out commands from a master. In the folklore of Haiti such zombies are widely believed to be creations of the black magic of Voodoo rites that originated with Palo Mayombe in Africa. Most of the serious literature distinguishes zombies from ghosts, mummies, ghouls, cannibals, individuals possessed by demons or other creatures (including spirits or even humans), and artificially created monsters as depicted in Shelley's *Frankenstein*. Zombies definitely occupy their own well-defined niche as the undead in human experience.

The creation of zombies is forbidden in the Haitian penal code. According to Article 249, "It shall also be qualified as attempted murder the employment which may be made against any person of substances which, without causing actual death, produce a lethargic coma more or less prolonged. If, after the person had been buried, the act shall be considered murder no matter what result follows."

The prohibition assumes that there are known procedures for creating zombies. And, whether effective or not, there are such procedures. But of course the issue is whether any of these folklore and movie theatrics are grounded in real experiences. At least a few are presented as genuine. Gino Del Guercio relates the case of Clairvius Narcisse, a young man in central Haiti who reintroduced himself to his sister Angelina in 1981 after a hiatus of eighteen years that began with his burial in a cemetery close to his village. After convincing his sister that he was her brother by reciting facts and a nickname known only to close family members, he told her that he remembered his burial quite vividly. He was fully conscious but paralyzed, unable to speak or move.

The story Clairvius told is riveting. That night, after the mourners had departed, a voodoo shaman raised him from his grave and took him to a sugar plantation in northern Haiti where he was forced to work as a slave. After almost two decades the zombie master died and Clairvius was able to escape and return home. The key evidence in this case is the fact that Clairvius was pronounced dead before his burial by doctors at an American-directed hospital. He had appeared at the emergency room spitting up blood with a fever and pain throughout his body. The medical staff at the hospital could not diagnose the illness. Three days later he "died." Clairvius reported that he could remember his sister crying at his bedside when the doctors declared him dead. The funeral and burial commenced shortly after.

Suppose we accept such cases provisionally as genuine. What is the causal mechanism that can explain them? This is the question raised by numerous Western researchers accustomed to scientific explanations. In 1981 Richard Schultes, a Harvard botanist, enlisted one of his former students, Wade Davis, a Canadian who at that time was pursuing a doctorate in biology, to travel to Haiti and identify the biological substances that might bring about conditions of the sort that created the undead state recounted in the story of Clairvius Narcisse. The Davis narrative is engrossing and Del Guercio tells it well. The young man arrived in Haiti a skeptic with little or no knowledge of the culture, history, or language of the country. But he had a hypothesis, a provisional belief that he was prepared to falsify. As a good empiricist of material bent he proposed that the belief system in Haitian culture was not the source of the voodoo spell, that instead a substance existed that rendered the victim incapacitated. The equilibrium needs of such a substance were and are considerable.

Western cultures possess hallucinogenic and paralyzing drugs, including LSD and various medical substances used in surgery and executions, such as pavulon or pancuronium bromide, two drugs that paralyze the entire muscular system. In executions pavulon seems to give comfort to those witnessing the event by (on most accounts) preventing the prisoner from moving (writhing) while s/he suffocates. In surgery the drug suspends respiration so that a ventilator can take over breathing for the patient. The drug that Davis sought had to paralyze the victim without somehow asphyxiating him, and destroy or at least provisionally suspend those parts of the brain that enable free will. The powder he found was a concoction of "parts of toads, sea worms, lizards, tarantulas, and human bones. . . . The poison is to be rubbed into the victim's skin." The mix was uneven across several batches Davis collected. In a second consignment of the powder Davis found traces of tetrodotoxin, a lethal poison produced by (among other species of life) the puffer or blowfish, the notorious fugu considered a delicacy in Japan. Chefs there remove most of the poisonous parts of the fish yet leave enough of the toxic sections to instill tingling sensations, prickling of the tongue and lips, and a feeling of euphoria that is probably one part the effects of the toxin and another part elation at having skirted death in a succulent meal. Davis felt that his hypothesis had resisted falsification. It could serve as an explanation for the zombie state.

But he had not explained it. The fact was that the drug alone, while occasionally fatal, did not create zombies. People who took the drug sometimes died, were paralyzed, at times crippled mentally for life, but did not become zombies from just ingesting the drug. (For example, there is no record of any Japanese diner becoming a zombie from eating too large a portion of the toxic sections of the puffer fish, though more than a few have died from the culinary excess.) So Davis did what all cultural anthropologists do. He looked for a cultural antecedent. He found it in the Haitian secret society of voodoo priests. The priests use the threat of zombification to police the society, relying on the drug to weaken the will of a transgressor and make him vulnerable to the considerable powers of spells and curses in a culture that believes in their efficacy. The drug amplifies the deep background culture of mental control that is used as a form of punishment by the voodoo priests. Davis, who eventually participated in the rites of the vodoun culture, explains zombification as a real phenomenon created by a template of drug administration on which cultural forces are amplified. The book Davis wrote about his experiences was *The Serpent and the Rainbow*, published in 1987. It became a controversial and global best seller.

More recent though still informal investigations identify Scopolamine as the zombie drug. Journalists report that it is a substance commonly referred to as "Devil's Breath" in Colombia, where it is a common street drug. Those who take the drug supposedly appear completely sober and rational, but they are really just automatons. A documentary by VBS, an online television network, reported that the drug is real and available. According to Ryan Duffy in the documentary: "This stuff is as close to pure evil as it gets. A tiny amount of the powder administered to the victim causes one of two effects, (a) death, or (b) complete loss of free will. Criminals are usually hoping for the latter, as it enables them to tell victims to empty their bank accounts, give away their car, perform sex acts, basically whatever the criminal dictates."

Duffy also reported that a legal drug cocktail known as "ScopeDex" (Scopolamine + Dexedrine) is sometimes taken by astronauts and those in training to prevent nausea and vomiting in altered gravity environments. Scopolamine, also known as hyoscine, is a tropane alkaloid drug obtained from plants of the family Solanaceae (nightshades), such as henbane or jimson weed (Datura species). Standard medical takes on this drug warn that it can be highly toxic and should be used in minute doses. In the treatment of motion sickness, the dose, gradually released from a transdermal patch, is only 0.33 milligram of scopolamine per day. An overdose can cause delirium, delusions, paralysis, stupor, and death.

ZOMBIES REVISITED

Both medically and philosophically, there is ample room to be skeptical of zombies and question their reality. In some (very) limited field research on individuals in Haiti that friends and family regarded as zombies, anthropologists have found that the said individuals suffer from maladies well documented in Western medical literatures. In 1997, Professor Richard Littlewood from the Department of Anthropology and Psychiatry at London's University College, London, and Dr. Chavannes Douyon from the Polyclinique Medica in Port-au-Prince, Haiti, published a paper in *The Lancet* summarizing their investigations of three individuals in Haiti who were considered to be zombies. The first individual seemed to be suffering from catatonic schizophrenia, the second from brain damage and epilepsy, and the third from a learning disorder they thought was possibly due to fetal-alcohol syndrome. The researchers speculated that the zombie appellation was assigned to a variety of mental illnesses in Haiti as a useful designation meant to bring mentally dysfunctional individuals into the vodoun culture of Haiti where a traditional and widely understood vocabulary could account for the deviant behavior.

The philosophical take is mainly in the form of intriguing thought experiments. A philosophical zombie is an individual who lacks consciousness but is identical to conscious individuals in his behavior. The idea of philosophical zombies addresses a widely known conundrum. Consciousness is obviously and unassailably located in individuals. Because of this, no particular individual can have access to another's conscious state. In some important sense we can know, feel, and acknowledge that we (each of us) are conscious in some ways but we cannot know in the same ways that others are conscious. Others may simply be engaged in a kind of machine-like mimicry of human behavior without the inner self marked by consciousness. Just a kind of metaphorical darkness, or silence, prevails. In the philosophical thought experiments it is easy to conjure a world populated by zombies, those behaving exactly like conscious individuals though without consciousness, except for the one who is intellectually exploring the possibility, of course. The ease is located in the admission—how could we know that others are conscious if we cannot infer an inner self from behavior? The thought experiments are generally deployed to draw conclusions about the nature of consciousness.

The neurology of actual consciousness is more complex, subtle, and imaginative. There is first the awareness among researchers that consciousness may be nuanced as to type and perhaps graded among individuals. The impact of these findings on zombification provides interesting contrasts. Individuals with mild cases of autism, for example, have reported that they learn how to act correctly, in terms of cultural expectations, by studying and imitating the behavior of others who are considered "normal." That such individuals are conscious is not disputed. But at least some parts of how they act spring from imitation, not from instincts and impulses. This is the opposite of the philosophical zombie. Autistics who imitate behavior are using the conscious powers of the brain to observe and learn how—consciously—to compensate for neurological deficiencies. In some remarkable way these individuals are consciously initiating a type of behavior that does not resonate or sympathetically identify with others, except that the response is driven from the conscious parts of the self mimicking patterns of behavior where the actual mimicked behavior is not conscious in any intentional or volitional sense.

One parallel would be the actor trained in a behavioral tradition of acting who does not mentally become the character he plays but convinces the audience of an internal life for the character through external behavior. This approach to acting does not require any of the internal emotions that the audience ascribes to the character. The autistic individual imitating others is playacting in this external sense of creating character without creating the inner self of the character. By contrast the Method actor who enters or re-creates the inner state of the character in the acting performance is, or tries to be, conscious as the character is assumed to be conscious. The Method actor does not create zombies on stage or in film as the traditional actor does, but rather aspires to the re-creation of the inner self imagined for the role, to be the inner self of the character at least for the dramatic presentation.

Also, it is abundantly clear from research that the brain is not conscious in most of its activities. Consciousness is a recently developed power historically (presumably through natural selection conjoined with biological laws) and is now generally acknowledged as occupying only a very small part of the bicameral brain. We know, for example, that the brain can process information at an unconscious level and that we can know without knowing that we know until a tripping event occurs. The robust view of the subconscious identified by Freud does not need the imprimatur of psychoanalysis to underwrite its existence. A variety of works, extending from the physiological orientations of a John Eccles to the philosophical meditations of a Michael Polanyi, have elaborated the many ways in which forms of thinking occur as a substratum of full consciousness. We do repress experiences, forget or bracket them until they are recovered in some way, rely on forms of tacit knowing that cannot be expressed visibly or explicitly but which yet conjure states of mind (like the "zone" in sports) where something other than the cerebral cortex is driving the action, thoughts, and perceptions. The vocabulary of intuition, gut feeling, blink decisions, tacit knowing, unconscious mental causes, symbolic or metaphorical languages without explicit meaning, all have entered the formal lexicon of human experience. The noncognitive self, the limbic system, is widely celebrated today in all parts of the world. What the philosophers call the zombie within, a local neurological area lacking consciousness, is almost a given in understandings of the human brain. But all this intuitive thinking presupposes a fully functioning brain, which, we know now, does contain a region of active unconscious life.

The film industry seems at times fixated on these phenomena. So many popular films negotiate various in-between states of life populated with creatures that are neither exactly alive nor dead. George Romero's classic 1968 horror film says it succinctly in the title: Night of the Living Dead. In the film some pretty horrible looking individuals tromp around at night trying to kill and eat those who are, well, really alive in the conventional sense. The really alive persons, those trapped more or less in a farmhouse who are the focus group for the film's plot, try to kill the living dead beings in self-defense, but they have a classic problem. The living dead are not really alive (a fact that the live persons seem never able to grasp in its entirety). The tripping event is a fallen satellite that releases radiation that activates the brains of the dead (even those who are buried) and turns them into ravenous creatures who must feed on human flesh. At some early point in the film the alive people discover that the living dead can be rendered really dead by a blow to the head (destroying, one presumes, their newly activated brains). The main activity in the film revolves around the efforts of the alive folks to get gasoline from a nearby pump to fill the tank of a pickup truck that will allow them to speed away to safety. In a later treatment of this theme in the 2003 film The Undead, a small fishing village in Australia is bombarded with meteorites that somehow cause the dead to awaken with a need to eat living human flesh. A young woman escapes to (yes) a farmhouse where she and other survivors battle with the undead creatures and begin entertaining the possibility that higher powers have created the problem.

The undead are usually presented in the movies as a bunch of unfeeling amoral thugs who wreak havoc without second thoughts or reflections on their deeds. In Dawn of the Dead (2004) the undead duke it out with alive people in a shopping mall. The zombies are still ravenous exclusively for human flesh even with fast-food joints all around them. Occasionally the undead become free spirits. In one computer game in the World of Warcraft series, a renegade group of the undead breaks from a tyrant and seeks to regain free will. But this is the exception. In film after film, book after book, the undead are devoid of any kind of will.

The hordes of undead slaves in Mordor in the book and film *The Lord of the Rings: The Two Towers* and the undead army (the Scourge) in the film *Bloodpayn* simply carry out the commands of their rulers or their own unconscious impulses or are driven by overpowering lusts (consuming human flesh). In no sense of the phrase are they moral agents. In *Bloodpayn* the undead are more heterogeneous, a pluralistic group consisting of "thousands of walking corpses, disembodied spirits, damned mortal men and insidious extra-dimensional entities." The undead in this more recent cinematic venture are the wasteland of the human genre, failed or condemned or deformed types of life that represent flawed possibilities in human forms of being.

Among the latest zombie movies are the twin-pack films *28 Days Later* and its sequel, *28 Weeks Later*, both set in a future post-apocalyptic London where a mysterious virus has ravaged England and turned the infected humans into monsters who kill everyone they can. Technically they are not zombies in the Hollywood sense, meaning that they are not called zombies, except that they do lack all human feelings and thoughts and cannot be killed except by dismemberment. The tripping event in the film, ironically enough, is a break-in at a laboratory by an animal rights group to free animals who are the subjects of experiments. In liberating them they free chimpanzees infected with the Rage virus, who then turn on their liberators, killing and infecting them and anyone else they encounter. The infected humans then become the new killer monsters. The sequel is set in the same London six months later with occupying troops establishing order. But all hell breaks loose as they are also subsequently infected. The DVD version of the first film provides three alternative endings, in all of which the male protagonist dies. What did you expect in a horror film?

In all the films and books the undead monsters are created or occasioned by freak, random, or planned events, mad scientists or advanced denizens of evil, incompetent and greedy political leaders, extraterrestrial interventions, spontaneous mutations, inexplicable diseases, misguided idealists who screw things up, or failed scientific experiments (as in each of the three *Return of the Living Dead* films [1985, 1988, 1993]: a failed scientific experiment affecting a graveyard is the event that summons the corpses, similar to the NASA satellites that fall back to earth with unwelcome radiation in *Night of the Living Dead*). Generally some actions and events cause a break with acknowledged natural laws, and this break turns out to be a fissure that releases forms of life occupying an area between the living and the dead, utterly immoral and given extraordinary strength.

Nearly everyone concedes, from a distance or through actual experience, that a brush with death is exhilarating. To come close to the threshold event without slipping over has been a literary fixation among writers from Homer to Hemingway (who famously called the orgasm the "little death"—the man obviously never had great sex if all he experienced was analogous to a "little death"). But to slip over the edge separating life and death without consummating the full act of death must be, what? Maybe it's like sex without orgasm (Hemingway inverted), coffee without caffeine, cognac without alcohol, a joke without a punch line, a concerto without the promised cadenza, odd but unrequited love, or a locked room with no exits (Sartre's hell *without* other people). Whatever it is, the signature defining statement of flat near death, that transitional state—Nancy Cruzan, Sunny von Bülow, Terri Schiavo—is that the person occupying it has no, repeat, *no* awareness of the experience.

Yet we do seem fascinated by these states of life. The view of these transitions from the outside is a gaze at the mysterious, the invisible, much like pregnancy and the solar system were inaccessible to direct visual experiences until the twentieth century. The lay public typically relies on experts to render such inaccessible phenomena intelligible. Indirect information drawn from autopsies of pregnant women, sketches from the partial data acquired from limited telescopes, allowed epistemic authorities to present experiences that in total, as a whole phenomenon, were not visible but could be made understandable by authorities in the relevant fields. The development of microscopic cameras, CAT and MRI scans, has provided a full rendering of gestation from the nanosecond of fertilization of the ovum to birth. Broad and powerful telescopic lenses and cameras on space probes have photographed most reaches of the solar system, allowing astronomers to develop a complete visual structure of our heliocentric system. In these two areas we now see directly what could not be seen for most of human history.

The inaccessibility of the brain is a more complex matter. Within the brain, states of conscious and unconscious activity are inaccessible, or based on indicators imperfectly correlated with consciousness. Not only is the brain the last organ of the body to be mapped, but consciousness, defined somehow by the properties of the brain even as it seems to extend beyond the purely physical, is itself one of the last great mysterious items in human experience. No one is certain where consciousness can be located in the brain, or even whether the concept of a region is the right approach to be used in neurological research into consciousness. Traditional (Cartesian) conjectures have postulated a self, a homunculus inside the brain that directs its activities. This "ghost in the machine" is the popular version of property dualism, the thesis that a noncorporeal being, a mental or epiphenomenal self, is the locus for a person's identity, not the physiology of the body or the brain as such.

If one subscribes to either substance (the homunculus is a soul) or property (the self is a mind) dualism, then the transitional state between life and death is open to amazing and impossible conjectures. Unlike pregnancy or the solar system, efforts to unlock the mysteries of the brain would track along two levels: the self and the biological brain, a binary framework in which the real identity of the person is located in a mental stratum, and the physical brain stuff which does *not* identify the self. The difficulty and challenge of such a conjecture are that, on its terms, even a fully visible intact brain would not provide a complete account of consciousness and the self. The mysteries of the brain would have to include layered divisions between the self as ineffable mind and physical body. It would be as if full descriptive renditions of human gestation and the solar system were yet incomplete, that an invisible substratum was the real venue for the identity of these two phenomena. This line of thought opens the possibility that there was or is a vibrant Sunny von Bülow, Nancy Cruzan, and Terri Schiavo living within the stricken body and brain of these individuals. The person may still exist as a whole ineffable being even with a badly damaged brain. In practical terms, this view could maintain that the zombie state might still house a sentient human creature.

Sunny von Bülow existed for almost twenty-eight years without any sign that she was even marginally conscious. She was completely passive, a life form utterly dependent on caretakers. There was never any prospect for any kind for recovery. Terri Schiavo was without any significant cognitive functions for fifteen years (almost eight years longer than Nancy Cruzan's ordeal). She could not speak or communicate in any way and had reflexes that only mimicked interaction with others without the reality of human contact. No legitimate medical authority believed that she had any chance for recovery or substantial improvement in her condition. She was washed and dressed by caretakers, received nutrition and hydration artificially through tubes (she could not swallow or "eat" food), and from all indications was unaware of her dependency or anything else about herself and the world. The question suggested by Justice Brennan reverses the burden of proof: Why not require compelling and credible evidence that individuals in these conditions would have wanted to be kept alive? If we shift the burden of proof in this way, then we would have allowed Nancy Cruzan, Terri Schiavo, and Sunny von Bülow to die at some early stages in their tragic conditions absent any evidence that they would have wanted to live in a permanent vegetative state. This reversal of the burden of proof relies on the standard understanding that the person who was Sunny von Bülow, Nancy Cruzan, or Terri Schiavo is no longer in existence, that the severe neurological damage that a PVS represents has extinguished the identity of these persons.

As an aside, it is a melancholy experience tracking and surveying the pro-life agenda from Cruzan to Schiavo, especially since one might expect a traditional religious perspective to support a Brennan-like shift in the burdens of proof. The reason is not because of the predictable observation that the Religious Right's delay of inevitable death makes no sense since the event is regarded as a union with God in the afterlife (for even if the observation is accepted, who knows the state of anyone's soul or relationship to God at the moment of death), but rather the fact that core beliefs in any religion typically contain a reverence for nature, which is often regarded as God's word made manifest. Hence the importance of natural law and process in resisting artificial insemination, chemicals that prevent the natural processes of ovulation or implantation, even prophylactics that impede the natural introduction of sperm in copulation and the destruction of the life process in human embryos to harvest stem cells. Catholic reverence for rhythm methods of birth control derives from a respect for natural laws in reproduction and birth.

Yet (can we say the obvious?) nothing is more natural than death. Individuals like Sunny von Bülow, Nancy Cruzan, and Terri Schiavo lived in their extreme conditions because of artificial techniques developed by contemporary medicine in the West. These techniques, including the injection of nourishment into Nancy Cruzan's and Terri Schiavo's bodies through a tube surgically implanted into their stomachs, allow for a kind of override of the death process, a suspension of nature and natural law at the cost of conventional human standing, and, we might say, the dignity attending a natural death. If we editorialize, one might point out to the pro-life movement that a true respect for God in these cases, and the proper reverence of nature that accompanies this respect, might allow for the dying process to continue to its natural conclusion as a default position (unless definitive evidence is offered that indicates contrary wishes from the patient). Still, and oddly, for the pro-life movement any semblance of human life is worth maintaining, no matter what the state of morbidity might be or the artificial sources of its maintenance. Transitional states must still be maintained on the pro-life program without considering what they are or how many human powers are missing in the conditions that define them, or without reflection on the robust array of artificial, non-natural devices and techniques employed to prolong transitional states between life and death.

Here is an unassailable observation from a secular perspective. A full human life depends on the neurological capability for thought. Or, in the harsher maxims of ancient Rome, one truly lives only so long as one has the powers that allow us to be human and not one moment more. Ample evidence demonstrates that individuals without a full range of powers can lead a full life (Ray Charles is but one striking example). But no one leads any semblance of a human life with the minimal cognitive powers associated with a permanent vegetative state. Sunny von Bülow, Nancy Cruzan, and Terri Schiavo were in that twilight zone where human life is not possible even in minimalist terms. There is also anecdotal evidence that at least the latter two individuals would not have wanted to live in those states. (The reports from Terri Schiavo's husband and friends that Terri would not have wanted to be maintained in such a state were accepted as genuine evidence in a court of law.) The secular perspective is that no one can successfully argue that it was in their interests to be maintained in that zone. If any interests were being served (on this view) they were the needs of some members of the family to see and visit with them, and the interests of the pro-life movement in pursuing an agenda that maintains levels of life secured not obviously by God or nature but by the powers of medical technology.

There is an obvious counter-question here. If transitional-state persons are not aware, why be concerned with them? From all the medical evidence they themselves are not and cannot be concerned. But unseen and future prospects can be sources of comfort or despair. Daniel Dennett once wrote that there are many kinds of different wild animals living in the woods behind his farmhouse in Maine that he only rarely if ever sees. Yet the knowledge that they are there is a source of pleasure and satisfaction for him and he "would be very unhappy to learn that they had left." For many people it is a source of comfort to know that they will not be remaindered like a used book in the unthinking conditions defining the transitional state. The existence of, say, a Sunny von Bülow is disturbing in compromising the prospect of a timely and natural death — even as we know that the person in that state is unaware. It is this uneasiness over the passage to death that, one might argue, drives the need for physician-assisted suicide. One wants to be in control of the time and manner of one's death. This is the platform that maintains the heretical secular hope that the burden of proof in these cases will somehow shift, in law and public opinion, toward Justice Brennan's suggestion before the next right-to-die tragedy unfolds.

Note, however, the qualification. If one is working with a strong version of property dualism that would allow human identity to persist in the zombie-like state, and if this view is framed with uncertainty about the needs of this homunculus, then one could argue that the interests of the self within, the spiritual or mental person, might be served with a preservation of the incapacitated body. I repeat the critical point. If one believes that the self, the person, is maintained somehow in those zombie states, that neurological compromises of the most severe variety can mask a sentient self that fully exists somewhere within or as an extension of a flawed human body, then the cessation of life support in these cases is much more complicated. So much of the dynamics of these events invite a discredited philosophical doctrine that Gilbert Ryle dismissed as the "ghost in the machine": the conviction that a homunculus exists as epiphenomena in the physical body, that we are spirits within bodies. But one can entertain the prospect of such an entity, even as one can't cash in on the prospect with real palpable evidence for such an existence.

There is anecdotal evidence of a non-physical self from what I am calling vivid NDEs that suggests this possibility. For example, Michaela Roser was in a severe car accident in 1994 that left her in a coma for fourteen days. Roser reports that during this unconscious state she was able to move outside her body, seeing her stricken physical self below, viewing friends and family who visited with her in the hospital room, and throughout this comatose time feeling "at one with the universe," a universe that she recalls as enveloping her in love. Her severe closed head injuries rendered her body inert, unable to move or think. Yet she recalls that her soul, her psyche, some essential *self*—something that was Michaela Roser—was a conscious moving entity in the vicinity of her motionless body. She awakened and eventually recovered. She now no longer fears death and, in a way, longs for that sense of oneness with the universe that characterized her spirit during the ordeal. In Roser's own words, "Death has a story to tell. It colors the world in its own way." These are familiar words uttered by those who have come close to dying and believe that they have entered a dimension of reality beyond the temporal span of human life. But in this case it is a narrative of someone recalling a fully conscious existence while in a prolonged comatose state.

This case, like so much else in this area, is a conjecture drawn from evidence that is both incomplete and uncertain. But these conjectures do speak to the dreams and nightmares we have about passing to a life after death, or to the nihilist state of nothingness that atheists believe is the destination following the final death of the human body. Also, if, as recognized today, death finally is a process, not an event, then we must realize that the process can naturally and through intervention accelerate, slow down, reverse itself, conclude. And this much we also must know: death is a process with radically different rest stops along the way to its conclusion. We have PVS individuals in arrested states, individuals (real or fictional zombies) who are the near-dead through conscious efforts by others, and vivid NDE individuals in a slide toward death that is interrupted somehow and turned around. Here is a curious thing: vivid NDEs and zombies are the stuff of dramatic portrayals, while PVS experiences (also a version of near-death) are the material for tragedies. What's more, we are fascinated with all the transitional stages that precede death, whatever this final state is that we call death. A culture so fixated—and consumed—by the *passage* to death is unlikely to reach a satisfying consensus from inquiries into a life after death.

VIVID NEAR DEATH: CASES

The subject of life after death finally may be approachable in complete form only by metaphorical lines of inquiry. Science cannot navigate through the metaphysical conjectures nor get to the alternative realities suggested in death-survival literatures. Nor will faith do the job of negotiating these matters. Thinking about alternative realities may be more effectively carried out with oblique methods of inquiry that exist somewhere between science and religion. It is a venerable method of knowing. At a surface level it is clear that fiction sometimes provides better insights into social conditions than can sociology or anthropology. Everyone has favorites here. Mine include Lampedusa's *The Leopard* for pre-Garibaldi Italy, Tolstoy's *War and Peace* for the true chaos of battlefield conditions (Pierre wandering across the lines of combat), Don DeLillo's *Libra* for the ambiguities of the JFK assassination (followed of course by the documentary treatment in Gerald Posner's book, *Case Closed*) — the list is rich and long. Then there are the powers of myth, allegory, parable — those versions of fiction that suggest or point to alternative realities that are fugitive to linear texts. The allegory of the cave in Plato's *Republic* is a device of entree into a reality that cannot be presented in literal or linear terms. Even though Plato is known for critical and formal thinking, the celebrated rational philosopher segues unabashedly into a story line rather than any of the mathematical systems revered in parts of ancient Greece. Why? Because some topics cannot yield to formal or (more recently) computational methods of thought. On the topic at issue here: absent a full access to the aftermath of death, and with the only palpable evidence the death of the body, science cannot address the topic successfully. Or, at least, without forays into negative metaphysics, i.e., that materialism exhausts the nature and scope of reality (which science cannot prove).

Vivid near-death experiences present exactly such narratives, and in doing so offer a different account than a flat NDE, one that seizes and expands on the fantasy that life can continue in a PVS individual, that the person is never extinguished but rather persists throughout all degrees of physical destruction. Vivid NDEs are light contrasted with the presumed darkness of the flat NDE. Vivid NDEs promise life, not death. Sometimes the narratives offered as evidence for a life after death are striking, and quite dramatic — as we would expect from events suggesting the possibility that individuals may survive death.

Stories about such experiences are legion across almost all of history, and include the ordinary person as well as the famous. In *A History of the English Church and People* by the Venerable Bede, we find an eighth-century account of an NDE. A man pronounced dead and who was being mourned by loved ones suddenly sat up. The effects on those weeping around the body were predictable: Bede reports that "they were very upset and ran away." Bede quotes the story told by the recovered man: "I was guided by a handsome man in a shining robe," he said. "When we reached the top of a wall, there was a wide and pleasant meadow, with light flooding in that seemed brighter than daylight or the midday sun. I was very reluctant to leave, for I was enraptured by the place's pleasantness and beauty and by the company I saw there. From now on I must live in a completely different way." He later left all his worldly responsibilities and entered the Melrose monastery.

Montaigne, in his *Essays*, describes his near death in similarly attractive terms, though without a narrative to describe the experience. He had slipped into a kind of coma while away from his home. His attendants tried in vain to revive him, and "thinking I was dead, they began to carry me with great difficulty to my house." Montaigne reflects on the experience:

> On the way, after having been taken for dead for over two hours, I began to move and breathe. It seemed to me that life held only from the tip of my lips and I was closing my eyes to keep life out: I was taking pleasure in letting myself go. My life was merely a perception passing fleetingly through my soul, which was as weak as the rest of me, although the whole experience was not only truly free of pain but was reminiscent of the gentle sensation felt by those who abandon themselves to sleep. I believe that this is the same state that people find themselves in whom we see fainting in death agony, and I maintain that we pity them without cause.

In 1995 a six-year-old boy named Scott was in an auto accident in front of his house. He had run out in the street to buy ice cream from a vendor driving slowly through the neighborhood. It was a common sight on a summer afternoon in the area. But Scott was struck by a passing motorist. The impact threw him in the air more than twenty-five feet. His mother ran over to him and found that he was limp, "like a rag doll," in the words of a hospice nurse who had witnessed the accident, and he had no pulse. Scott's father, who had seen the accident from inside his house, called 911 and ran out to hold his unconscious son. Scott regained consciousness eight hours later in the hospital's intensive care unit and described to his parents what he had experienced while unconscious. He told them that he had left his body and saw himself making three somersaults in the air before landing on the pavement. Then he felt himself being thrown into a tunnel, which looked to him "like a tornado laying flat on the ground," and in this unwelcome place he had a terrifying encounter with the devil, who tried to grab him. Scott found himself somehow whisked away by an angel to a safe house, a distant point of light filled with what he felt was goodness and security. He had seen his deceased uncle on the trip away from the tunnel and came to know that the angel's name was Susan. The sanctuary was his last memory before regaining consciousness in the hospital.

These are dramatic stories. Both types of NDEs — flat and vivid — offer perspectives that influence our understandings of the rules of evidence, inference, and argument that frame inquiries into life after death. But vivid NDEs encourage an open state of mind on survival after death based on the evidence of reported experiences. The vivid NDE cases are narratives that present no less than strong, nuanced, and complex promissory notes for a life after death. They are the subject of the next chapter.

the migratory self, no. 2

"The nature of the self." Frank is trying to concentrate and direct the conversation with what can only be called academic distinctions. "Lupe's story requires a self so integrated and well defined that it—he, she—can move somehow across time and reside in different bodies. A spiritual self, one not defined by physical forms, or bodies, nor governed by known laws. And this self—Lupe—has knowledge of the different vehicles that contain her identity. Paul's story is in one way even more ambitious. The self can enter a physical form that is not human, or is not a human body. In both stories a noncorporeal self is the locus of human identity and this self is migratory."

"True," David observes. "And obvious. So is there a rival theory?"

"David Hume, teacher," Mark Hiller answers.

"Oh, no. I hate that asshole philosophy. Empirical bullshit." David grimaces and tries to appear nauseated.

But Mark begins anyway. "Hume's observations are actually more defensive than they are usually taken to be. He did not deny the possible existence of a unified, irreducible self. He just maintained that we have no knowledge of such a self, that when we think of the self we think always of perceptions—heat, light, cold, love, pain—and that empirical knowledge can proceed without the concept of a unified or simple self. So Hume relied on the idea of the self as nothing more than a collection of perceptions. We are, in a word, sensations and no more than that."

"Fuck Hume." David starts laughing. "Let's hear it from the crowd."

"And this self, I gather, is not transferable." Frank is on a role toward conclusions. He is also oblivious, it seems, to the obscene or ironic. "Yes." He begins responding to his own speculation. "If we are no more than the empirical sum of our sensations, then there is—literally—nothing that can move from one body or physical vehicle to another. The body is, must be, at least the parameters of the self, and perhaps the self."

"Let's assume that Hume is wrong," David replies. "That's a first step to getting somewhere in this discussion."

Frank spreads his hands. Maybe a subtle supplication? He continues in the sonorous voice of the methodical teacher. "But I am still having problems imagining how these—what shall we call them—cross-body experiences can be known. Especially the transference of the self to the hawk. Since the neurological endowment of the hawk is radically different from that of a human, how could the boy, the human, become the hawk? Did he experience what the hawk experiences? I maintain that this is impossible. The hawk has a neurological system so radically unlike a human system that its reality must be inaccessible to humans. Or did the boy see the world as a human from the spatial perspectives of a hawk, flying up there above the earth, and so forth? I suppose this is possible, though requiring unusual—no, extraordinary imagination if it is to be anything more than a circus trick or a visual exercise from a different vantage point." Frank slowly, very slowly, sips his cognac. "Of course this objection does not bear on the reincarnation story that Lupe told."

"Listen. Stop. I have a report—I won't call it a story. It may help. No—it will probably make things worse." Mark is speaking. His voice is excited. He speaks quickly. But he had been a radio announcer part-time while in college, and since then has had this sonorous quality in the way he talks that makes every sentence sound like a pleasing announcement, no matter how rapid the delivery. "Still, I want to tell it."

"Proceed," Frank says.

"It happened when I was young. In this sense, and only in this sense, it's like Paul's story."

"But is it history?" David asks.

"Shut up, David," Lupe says.

"I am, as you know, a child of the sixties," Mark continues. His voice is more modulated now. Under control. "Meaning that I identify with certain dates. I was just entering college when John Kennedy was elected president, a senior when he was assassinated, in my dissertation year when Robert Kennedy was killed. I was a minor part of the civil rights movement in the South, most intensely in joining the demonstrations there in the summer of 1964 when Chaney and friends were killed. I missed Selma by chance, bad luck, but was there at Martin Luther King's 'Dream' speech in D.C.—along with about 50,000 others, I hasten to add. My friends and I were anti–Vietnam War before it was fashionable.

I think three of us demonstrated outside of the White House after Kennedy announced on television that he was sending advisers there, in 1961 I think."

Several members of the group smile at this last confession. No one in the group escapes the expected feelings of melancholy that afflict those who were American adults during the history that Mark is recalling. It is a curious and touching phenomenon that we are observing here, a collective acquiescence in the power of political violence to restructure perceptions. Where are Hume and Kant on this point?

"Drugs were part of the counterculture, as we all know. I took them in abundance at one stage in my life. On the night that Robert Kennedy won the California primary I was smoking joints with friends in celebration. When I got the call early the next morning that he had been shot, however, I felt the drugs bleed right out of my consciousness. We all stayed cold sober for days, right through his death and the funeral. And even through the moment when Ted Kennedy's voice broke during the eulogy he gave for his brother.

"But we went back to drugs in fairly short order. Mainly marijuana, benign enough, and some Quaaludes, a bit of speed from time to time. Then, in 1969 I started taking LSD. One member of our political cell was a chemist and he found a way to make the drug right in the university lab. I knew the warnings. That it was like shooting a bullet into the brain — the effects are random but all bad. I thought that was bullshit then, and still think so today. For me LSD is still a transient alteration of consciousness, short-lived and without permanent effects. Though I must confess that some of my friends were not so fortunate. One, I admit it, is still in therapy after all these years. But then he might have ended up there anyway, who knows. Remember that Hume's attack on causality invites especially self-serving counterfactuals.

"There was one experience with LSD that was unusual, however, in extreme ways. It was on a night that my brain felt like it was raining inside on itself, my thoughts were so moist and sluggish. I think I had been doing too much weed or ludes. Anyway, I wanted to sharpen and adjust my perceptions, or just escape the memory of a fight I had just had with my girlfriend. Believe me, I was not your standard survivor back then, no bearer of integrated coping skills. Now I am just grateful I made it through those years and introduced some order to my life.

"I took the drug sitting on a sofa in a friend's apartment. The one who is still in therapy, I now suddenly remember. Absorbing the drug was easy, nothing to it, you just put the fragment in your mouth and let it dissolve, doctor. When the effects started in I knew something was different. Maybe my friend had made a mistake in fixing the dosage, or something else had contaminated the drug, I don't know. But I do know, I do remember, that reality started coming apart. Things partitioned. At first everything I looked at was split horizontally, the tops and bottoms not quite in alignment, so that objects appeared to be on two disjoined planes.

"Then things got really interesting. The backs and fronts of objects began to get mixed up. I could see all at once the front and the rear of the piano that was placed ten feet in front of the couch where I was sitting. The insides of things next. The wires, which I could not possibly see without raising the lid of the instrument, became surface features, competing in my vision with the wood encasement of the piano. It was like being in a Picasso world—maybe 'Les Demoiselles d'Avignon' or something—with extraordinary insights replacing ordinary reality.

"The drug kept going, crawling through my body with more visual surprises. Things came alive. This part I still have problems describing, much less explaining. It was as if every object I saw was pulsating slightly with some vibrant force. Chairs, tables, everything seemed to have an interior dimension, some spiritual status. You know how you can often tell the difference between a completely immobile human and a perfectly rendered mannequin? Something about the human, some life force that you sense, marks him off from the dummy, the artificial form. Under the drug the world lost its inert status for me. Every item I saw seemed to be alive. Everything had a soul. The world was animated. I could see each molecule in objects, see the moving life in every object.

"The interesting thing was that I had no problems with this world that I was viewing. I was quite comfortable with it. Obviously I had been a closet vitalist all those years, secretly believing, or at least wishing, that the entire universe of objects was suffused with a life force that placed physical things on the same ontological plane that biological entities occupied. I felt a kinship with the objects around me, a kind of fellowship you might say. I was right at home.

"The problems came as the drug's effects intensified." Mark lifts his hands to his face. "I began to lose parts of myself. I felt myself partition and drift. First a kind of layering effect, which I was still able to explain to myself. I believed, or imagined, that regions of the brain that normally remain unconscious were being activated to a conscious level by the drug. That the long dormant reptilian brain, primitive core yet within the neurological levels of cerebrum and cerebral cortex, was being summoned to help this poor bastard order his sensations. More metaphor than possibility, I know now, but it made sense to me in that chemical state I was in. Reflective and reptilian modes hand-in-hand in joint orderings of empirical data. What a partnership.

"Then the partitions split laterally—there is no good word to describe what I experienced—so that I was talking across myself to myself. My identity divided, and subdivided. I drifted away from whatever made me what I was. May I assign the 's'-word in this company? My soul, indestructible and indivisible in metaphysical doctrines, separated into parts that floated away from each other. I swear I saw a portion of my spirit, maybe my actual brain, in my visual field, there in front of me just out of reach. I was terrified. I knew that if I did not retrieve that drifting part I would never regain wholeness, sanity.

"The next moment it did not matter. I lost all understanding, all awareness of myself as an individual. I simply dispersed, became the world that I had previously perceived from my location on the sofa. All fear vanished, all emotions, all thought—my identity was lost. There was just a single uniform wholeness, a reality that did not include me—or anyone—as a separate aware self. I no longer existed."

Mark spreads his hands on the dinner table. "It is impossible for me to describe this experience any better. If ever language is inadequate, and just plain distorting, it's when I try to assign it to that experience I had with LSD. One colorless fraction of a gram, a tiny fragment smaller than the point of the pen there on the table, placed under the tongue. Then a set of experiences that no adjective, no vocabulary can adequately describe. Even to think about it is not very helpful. It just happened. It was. Period.

"The best I can do is describe what it was like to come out of the experience when the drug wore off. It was like waking up episodically from a dreamless but still troubling sleep. Like emerging from nothing to something, with many regressive stops along the way where I slipped back spontaneously into complex delusions. That was what it was like. I do not know what it was. I do remember one powerful image that entered my consciousness as I was restored to whatever it is I am. Three computers seemed to turn on and rearrange themselves within my head in tandem fashion. Click, click, click, very rapidly. Then the thought that all is well again with my brain. Power is restored."

"We are happy for you," David remarks. "But what do you conclude from this story?"

"That the self is malleable, David. That while we resist its migratory powers described in the stories that Lupe and Paul have told us, we have abundant evidence that the self can merge with reality, be extinguished for a period of time as it becomes one with the world. Now can anyone tell me why reincarnation and the momentary occupation of another physical form by the self is any less credible than the self fusing with the cosmos? Anyone? I am waiting."

CHAPTER FOUR

a catalog of vivid
near-death experiences

DEFINITIONS

The vivid near-death experience (NDE), whatever it is in fact, is presented by those who experience it as a journey across the threshold of death, and a return to full life before morbidity is transformed into that permanent state acknowledged as death. In an odd sense the NDE is yet another transitional state in the journey to death. No one dies and returns from a death state in these experiences. The dying process is arrested; the individual is resuscitated or recovers spontaneously before the final stages of death commence.

There is no deep account, no definition-in-detail that all researchers accept. There is disagreement on the causal variables triggering the experience and (for want of a better term) the nature of the experience itself, most notably whether it is a genuine glimpse of a life after death or a strictly physical response of the brain to death. But minimalist and of course partisan definitions abound. The sparest and most succinct definition is that an NDE is the experience of being close to death but surviving with stories to tell about an afterlife. A bit more elaboration that attends to the survival part of an NDE is "a lucid experience associated with perceived consciousness apart from the body occurring at the time of actual or threatened imminent death" (from *Near Death Experience Research Foundation* [June 2003]). Or, from Wikipedia: "A near-death experience (NDE) is an experience reported by a person who nearly died, or who experienced clinical death and then revived." In *The Dictionary of Modern Medicine*, an NDE is defined as "a phenomenon of unclear nature that may occur in patients who have been clinically dead and then resuscitated; the patients report a continuity of subjective experience, remembering visitors and other hospital events despite virtually complete suppression of cortical activity; near-death experiences are considered curiosities with no valid explanation in the context of an acceptable bio-medical paradigm; the trivial synonym, Lazarus complex, refers to the biblical Lazarus who was raised from the dead by Jesus of Nazareth."

Or, from the Division of Perceptual Studies at the University of Virginia,

> A near-death experience, or NDE, is a common pattern of events that many persons experience when they are seriously ill or come close to death. Although NDEs vary from one person to another, they often include such features as the following:
> - Feeling very comfortable and free of pain
> - A sensation of leaving the body, sometimes being able to see the physical body while floating above it
> - The mind functioning more clearly and more rapidly than usual
> - A sensation of being drawn into a tunnel or darkness
> - A brilliant light, sometimes at the end of the tunnel
> - A sense of overwhelming peace, well-being, or absolute, unconditional love
> - A sense of having access to unlimited knowledge
> - A "life review," or recall of important events in the past
> - A preview of future events yet to come
> - Encounters with deceased loved ones, or with other beings that may be identified as religious figures

CASES: A SAMPLE

Hemingway's description in 1918 of a brief exit from his body after a mortar explosion at the front that almost killed him is presented in chapter 9 of A Farewell to Arms when the main character in the novel, Frederick Henry, is wounded:

> I heard a cough, then came the chuh-chuh-chuh-chuh—then there was a flash, as when a blast-furnace door is swung open, and a roar that started white and went red and on and on in a rushing wind. I tried to breathe but my breath would not come and I felt myself rush bodily out of myself and out and out and out and all the time bodily in the wind. I went out swiftly, all of myself, and I knew I was dead and that it had all been a mistake to think you just died. Then I floated,

and instead of going on I felt myself slide back. I breathed and I was back . . .

In 1918, the year that Hemingway had his NDE, a twenty-eight-year-old Katherine Anne Porter contracted the flu virus that ended up killing twenty to forty million people around the world in the worst flu pandemic in recorded history. Her fever spiked at 105 degrees. She was dying. The newspapers prepared her obituary and her family made burial arrangements. The doctors gave her an experimental shot of strychnine (a deadly poison) and she inexplicably recovered. Afterward she described to friends and family the near-death experience she had during her ordeal. Like all great short story writers and novelists Porter used the experience in her fiction. In one of her most famous novellas, *Pale Horse, Pale Rider*, a young woman, Miranda, who is a reporter, contracts the flu and almost dies. When she becomes ill her fiancé, Adam, takes her to a hospital, where she slips into a coma. In her near-death experience she sees a "minute fiercely burning particle of being that knew itself alone. . . . Trust me, the hard unwinking angry point of light said. Trust me, I stay."

Then the light "grew, flattened, thinned to a fine radiance, spread like a great fan and curved into a rainbow." Miranda is transformed by the experience, at the end "questioning nothing, desiring nothing, in the quietude of her ecstasy, stayed where she was, eyes fixed on the overwhelming deep sky where it was always morning." But a "vague tremor of apprehension" sets in, a realization that "she had left something valuable in another country." She realizes that she must go back. Her return to life brings her back to the pain and smells of the sick, to a hypodermic needle inserted in her arm, and at last an awakening to horns and whistles outside the hospital. The nurse tells her, "They're celebrating. It's the Armistice. The war is over, my dear." Miranda has recovered just as the First World War has ended and discovers in a letter from one of his army buddies that Adam had died of influenza in the camp hospital a month earlier.

These two events obviously precede the resuscitation techniques of contemporary medicine.

Three more recent NDEs, within the folds of the newer recovery techniques in medicine, have captured headlines. The difference today is that medicine can now routinely retrieve individuals from more extreme conditions, those that would have led inevitably to death at any time in the past. The results have sometimes been the tragedies of prolonged transitional states of the undead (represented by the cases of Nancy Cruzan, Sunny von Bülow, and Terri Schiavo), and the triumphs of persons brought back from presumably the last thresholds of the death process to resume a full life.

Roy Horn, one half of the Siegfried & Roy illusionist duo, was attacked in 2003 by a 380-pound tiger during a live performance of his act in the Mirage hotel-casino in Las Vegas. The tiger, a favorite animal in the entourage, bit into Horn's neck and dragged him offstage in an apparent attempt to help the performer after he fainted during the act. The wound to his neck caused Horn to suffer a stroke immediately after the tiger's jaws were wrested from the performer's neck and throat. The tiger's teeth had cut into an artery carrying oxygen to Horn's brain and crushed his trachea. Horn's heart stopped beating for a minute. On the operating table Horn had his NDE. "I saw a bank of white light," he reported later, "and then I saw all my beloved animals. For a moment I stepped out of my body."

Former U.S. president Bill Clinton had quadruple heart bypass surgery in October 2004 to correct severely blocked arteries. In a television interview with Diane Sawyer on *Primetime Live* shortly after the surgery, Clinton described an NDE that he had while under the general anesthetic as "profound and lasting" visions. One vision "clearly connoted death and images that clearly connoted life." As Clinton elaborated the experience, he said, "I saw dark masks, like death masks, being crushed in series. And then I saw great circles of light, and Hillary's picture or Chelsea's face would appear in the light. And then they would fly off into the distance." Hillary Clinton reports that the experience had a profound effect on the former president; he feels his tasks are now a bonus and seems to be more concerned with everyday life.

Bob Woodruff was an ABC anchorman on assignment in Iraq on January 29, 2006, riding in a tank with his head and upper body outside the vehicle when a roadside bomb went off. The explosion tore off part of his skull. He immediately had a brief NDE. As he reported later, "When [the bomb] actually exploded, I don't remember that. But I do remember immediately at that moment that I saw my body floating below me and a kind of whiteness." He collapsed back into the tank and lost consciousness. He woke up after a few minutes spitting up blood and, in his words, "I looked up at Doug [cameraman Doug Vogt] and

I saw his eyes big and afraid and just asking him if we were still alive and that's the last thing I remember." Woodruff slipped into a coma that lasted thirty-six days. When he woke up he could barely remember the bombing. During the coma he had no near-death experiences. It was simply lost time. He has since begun a slow process toward recovery of his physical and mental powers. In a sense Woodruff had both a (brief) vivid NDE followed by a flat NDE of thirty-six days, followed by a return to full consciousness.

NONSTANDARD CASES

Researchers have also collected a number of near-death experiences that do not fit the standard model. Like string theory in physics they challenge conventional thinking, in this case the belief that NDEs are all very much alike. Here are three reported by Dr. Dhebhanom Muangman, president of the Bangkok Institute of Psychical Research in Thailand. The reader will notice as we move through this chapter that the neat perimeters that border the traditional Western out-of-body-experiences are missing or porous in these accounts, which are driven by rich imaginative forays.

A forty-three-year-old woman with twelve years of education, married to a college-educated man and mother of four children, died of unknown causes, possibly related to anemia. Her NDE began with a visitation by two white-robed young men not known to her. They informed her that it was her time to die, and that she was to be taken for judgment. She did not want to go. One of the figures touched her arm, and she then had an out-of-body experience (OBE) in which she flew while holding the figure's arm. She saw the roof of the hospital as she felt herself fly upward. She reached the clouds and found herself able to walk on the clouds. Shortly thereafter, she found herself in front of a desk. The figure behind the desk told her that she was the wrong person, and the right person was in the same hospital, in a room three doors down from the room in which she had "died." The patient revived. Shortly after, a nurse working in a room three doors down from her collapsed and died. The nurse's family refused to allow an autopsy.

Another woman, fifty-eight years old, a U.S.-educated university professor, had an NDE that began in her kitchen when a cobra bit her after she had reached down to turn on the propane that fed her stove. The patient was put in a coffin, which was placed in a Buddhist temple. She remained there for three days before reviving. Her NDE began with an autoscopic OBE. She then found herself in front of her house. Two men in western clothes appeared and told her to get up. They said they wanted to take her for a walk. She looked back and found that the house had disappeared. The path in front of her was misty. The weather was cool and pleasant. She saw crowds of people from which emerged an older man whom she referred to as Uncle Pong (her father's elder brother).

Pong told her that he was dead and was there to welcome her. (He had, in fact, died the day after she was bitten by a cobra.) Two men, not described, came to take her for judgment. She came before a judge (not described) who told her that although her name was the right one, it was actually another person of the same name who was to have been taken. He instructed the two to take her back. The patient resisted and asked to know, before she went back, if heaven and hell were real. The judge instructed the guides to take her on a tour of heaven and hell. She was taken to heaven first. Her experience there was of a cool place where birds, flowers, and beautiful houses were found in abundance. Hell was a place where souls were tortured in various ways, with whippings specifically mentioned. After her tour was over, she revived and began to beat on the lid of the coffin. The monks in the temple ran away, frightened, thinking that she was a ghost. One of her family members opened the coffin and let her out.

The following is an adaptation by Phra Bhavana of a first-person story related by a woman, Boonchu:

On February 5, 1952, I came home from work feeling very tired and sleepy, after feeling run-down and fatigued all day. I lay down to take a nap, and when I awoke, I got up and found that, although I was standing up, my body was still sleeping. I went outside the house and stood under a coconut tree. I experienced a deep sense of beauty. I did not know where I was. Looking around, I saw a road and wondered where it went. I walked along the road. Suddenly, I heard two people talking very loudly. I looked and saw that they were Yamatoots (servants of Yama, The Lord of the Dead). One of them spoke to me saying, "We've come to take you to hell." I said, "I'm not going," and I tried to escape. I turned and repeated that I was not going to go to the house of Yama. I soon realized that I could not escape. I asked the Yamatoots to wait a while, because I had to tell my family that I was dead. I told them, "Nobody knows I'm here." I walked to my house, stood in front of it for a minute, and then went inside. I saw there were a number of people there, and all of them were crying. I saw my wife and daughter sitting together. I tried to run to them, but I tripped on something. I fell. As I hit the floor, I revived.

IMPLICATIONS

The striking feature of vivid NDEs has been the unexpected stories that the survivors tell. They describe leaving their bodies, often seeing their bodies as they depart the scene in which they have "died," sometimes being greeted by dead family or friends, occasionally encountering a guide who reviews their life with them, beginning a journey characterized by movement through a tunnel or across a field, over a barrier such as a fence, and then—always in the good versions—approaching a light radiant with a fulfilling love that promises redemption and a completion of the self. Not all near-death experiences are benign or satisfying. Some recent stories describe privation, loss of love, demons who promise harm. But three things about all these experiences seem fixed. One is that they are reported across all cultures on the earth, though not among all those who have nearly died. Second, while the descriptions contain different symbols in different cultures, they converge toward a small set of models that are generalizable in important though not identical ways. Third, NDEs are eminently credible to those who experience them. People who return from thresholds of death and near-death experiences believe that there is life after death.

Western studies indicate that those who have had NDEs are more sanguine about death than they were before the experience. But in general attitudes toward death are surprisingly benign among those who are close to dying. Karlis Osis conducted a large study of the deathbed observations of doctors and nurses. He sent out 10,000 questionnaires, of which 640 were returned. Those answering claimed a total of 35,540 deathbed observations. As summarized in *The Natural Death Handbook* (1993):

Osis found that about 10% of dying patients appeared to be conscious in the hour preceding death. Surprisingly enough, fear was not the dominant emotion in these individuals, according to the physicians and nurses in the sample. They indicated that discomfort, pain and even indifference were more frequent. It was estimated that about one in twenty dying persons showed signs of elation. A surprising finding in this research was the high incidence of visions with a predominantly non-human content. They were approximately ten times more frequent than one would expect in a comparable group of persons in normal health. Some of these visions were more or less in accordance with traditional religious concepts and represented heaven, paradise, or the Eternal City; others were secular images of indescribable beauty, such as landscapes with gorgeous vegetation and exotic birds. According to the authors, more of these visions were characterized by brilliant colors and bore a close resemblance to psychedelic experiences induced by mescaline or LSD. Less frequent were horrifying visions of devils and hell or other frightening experiences, such as being buried alive.

Moving across all definitions of the NDE is uncertainty about the truth or reality of the experience, best expressed by Susan Blackmore:

> For many experiencers, their adventures seem unquestionably to provide for evidence for life after death, and the profound effects the experience can have on them is just added confirmation. By contrast, for many scientists these experiences are just hallucinations produced by the dying brain and of no more interest than an especially vivid dream. So which is right? . . . Neither is quite right: NDEs provide no evidence for life after death, and we can best understand them by looking at neurochemistry, physiology, and psychology; but they are much more interesting than any dream. . . . Any satisfactory theory . . . leads us to questions about minds, selves, and the nature of consciousness.

The occasional negative NDE raises the question of whether the entire experience is merely a psychotic episode with various causes and implications. The functional role of psychosis in religious life is well known. Stanislav and Christina Grof demarcate *spiritual emergence* (a transformation that involves one's entire being extending to the spiritual dimensions of one's life) and *spiritual emergencies*. The latter are

> critical and experientially difficult stages of a profound psychological transformation that involves one's entire being. They take the form of nonordinary states of consciousness and involve intense emotions, visions and other sensory changes, and unusual thoughts, as well as various physical manifestations. These episodes often revolve around

spiritual themes; they include sequences of psychological death and rebirth, experiences that seem to be memories from previous life times, feelings of oneness with the universe, encounters with various mythological beings, and other similar motifs.

The spiritual and the psychotic can dramatically intersect in practice. In one memorable (anecdotal) event in the history of the Syracuse Hutchings Psychiatric Center (a publicly funded mental health facility of excellent standing), an elderly man who had been brought in off the streets was diagnosed as a classic schizophrenic and given treatment. The next day a large crowd of people from a Native American community gathered at the door of the Institute. It seems that the man was a revered spiritual leader in their community and they wanted him released so that his presence and visions could continue to serve the community. He was subsequently released and returned to a setting where his "illness" was respected and highly useful. Are NDEs peculiar forms of psychosis that serve the individual well in providing comfort before death? Are they perhaps an iconic and very dramatic representation of the ancient conviction that we live on after death?

The answer is no if we allow that psychotic episodes must provide signs and leave traces of a damaged psyche, even when healing of the psychosis occurs. NDEs seem to escape even the most encompassing criteria for depicting mental problems. The individuals who have NDEs typically are mentally sound before, presumably during, and after the experience. No mental disorders seem even remotely connected to the experience. As summarized in Wikipedia: "The effects of near-death experiences are often great for those who have them, their friends and families, and medical workers." Kenneth Ring discovered what has become the standard mantra on NDEs and mental health, that values and beliefs change for the NDE individual but the changes are beneficial. The personality changes include a greater appreciation for life, higher self-esteem, greater compassion for others, a heightened sense of purpose and self-understanding, a desire to learn, elevated spirituality, greater ecological sensitivity and planetary concern, a feeling of being more intuitive (sometimes psychic), increased physical sensitivity, diminished tolerance to light, alcohol, and drugs, a feeling that the brain has been "altered" to encompass "more," and a feeling that one is now using the "whole brain" rather than just a small part. Bruce Greyson, professor of personality studies in the Department of Psychiatric Medicine at the

University of Virginia, and editor-in-chief of the highly respected *Journal of Near-Death Studies*, reports that near-death experiences "are associated with enhanced purpose in life, appreciation of life and with reduced fear of death, but also with adverse effects, such as posttraumatic stress symptoms. Some subjects also report internal feelings of bodily energy and/or altered states of consciousness similar to those associated with the yogic concept of kundalini." As the saying goes, what's not to like about these changes?

The antecedent conditions for NDEs present a more mixed picture. Greyson has found that "people who reported NDEs also reported significantly more dissociative symptoms than did the comparison group." Disassociation is a separation of thoughts, perceptions, feelings—the desiderata of the self—from the ordinary streams of experience. It can range from the extreme to the benign. Victims of assault sometimes report an imposed dissociation. One rape victim described her ordeal in this way: "When a bearded stranger kidnapped me and stole my virginity, I witnessed his brutal act from outside my body, detached from the pain." By contrast, Greyson presents the dissociative tendencies of NDE experiencers as benign, a product of temperament or personality traits, not the result of trauma. "Among those who reported NDEs, the depth of the experience was positively correlated with dissociative symptoms, although the level of symptoms was substantially lower than that of patients with pathological dissociative disorders." It may be that certain types of individuals, those who are inclined toward a variety of dissociative experiences, are more susceptible to NDEs, more likely to have them and have them at greater depths.

There is one important change brought about by NDEs that, by virtue of its risk inclinations, might be singled out as a mental issue. This change is the augmented indifference of NDE survivors to death itself, with the attendant lack of concern for protecting the self against death. This is not to say that NDEs incline individuals toward suicide, but it follows that the common revulsion and fear of death have inspired some remarkable avoidance tactics. If one views death as simply a transition to a different and perhaps better state of affairs, then it raises the question—why avoid it? Of course an increase in one's inclination to risk life, to take death casually, can be viewed as a pathology only if one views death in the traditional way, as an end to one's existence. If death leads to a better world that one has actually seen and personally confirmed, then an indifference and even risk-inclined approach to death is rational and hardly pathological. So whether the pathology predicate can be assigned to post-NDE behavior toward death is entirely a function of how one views death in the first place.

RIVAL MODELS

If we were diagramming the NDE, we would sketch two ineluctable and basic components. One is the objective side represented by the "clinical death" condition, which, by the way, is a traditional definition of death that relies on a cessation of cardiopulmonary activity. The other is the subjective side represented by the accounts provided by the one who has nearly died and claims to have entered a sphere of existence that awaits us after we die. The temptation is to view the objective side as firm, precise. But that is not so clear. So-called "clinical death" refers to the traditional perspective that a person is dead if all respiratory and cardiac functions stop. The Hollywood gesture of placing a mirror in front of the mouth to see if the "dead" person is breathing or not is a rough cinematic representation of informal tests for clinical death. The obvious suggestion is that the concept of clinical death tracks to an earlier period in medicine, a bit like "quickening" was used in the common law to determine the point in pregnancy when abortion was no longer permitted, meaning a test that predates high-tech medicine.

The problem is that high-tech medicine has shifted the playing ground to tests of brain death without the sharp demarcation between life and death that one might want. A flat EEG test indicates no brain activity and is considered the gold standard for proof of death. It is also a documented fact that the brain begins to deteriorate and die after just a few minutes without the oxygen and blood flow supplied by respiration and the actions of a beating heart. Yet children and adults have recovered even after a short but very flat EEG reading, and heart and lung machines can reproduce the functions needed to keep the brain alive, at least for a time, thus maintaining the zone between life and death for extended periods of time. In this way a clinically dead person can be resuscitated to a form of life that defeats the traditional tests for death. Also, certain radical forms of surgery involve stopping the heart and literally draining the body of all its blood, turning the brain off, in effect simulating death in all respects except for its permanence, and then restoring the patient from this dead state to life.

Do such states represent life or death? Do not misunderstand the point. We have polar extremes where a person is definitely alive or definitely dead. The corpse buried in the ground for prolonged periods of time is the body of a dead person. That person is definitely dead. The vibrant active individual living life large is a live person. But note the definitive sense of death at the margins of life: death is an irreversible condition in which the heart, lungs, and brain are not functioning and these functions cannot be restored. This is the easy definition of death, except that it can be established only retrospectively. The defeat of this form of death is the condition for the near-death experience, meaning resuscitation after a cessation of vital signs. Or NDEs occur and the individual is retrieved as clinical death is reversed. Or, put succinctly, the subjective side of the NDE is a direct product of the defeat of the objective, traditional, and clinical definition of death.

In a report to a group at the Esalen Center studying life after death, Greyson summarized two early twentieth-century models used to explain NDEs. One, the "perceptual release theory," maintains that NDEs are forms of hallucination, essentially projections of the thoughts of the one having the experience. In an enchanting illustration the proponents of this theory ask us to imagine a fire in a house. Looking out of windows in the house during the day we can see the trees, grass, and animals playing in the fields, but at night we would see the fire reflected in the window pane. NDEs, they argue, are like seeing the reflections, which in the analogy are the result of sensory deprivation represented by the onset of night. The onset of death reduces our sensory loads and causes the brain to project thoughts as perceptions. This theory is properly seen as skeptical of NDEs. Like all skeptical theories it accepts NDEs as experiences (people do see what they claim to see) but denies their reality (the visions are hallucinations, meaning thoughts mistakenly accepted as perceptions).

The second theory, "the alternative reality theory," accepts NDEs as veridical. This is the theory developed by William James that regards NDEs as authentic access to a dimension of reality denied to us when we are fully alive. James proposed a different analogy. Here we are asked to imagine our perceptions of the sky during the daylight hours. We cannot see the moon and stars because they are obscured by sunlight. But when the sun sets and the sky is darkened we can see the moon and a rich array of stars. James proposed that the brain filters out a wide range of experiences when it is functioning at full strength in monitoring and framing sensory data. But when we are dying the brain's powers are reduced and we are deprived of the usual vivid assortment of sensory experiences. Then the hidden dimensions of reality become more fully visible to us, not as hallucinations but as a real world that we cannot see until we are near death. This theory is obviously a believer's account. Individuals having NDEs are seeing dimensions of a world that is hidden from us while we are alive but appears to us in the dying experience as a reality we are to enter when we die.

Versions of both theories have endured to the present day. One reason for their long shelf life is that both accommodate the NDE. The evidence that we have for the experience, and our current knowledge and conjectures on how the brain works, supports both models. Neither the skeptic nor the believer carries the day, in part because we do not know enough about the workings of the brain to rule out, to falsify, one or the other depiction of the NDE. Attempts to provide hard evidence for the near-death experience rely on the possibility that the intact self, replete with identity and memories, is not destroyed by death but in fact leaves the body at the moment of death for another dimension of reality. The central expectation of the veridical understanding of NDEs is that, if the experience is true, the external though still intact self should be able to see things that are outside the visual field of the body that has been left behind. Also, on the veridical interpretation it does not matter that the brain is producing abundant natural chemicals at the time of death, or, rather, it matters but in different ways than the skeptic thinks. Like the activities of the brain in ordinary perceptions—the seeing of real objects in the visual field (visible through MRIs)—the NDE activities of the brain may simply be the neurological correlates of another type of real experience, in this case access to an alternative reality. Or, the onset of death may simply be the triggering event for the brain to begin scanning and providing entrée to the life we are to enter after we die.

NDES: SENSORY EXPERIENCES

There have been impressive visual experiences reported by individuals who are unconscious, under strong anesthetics during surgery. Many involve what is called autoscopy, "an experience in which a person while *believing to be awake* sees her/his body and the world from a location outside her/his physical body" (Wikipedia). Greyson reports several such instances. In one,

Al Sullivan, a 55 year old truck driver who was undergoing triple bypass surgery, had a powerful NDE that included an encounter with his deceased mother and brother-in-law, who told Al to return to his life, to tell one of his neighbors that their son with lymphoma will be OK. Furthermore, during the NDE, Al accurately noticed that the surgeon operating on him was flapping his arms in an unusual fashion, with his hands in his armpits. When he came back to his body after the surgery was over, the surgeon was startled that Al could describe his own arm flapping, which was his idiosyncratic method of keeping his hands sterile.

Or this story (from the work of Raymond Moody): One patient told Moody,

> After it [his surgery] was all over the doctor told me that I had a really bad time, and I said, "Yeah, I know." He said, "Well, how do you know?" and I said, "I can tell you everything that happened." He didn't believe me, so I told him the whole story, from the time I stopped breathing until the time I was kind of coming around. He was really shocked to know that I knew everything that had happened. He didn't know quite what to say, but he came in several times to ask me different things about it.

In another story, this one in Moody's documentary *Life after Life*, he interviewed a Russian scientist named Dr. George Rodonaia, who had a near-death experience during which he observed an infant crying in a nearby room. George observed that no one could figure out why the infant was crying so persistently. But George learned while out of his body that the infant had a broken arm. When George returned to life, he told the infant's parents about the broken arm. An X-ray revealed that the infant's arm was indeed broken. It seems the Russian scientist visited and talked with the baby while having the out-of-body experience and saw in a kind of X-ray vision that the baby's arm was broken. It is hard to know what to do with these cases. In this instance a scientist in close proximity to a crying baby has to have an OBE and a psychic connection to the baby to disclose what standard medical tests could easily reveal. Not even the totally faithful can count this report as a veridical perception confirming the truth of the NDE.

Then there are the straightforward metaphysical experiences, for example, the suggestion of ESP in a near-death experience (again from the work of Moody):

In another instance a woman with a heart condition was dying at the same time that her sister was in a diabetic coma in another part of the same hospital. The subject reported having a conversation with her sister as both of them hovered near the ceiling watching the medical team work on her body below. When the woman awoke, she told the doctor that her sister had died while her own resuscitation was taking place. The doctor denied it, but when she insisted, he had a nurse check on it. The sister had, in fact, died during the time in question.

The absence of controls on the reports of veridical perceptions in NDEs, the tendency to rely on observations confined to and confirmed within the site where the individual is located while having the NDE, and the reliance on strictly metaphysical stories of OBEs lodged in a strictly spiritual dimension suggest one of two things once one examines the evidence for veridical perceptions: either these perceptions do not occur as actual perceptions, or if they occur they are lodged in a dimension of reality that does not intersect in strong ways with the ordinary worlds of sense experience. Both possibilities are important, but they speak against the access of the NDE individuals to the normal perceptual powers of an ambulatory spiritual self. There are some experiments designed to test the veridical perception hypothesis, meaning accurately seeing and hearing events from outside one's body during an NDE. But these accounts are not conclusive. For one thing, the exogenous "spirit" has no powers of psychokinesis. No item can be moved across a table, no blinds drawn shut, nor has anyone even turned a page in a book while in an out-of-body state. For another, even the strongest instances of veridical perception seem always to occur in the vicinity of the body putatively left behind.

Many of these cases are consistent with a kind of attenuated perception that might be triggered, or at least not blocked, in the surgical experience. Again, we know that our brains are the instruments that organize sensory data and are our main resource for knowing reality. We also know that we can hallucinate on occasion, that a sick or impaired brain can conjure false realities, and that the brain produces a wide assortment of chemicals, including endorphins, when it is under stress. We may also assume that death is a stressful experience for the brain since it is dying along with the rest of our bodies. The NDE may be a hallucination conjured by the brain as a direct or indirect byproduct of natural selection. On the other hand, we do not know the full range of real experiences that the brain can access. As an organ that may be the most complex entity in the universe, the human brain may have the power to see, to enter, alternative realities that are not joined in ordinary experiences. Our neurological powers, expressed in physics, have given us renditions of worlds far beyond the ordinary. The capacities of the brain to know more than we normally experience may be activated in different and even more dramatic ways in the NDE. Patients in surgery can occasionally repeat, almost verbatim, the conversations of the medical team performing the surgery, see the actions of the surgeons and nurses, and so on. The documented fact that the brain processes information at an unconscious level is likely the better start for an explanation of this type of event represented by the Al Sullivan story. We may simply retrieve and collate data even when unconscious at deep levels.

More interesting are those events in which a person "sees" things that s/he could not (by definition) see in the lived life. For example, this case, again from the work of Raymond Moody: "An elderly woman had been blind since childhood. But, during her NDE, the woman had regained her sight and she was able to accurately describe the instruments and techniques used during the resuscitation of her body. After the woman was revived, she reported the details to her doctor. She was able to tell her doctor who came in and out, what they said, what they wore, what they did, all of which was true." The true mystery of this story, and its singular importance, is the blindness of the woman recounting the events with a mental acumen and visual confidence she could not have had throughout her life.

There are other cases of perception during NDEs that common sense and medical understandings tell us cannot be secured by a brain exercising even extraordinary powers. For example, there is the case presented in Dr. Michael Sabom's book, *Light and Death* (1998),

the NDE account of a woman named Pam Reynolds who underwent a rare operation to remove a giant basilar artery aneurysm in her brain that seriously threatened her life. The surgical procedure used to remove the aneurysm is known as "hypothermic cardiac arrest" or "standstill." Pam's body temperature was lowered to 60 degrees, her heartbeat and breathing were stopped, her brain waves were flattened, and all the blood was drained from her head. For all practical purposes, she was put to death. . . . When all of Pam's vital signs were stopped, the doctor turned on a surgical saw and began to cut through Pam's skull. While this was going on, Pam reported that she felt herself "pop" outside her body and hover above the operating table. Then she watched the doctors working on her lifeless body for awhile. From her out-of-body position, she observed the doctor sawing into her skull with what looked to her like an electric toothbrush. Pam heard and reported later what the nurses in the operating room had said and exactly what was happening during the operation. At this time, every monitor attached to Pam's body registered "no life" whatsoever. At some point, Pam's consciousness floated out of the operating room and traveled down a tunnel which had a light at the end of it where her deceased relatives and friends were waiting including her long-dead grandmother. Pam's NDE ended when her deceased uncle led her back to her body for her to reenter it. Pam compared the feeling of reentering her dead body to "plunging into a pool of ice."

Sabom noted that "while this woman was dead, as defined by silent EEG, absence of brainstem response, and lack of blood in the brain, she had the deepest NDE of any patient in his study; her NDE scored 27 points on the NDE Scale, almost 2 standard deviations above the mean for near-death experiences."

GENERAL ASSUMPTIONS AND THINGS WE KNOW

Near death experiences are commonplace events throughout history, though more frequently reported today. The best figures indicate that seven million people worldwide have reported near-death experiences, a large number even if some significant part of that figure is bogus. In an interview with journalist Lese Dunton, Greyson, acknowledged as the preeminent scholar in the field, summarized much of what we know about the phenomenon:

> Dunton: What would you most like people to realize as a result of this research?
>
> Greyson: I think the most important thing for people to realize, for the average person to realize, is that having a near-death experience is a very common, very normal experience. They happen to everybody. They happen to presidents, they happen to psychotics, religious people or atheists. They are a normal part of living. They have nothing

to do with mental illness. They're nothing to be afraid of or worried about if you have them. Nothing to be ashamed of, either.

Dunton: And it results in a tendency to not fear death anymore.

Greyson: Right. And people tend to think that if they weren't afraid of dying, or they thought dying was beautiful, they'd become suicidal. That does not seem to be the case. What happens is that when they lose their fear of death, they also lose their fear of living life to the fullest because they're not afraid of taking chances anymore. They're not afraid of dying. So they actually get more interested in life and enjoy it much more than they did before.

Dunton: Do you study what children say and what adults say; the differences and similarities?

Greyson: Children don't have the same cultural indoctrination that adults do. So in that sense, their experience is a little more pure. There are also ways in which children are *biologically* different from adults and that kind of confounds the issue. Generally speaking, they tell the same types of stories that adults do. They tend not to have the elaborate life review that adults do because they don't have as much life to review. They don't tend to see deceased relatives because they don't have as many. There are some striking stories of children who've talked about "guides" in their near-death experiences. As they described the guides, their parents recognized them as deceased relatives that the kids had never met.

While the rudiments of the experience converge to a single generalizable model, we have seen that there are intriguing variations on the experience that suggest it is what's called a cluster concept rather than a strict rote experience. If nothing else, the reports of Thai near-death experiences illuminate the effects of culture on NDEs, both as to descriptions and criteria for validity. There are also unremitting and uncompromising skeptical takes on the experience housed within that cluster that qualify the seemingly unbroken confidence of those who have NDEs. For example, more than a few individuals who experience NDEs are skeptical about their validity. For example, in a letter to the *Skeptical Inquirer*, a woman who had an NDE wrote:

I died a few days ago. I was on the operating table, conscious and aware, as is the procedure in angioplasty, and all of a sudden I felt incredibly sleepy—sleepier and sleepier until I faded out entirely.

What happened on the table was that my heart fibrillated, stopped, and then I passed on to oblivion. An eternity later, which was only a minute or so in real time, I came back. What I experienced, as a skeptic and one who doesn't believe in the survival of personal identity, was awesome.

Looking back on it I realize that as my conscious brain had slowly closed down, the surface gave up its energy before the lower layers did, and it gave me the impression that I was starting down a long tunnel, a tunnel that closed upon me even as oblivion embraced me. Then, totally unbeknownst to me and without any sensation of pain, the doctor hit me with the paddles. From out of the darkness, void and dead, the tunnel reappeared, and at the end I could see a light. I struggled toward the light, and the tunnel pushed back and back until I heard the doctor say: "Laura, we lost you, but it's all right now. We brought you back!" Opening my eyes I realized the bright light had been the bright light of the operating room. It was only then that I understood I had died. Lethargic, I didn't care; I almost wished I had been left alone.

I can understand how those who talk of NDEs and believe in some mystical power might misconstrue this happenstance; I cannot do the same. But I did find it moving and powerful, and I have recognized that the only thing that is important in life is what we do here and now. We won't be getting another chance! What we accomplish now, what we do in this life, is all that is important. We take nothing to the grave with us!

Another thing we know about NDEs is that their consequences are complicated. Even though most react to them positively afterward, it is difficult to integrate such a life-changing experience into one's life. Again, from the Greyson interview:

Dunton: And then children aren't afraid of death afterwards.

Greyson: Yeah. It can be very difficult for children to grow up with the knowledge that they get in NDEs. I had one young man who was referred to me as a patient a few years ago. He was a freshman in high school and was very active. He played in a rock band, was on the football team, and active in church. Then he had his NDE and all these things seemed sort of unimportant to him now. He came back with a sense of—there's something important in this life. And these other things seemed so trivial to him. He felt out of step with his peers;

school seemed unimportant. He started not going to classes. It was a very difficult period for him and it was years before he finally started to get back on track.

Dunton: I guess that happens with adults too. Sometimes people come back to their marriages or their jobs and think, mmm, some things need changing.

Greyson: There are some people whose lives are spiritual before the NDE, and then when they have it, maybe it doesn't change them very much. But people who were in very punitive or violent professions can be totally shaken up by the NDE and not be able to go back to their lives as they were before. There were a lot of people who had NDEs in Vietnam, who had been career military people. They just couldn't go back to it.

Some NDEs, however, are dark, negative experiences. The best, though still rough estimate is that as many as 25 percent of NDEs are scary, even terrifying, and so present an unwelcome prospect of life after death. It's just that the life after death may be miserable, not displaying that radiant bliss in which the NDE is typically presented. One such example comes from Barbara Rommer's *Blessing in Disguise: Another Side of the Near Death Experience*, which chronicles the negative dimension. Here is the story of one survivor:

Joyce Harvey, a 75-year-old retired CID officer from Essex, had a near-death experience when she was recovering in hospital from a chest infection. Ms. Harvey said that she was having problems breathing when she suddenly felt very cold and could not move. "I started going down and down in a lift, with someone pulling my legs which were really hot," she said. "There were terrible noises, discordant notes, and screaming. I could see thousands of faces without bodies beneath me; they were trying to pull me down further and further. I was terrified." Ms. Harvey said that she felt she was dying and fought to come back to life. "Suddenly I was coming back up in the lift and the nurse was standing in front of me," she said. "I had no particular beliefs and believe it was my body responding to lack of oxygen."

NEAR DEATH EXPERIENCES: TRUTH
OR DARE?

Death and dying are also areas of experience that lend themselves to artifice, simulation, and the inexplicable. The open and salient issue addressed here, whether there is a continuation of life after death, is a holding cell for enchanting anomalies. The moment of death, a real and compelling event in the lives of everyone, is also reproducible in controlled experiments. For example, the replication of that critical datum, the near-death experience, continues to cloud the validity, the truth content of this experience. The controlled experiments with ketamine (a short-acting general anaesthetic that has hallucinogenic and pain-killing qualities, presented first in experiments conducted by Dr. Karl L.R. Jansen beginning in 1990) have yielded striking results that simulate NDEs. The simulated experiences are every bit as vivid as the "real" experiences. Except that they are often more bizarre, less regulated by the standard model. And they are never completely absorbing, meaning that the participants in the experiment are always partially aware that they are in a conventional room in ordinary reality, not near death.

Then there are the experiments that mimic out-of-body experiences. For example, scientists in at least three countries (Switzerland, Sweden, and Britain) have successfully convinced subjects that they have left their bodies. These experiments take a variety of forms. For example, in one experiment led by Dr. Henrik Ehrsson at University College London's Institute for Neurology, subjects were outfitted with head-mounted video displays that allowed them to view themselves from behind in a number of locations. The purpose of the experiment was to determine if subjects who could see themselves from the outside would simply accept the odd viewing perspective from within their bodies, or if the self would move with the eyes outside of the body. The subjects reported that they felt they were actually outside of, behind their bodies, during critical parts of the experiment. The change in visual location shifted the felt locus of the self. In another experiment, a team of scientists led by Professor Olaf Blanke fitted subjects with virtual reality goggles, and, in a combination of visual and tactile sensations they were tested for orientations to their own bodily locations. Again, the controlled distortions affected their perception of bodily location. In all these experiments the sense of self can be tricked by the contrived sensations into feeling that the self, which is conveniently and conventionally located in the body, was outside the body to some degree, or not in harmony with a sense of the body as housing the self.

It's hard to know whether any conclusions about the validity of NDEs can be drawn from these experiments. One can concede that a variety of devices and controlled experiments can simulate in a rough and imperfect way the NDE. But what does that prove for the truth or falsity of NDEs? If weightlessness can be simulated in controlled experiments, does this speak to the validity or reality of weightlessness in real-world conditions (in outer space, for example)? Is the experience false because we can simulate its source in experiments? It does not seem so. Simulation is generally defined as an experience without the reality of the experience. But the success of a simulation usually does not compromise the reality at issue. If certain drugs can stimulate the brain into a spiritual experience, even perceived contact with God, the fact that the experience can be simulated has no bearing on whether there is a real experience of God in normal (noncontrived) human experience.

In fact the argument goes in the opposite direction. It would be counterintuitive for the genuine standing of religious experience if no stimulation of the brain could trigger what is called the "God experience." It is, after all, the brain that is the instrument to have experiences, and producing a simulated religious experience may be an informal proof of the brain's powers to have the real experience in the proper natural conditions, and a harbinger of NDEs at the moment when the brain is actually dying. Christian and Buddhist monks have a long history of seeking God or the cosmos with the help of fasting, prolonged meditation, and natural psychotropic drugs. That an exogenous substance conditions the brain to have certain experiences does not in and of itself discredit the reality of the experiences. That the brain produces indigenous drugs in the initiation of NDEs would seem to be a positive sign that something real may be happening for the dying individual, and that this real thing may be signals and indicators of a life after death.

Given the mixed and unavoidably inconclusive takes on life after death, and the melancholy fact that beliefs are always part of a constellation of thoughts, it often helps to ask what is entailed when one holds a particular belief. This intellectual style is often expressed in strident form as what I have always called a New York way of arguing, for example: "If you believe that—call it A—then you have to believe B. What? I am astonished. You actually *believe* B? But if you believe B then you have to believe C. No, that's not possible. You actually believe C? C? You are lost, hopeless." Well, let's pose the question—if you believe in life after death, what does this belief require of you in the way of other beliefs? (Note that I am negotiating a far more politic version of the New York way of arguing.) Put in stark terms, if you believe in an afterlife, you must believe in alternative realities that are invisible, only partially accessible in this life and only with the use of intuitions and formal systems of thought (like mathematics). After all, individuals must go somewhere if they live again after they die. But the odd thing is—this is the easy part. Of course there are alternative realities that we cannot see, attested to by contemporary physics. In the film *The Horse Whisperer*, Robert Redford's character expresses in two brief sentences the disjunction between knowledge and action that everyone in a doomed relationship has experienced: "Knowing is easy. Telling is hard."

It's the second step in NDEs, in this case rendering the external reality in sentient form, that is hard. The species of reality explaining an afterlife would seem to require that forms of life, guides or mentors who are something other than human, occupy an alternative reality—when the only reliable indication of that reality that we have is a mathematical representation occasioned by the need to make three-dimensional space intelligible. We need to construct a different way of thinking about experiences that is capable of revising understandings of life itself, coherence rather than a truth-driven approach, and one that is definitely not compatible with traditional ways of thinking through the issues of a life after death.

LIMITS REVISITED

Michel Foucault opens *The Birth of the Clinic* with the story of Pierre Pomme, the respected eighteenth-century French physician who famously saw membranous tissue on the human body "like pieces of damp parchment." These visual experiences were dismissed over time as medicine became more closely based on scientific evidence, meaning data that could be falsified through acceptable tests. But there is little doubt that Pomme saw the membranes. They were a realistic part of his visual experiences. The revisions in history that later dismiss what was real to earlier communities are as common as the experiences themselves. These "false" experiences are astoundingly commonplace, occupy places in both scientific and nonscientific practices, and are often grounded in theories that have acceptable standing for the time and place.

From the long lines of support stretching for almost a thousand years dating to the Ptolemaic or geocentric theories of what later became known as the solar system, a support that cut easily across both religious and scientific communities, through the witch hunts in the late seventeenth century in Salem, Massachusetts, through the bloodletting purges in medicine prior to the dominance of allopathic medicine, on to the red scares of the mid-twentieth-century in the United States and the first UFO sightings in 1947 that later morphed into reports of alien abduction—the human race has been absorbed from time to time with mass delusions or scientific errors taken as truth. The issue is how to sort out truth from fiction on the recognition that the distinctions themselves are culturally formed to a great extent and sometimes plagued by willful ignorance. This trait was caustically assigned to the media by Senator Adlai Stevenson, who once said that the press had an uncanny ability to separate the wheat from the chaff and inevitably printed the chaff.

We also know at this point in history that an individual under stress can hallucinate, sometimes in very imaginative ways. R. D. Laing once attributed the onset of psychosis, especially extreme dissociation, to Gregory Bateson's "double bind" situations in which an individual is confronted with alternatives, each of which is intolerable. Now we are more aware of the chemical disorders that underlie mental illnesses, but the pernicious effects of stress remain very real. The mind, or brain, can react (especially in children) by withdrawing from reality and conjuring a kind of alternative reality that does not contain the impossible, con-tradictory imperatives of the real world. Victims of trauma and violence often report finding and occupying a detached space outside their bod-ies where they watch what is happening to them with a definitely flat affect in the viewing arena. The paralysis reported as a prelude to what individuals describe as alien abduction is a move into an alternative re-ality populated by higher forms of life that might be constructed by a terrified brain, a dark reminder that the escape path from stress can be strewn with its own horror shows. From these documented experiences we might say that there is no greater source of stress than impending death. Perhaps NDEs are the artifacts of the dying brain conjuring a vivid set of images as the ultimate escape mechanism from the harshest of all double binds, the extinction of the self in death.

This reductionist approach to NDEs is in some ways consistent with Occam's razor. It avoids complexity by cutting out a dense assortment of terms and ideas that appear otiose in the modern world of technology that has occasioned NDEs: either substance or property dualism, mean-ing a soul or psyche, an incorporeal self in the body that escapes death by departing from the physical self, a metaphysical reality that transcends the temporal world, the very existence of life after death—this is the conceptual baggage that modern science is eager to jettison. If the NDE is a purely neurological reaction to the stress of death, then we remain safely within a world bounded by the parameters of ordinary empirical science.

The problem for this world is that NDEs are so irreducibly complex, so deliciously resistant to reduction, and so open to the dazzling worlds of recent physics and medical experiments that they compete successfully with all attempts to define them away. For one thing, we have to stretch the powers of the brain to new and unproven levels of achievement to negotiate a materialist approach to NDEs. It is possible that our neurological powers are up to the task, that they are so wonderfully complex and our mental powers so robust that we can attend to the minutiae of the temporal world while unconscious and clinically dead. But the weight of likelihood, of possibilities, seems to be in favor of the transcendent experiences reported in the NDE (though both alternatives test the limits of possibilities). An ineffable realm of the purely spiritual is not required for this view of NDEs. All NDEs may be both transcendent and part of the physical world. The brain may be the instrument that guides the self into a realm of existence as real and empirical as the dimensions we currently occupy. All we have to do to accommodate such an interpretation of NDEs is move the perimeters of physical reality out to more comprehensive dimensions. Death is as ordinary as birth, and may be the same kind of portal to another empirical stage of life.

Here is what the physicists tell us. There must be additional dimensions to reality in order to explain the reality we sense and know. The standard model of physics is dead and buried. The only hope for a unified theory that accommodates quantum theory with gravity is a redefinition of the basic items in the universe and a recognition that reality may be composed not of particles but of minuscule and vibrating strings. String theory postulates many more dimensions than the three that our brains are hardwired to see. Put simply, in the terms that all of us can understand, the universe is complex, multidimensional, and alien to human intelligence. What we experience is only a limited version of reality framed by our neurological endowments. Our limited powers of perception and thought cannot gain access to the true nature of the universe (if there is such a thing as a true nature to things). But among the interstices of this complex universe there may be an ordinary place for a human life after death. We simply cannot know this in any intelligible form, or with the certainty metrics of truth and falsity, with or without science.

order therapy against the wishes of the patient or, in this case, of the attorney who represented him."

"You, in other words." Frank has regained his voice.

"Yes, me. All attorneys are bound by law and professional ethics to provide the best possible defense for their clients. Here was my dilemma. If I allowed my client to resume therapy he would be tried and in all probability convicted of second degree homicide, and maybe first degree since there was ample evidence for premeditation. Since I was practicing at the time in a state with the death penalty, he could well have faced execution. At the very least he would have received a life sentence. If he was kept off therapy he would be condemned to the delusional world of schizophrenia and, at best, to a halfway house and, at worst, an asylum for the rest of his life."

"Wasn't there a 60 *Minutes* show on this case?" David asks.

"Similar. Mine had a different ending."

"What did you do?" Ellen asks.

"I consulted his family, the parents. Since he was not competent to make decisions I sought someone who could represent him. They opted for a resumption of therapy."

"Did he stay with the sanity option when he was restored with the therapy?" Ellen asks.

"No. His symptoms declined in intensity when the drugs were resumed, but on finding his sanity restored and understanding the charges against him, he refused any further medication and lapsed into schizophrenic delusions."

"And then?"

"I withdrew from the case. His new attorneys kept him off therapy, and perhaps out of the cyanide chamber. Wait—no discussion here. I know the specious arguments that schizophrenia may just be a condition providing access to an alternative reality, one with its own logic and rules."

"Where everything is a sign or symbol. Because the patient cannot filter reality like so-called normal people." The speaker is Janet's husband, Paul.

"My point is elsewhere."

"Your client may have been too aware of everything, Janet, love."

"I repeat, darling, my point is elsewhere. What I am saying here is that my client was sane in one set of circumstances and insane in another just because of the malleable chemistry of his brain. Sanity, insanity are jurisdictional terms, not universal features of human experience."

"I thought you were going to say something else." Frank has rejoined the group discussion. "It seems to me that the jurisdictions are not critical in your example. The state of the man's brain is. He was sane, then insane, not because the venue of his experiences changed, but because he did. Also, you have provided us with an excellent instance of insanity as resting on a delusional reality, one that is radically unlike the conventional reality that is the source and measure of our sanities."

"I am glad that you used the plural 'sanities,'" Paul responds. "Because I have seen people who did not change and were seen as sane in one setting, insane in another. One of my students was judged mentally incompetent—granted, a cut down from insanity—in the hospital where he was taken for the treatment of some injuries he sustained in a car accident. He had claimed in front of the medical specialists that God would heal his broken arm. But of course this belief was sane and even intelligent in the religious cult in which he held membership, a cult formed precisely on beliefs in divine intervention. But Ellen, come on. You must have some experiences along these lines in your practice."

"Well—I say this reluctantly," Ellen begins, "but, yes, I have had patients who were regarded as sane or insane depending on the circumstances they were in. One woman, over eighty years old, began giving her money away to street vendors. Her family came to me and wanted me to refer her to a psychiatrist so she could be committed. But are charitable impulses insane? Only from the point of view of this self-interested family. Then I get patients sometimes who seem to have minds at odds with themselves, parts of them sane, other parts insane. I had a middle-aged man in therapy, successful man with a lovely wife, wonderful children. The man was a paradigm of conventional sanity. His problem? He had a secret desire that was slowly taking over his life. He wanted to kill his children. Didn't know why. Only knew that he had come close to doing it on several occasions. My strangest and still favorite case, however, was a young man who was sane in all conventional ways until the conversation reached certain critical and hidden thresholds. He believed, quite simply, that he was from outer space. An alien on earth. All of this was quite structured, credible in its details. I confess that when he showed me photographs of his spaceship I felt the parameters of my reality shift ever so slightly."

Mark asks the one question everyone is thinking. "Photographs?"

"Yes." Pause. "Oh, I don't know what it was I was seeing. It just seemed so plausible, so natural, at the moment." Ellen laughs gently with a kind of rocking movement. "So I suppose I must back off from my harsh judgment. This group has not moved to an insanity domain. Though I still maintain that certain shifts away from conventional reality, especially the common sense understandings of time, are typical signs of some pathology."

"That's because mental therapists represent and enforce conventional reality," Paul remarks.

"No, I don't think that addresses the point. A society composed entirely of schizophrenics would obviously have a radically different sense of conventional reality. But believe me, the members of such a society, no matter how consensual or cohesive, would still be sick."

"In what way?" Janet asks.

"They would not be able to function successfully. They could not secure their prudential interests. Delusions are delusions. Reality is not the product just of social norms. Neurology counts, and maybe even psychology generalizable across cultures."

"I think Ellen is right," David says. "Now that I think about it, depriving children of security, of love, cripples the mature self in all societies. Pathology is not just an arbitrary product of conventional arrangements."

"All right." Janet puts her coffee down. "Now that we are dangerously close to an editorializing mood, I will tell a story. A briefer and less dramatic story than the ones told so far, but one that will break the neat equilibrium that seems to be developing here. When I was young—what a start. I might as well say 'once upon a time.' But, once, when I was young, I was in love with this older man."

"Love again." Paul buries his face in his hands. "Why does love inform so many stories of the supernatural?"

"You don't know?" David asks. He is still thoughtful, at this moment slowly rubbing the rim of the cognac glass he holds just in front of his face. From time to time he has tried to look through the glass to see his friends in hazy outline above the sliver of cognac he is sipping. One might also ask why a whimsical mood seems so often to accompany thoughtfulness.

"Let Janet tell her story." Frank has resumed his role as interlocutor.

"My career was going nowhere then. I had just graduated from law school and was working in the Manhattan District Attorney's office. An assistant district attorney doing grunt work, with almost no trial exposure. I wanted to litigate but was spending my waking hours managing the lowest level criminal cases—arraignments, misdemeanors, plea bargains, that sort of thing. I considered it a favorable break in the routine when the DA sent me to Rikers Island one day to get a deposition from a potential witness in a bank theft. Ironically enough, the man was in jail on an embezzling conviction. He had been an executive in a bank that was robbed by two masked men. It happened to be a bank in which he was quietly stealing money by cooking the accounts. The DA thought he was a part of the armed robbery, the inside partner."

"They say crime tends to cluster in odd lumps," Frank observes.

"Anyway, I go to Rikers one sunny Tuesday morning. The place is filthy, dark, a true collection of horrors. You go first to a depot where you are screened, IDs checked and then checked again when you leave the place. At the desk you sign up for a building and a prisoner. No purses, bags, anything allowed, just a note pad and a pen. Then everyone boards a bus—a class-structured arrangement, believe me, with all the lawyers in suits and all the families in other attire—for the ride to the different buildings. From the yard, by the way, you can see Manhattan across the East River, which is the view that the prisoners have when they are out for recreation. What a remote spectacle that must be, and how distant they must feel from the amenities of human life.

"Just inside my building I have to show my attorney ID to a guard behind a window on the left. I sign in and identify the prisoner I'm going to see, go through the metal detector, body also screened by the hand-held detector, back of hand stamped with an identification mark visible only under infrared. Then they open the doors and I can see the long hall that the prisoners must walk through to receive visitors. But I am quickly taken directly to the left to the famous room of cubicles where my client, witness, prisoner, whatever, is summoned. I swear I remember everything as painted yellow in that room. Small barred windows line the tops of the walls. You can't see through the bars but it doesn't matter because the windows are too dirty to permit any outside looks. The interview with the prisoner always takes place in plain view of the guards in one of the dozen or so partitioned cubicles with small wooden tables about the size of those desks you have in elementary school. Real privacy in Rikers doesn't exist.

"Let me tell you something. The first thing you do when you get back home after visiting Rikers is to strip off every shred of clothing and take the very hottest shower of your life. But the nightmare of the place always stays with you in one sense. Since the stamped ID is invisible in ordinary light you can't be sure—ever—if it has truly been washed off.

"But back to the horror compound where, at least at first, I have to talk to my witness with one of the guards right near the cubicle listening to everything, which is clearly against the rules and crazy since the searches you go through would discover a gnat on your third rib if the insect presented any risk to prison security. So I argue with the keepers. After talking with three flunkies I get someone in authority. With some irritation he removes the guard to the proper distance so I can talk to my witness more civilly, which is to say in a cubicle with armed guards present but with some modicum of privacy at last in communication. And this for a white-collar criminal, remember, who has probably never held any kind of weapon in his life.

"Well, the conversation goes slowly at first. He is this tall character right out of central casting, a stand-in for Gary Cooper. Gaunt handsome, lanky, knockout cheekbones, big knuckles in his hands. But he has seen some real bad things in prison, as who hasn't who has been there, and he is looking at three to five years inside. The DA has offered a reduction, unspecified, if he cooperates. He wants to cooperate, believe me. And he does. He gives me confirmation of the DA's intuitions. He and a friend arranged the heist to throw the books off with the removal of the cash, concealing the embezzlement by miscounting the money taken. It didn't work, but the key was the friend. He was a local loan shark, connections to organized crime and thought to be involved in some critical influence peddling at city hall. The DA wanted him—bad. So if Gary Cooper can give us what we need to get the friend, it's Christmas all around—real bad guy goes to jail, sentence reduced for cooperative witness.

"Gary—let's keep calling him that—feeds me the story bit by bit. The usual reasons. Two kids in college, the bills piling up, loans at the bank, then loans with the bad people, the sharks—bad mistake. Easy solution. Embezzlement take is split with the shark, and the armed robbery covers the losses. Then come the crucial bits about the meetings with the bad guy, times, dates, plans, the works. Nothing like a little prison time to make someone spill his guts. Plus Gary is credible, even when he is scared and nervous."

"Gary Cooper scared?" Paul asks.

"I know—an oxymoron, right? But remember *High Noon*. My Gary was even more nervous than the marshal character the real Cooper played. And not just from the usual prison horrors. It seems a real weird thing happened the week before I see Gary. A prisoner had been brought in on a possession charge, only they couldn't identify the drug. The guys in the lab were sure it was some kind of controlled substance with hallucinatory powers, but they had never seen anything quite like it. The arresting officer thought his perpetrator—I love the vocabulary of law enforcement—was high on something when he collared him. So he asks politely if the subject would furnish a blood sample—voluntarily, with all rights to refuse understood. The guy says yes. So they draw blood and take him to a holding cell while they analyze the sample and the substance. Only problem is the guy disappears in the holding cell.

"Now imagine this if you can. Three other offenders are in the holding cell with Mr. Strangedrug. Granted, all three are on various drugs, including alcohol, and one is even in a stupor and so oblivious to everything. But this is a jail cell. No one can hide anywhere. The sergeant in charge takes the subject to the cell, puts him in sans belt, tie, shoelaces and then shuts and locks the door. Returns two hours later and subject is gone. Vanished. The two conscious occupants of the cell have no explanation. They say subject knelt by one of the bunk beds and prayed. Then, at some later moment, they noticed he was gone. The officers turned the place upside down, searched the entire prison. The thing is, every exit was secure, from cell door out through every route. There is no way anyone could have exited that area. Yet the man was gone. He was not anywhere in that prison."

CHAPTER FIVE

science, religion, and the languages of faith

SCIENCE AND NARRATIVES

Someone once said that we are the apes who dream while awake. This simple observation suggests that we navigate experience in two disparate ways: indirectly (in waking dreams) with thick layers of language that frame events in metaphor, simile, allegory, parable, and myth that fold into the fictions of poetry, theater, film, and novels, and more directly (in lucid forms) with expressions that strive for precision, economy, and transparency, the requirements found in, say, predicate logic. Put in the odd precision of street talk, sometimes we are driven with fiction to say it like it's not in order to say what it is, at other times we are driven to state matters directly in more precise terms.

This binary frame for expressions (a riff on the distinctions introduced by the cognitive psychologist Jerome Bruner) helps locate religion and science as, in Stephen Jay Gould's phrase, "Nonoverlapping Magisteria," or synoptic practices that can occupy distinct and parallel areas in experience without contradicting one another. You might guess that religion, a lost art, according to the resurgent atheists of the day, is typically presented as narrative thinking, distinct from the iconic form of direct thinking in modern Western cultures known as science. The difficulty is that while the two practices rely on different methods of inquiry, the exact or even pragmatic distinctions between these ways of thinking cannot always be consistently maintained, with the consequence that religion and science, while seeming to track different brands of truth, are sometimes closer than the champions of either practice might concede.

The main problem with a sharp distinction between these two practices is that stories are . . . everywhere, even in and of scientific practices. We typically frame our lives not in the form of demographic data or market fluctuations or mathematical equations but rather in terms of a story. Trial lawyers discover very quickly that juries are not moved by mountains of exact data, but who saw Harry put the poison in the well, or does the glove fit the accused killer's hand, or is the prosecutor's narrative of the crime palatable on the visible evidence, and so on with one plot line after another. Therapists sometimes say that a marriage ends when the story line of the relationship can't yield another chapter, when neither partner can figure out how to go on in what is sometimes a chain novel written by multiple players. Ronald Dworkin has suggested that we look at the history of law (metaphorically) as a chain novel, with different chapters written by different legal players in succeeding time zones, all blessed with creativity in saying what the law is but also constrained by the plot lines that loosely govern the novel.

Champion chess players don't and can't compute to any impressive degree rival permutations of alternative moves, but they can use heuristics that indicate patterns, *plot lines*, from other games that carry promissory notes of success. Fictional or oblique expressions can sometimes even intensify experience, extract value from it, and provide a deeper intelligibility than found in direct expressions. Or sharpen understandings with humor lined with an invitation to interpret texts. In one burlesque story a mummy is unearthed with a horrid expression of disgust on his fossilized face and gripping a piece of parchment. What could he have seen that caused such a wretched facial expression? The archeologists unravel the parchment. It says, "100 drachma on Goliath." Score a point against gambling, or maybe losing. You have to interpret the story.

Many religious beliefs are little more than benign and unadorned stories about the intersections of mental and material planes, sometimes just direct conjectures about the scope of reality and the inventory of items in the real world gift-wrapped with moral instructions on how to live properly, at other times a story about experience that indicates an alternative reality with its own moral compass, all conditioned by faith. Science, though playing by different rules of evidence, inference, and argument, is as richly populated with stories and conjectures based on faith. Scientists have always postulated complete though provisional accounts of phenomena with hidden or unproved variables, invisible items, in order to explain visible events. The existence of these variables is often accepted on faith, at least for a time. Here are two chestnuts, stale in their retelling but worth trotting out to make the point.

In 1930, Wolfgang Pauli asserted the existence of a new particle to explain the loss of energy and angular momentum when a neutron was transformed into a proton and electron. The new particle was later named the neutrino by Enrico Fermi. By factoring the neutrino into the decay event, Pauli was able to account for the missing energy and momentum. Twenty-three years later, in 1953, with an experiment that would eventually earn the 1995 Nobel Prize in physics, Fred Reines and Clyde Cowan found direct evidence for Pauli's neutrino. Later calculations and better methods developed in the newer fields of technobiology refined Pauli's theories and conjectures to show that there are at least two "flavors" of neutrinos: the electron neutrino, which appears only in connection with electrons, and the muon neutrino. Pauli's faith in the existence of the neutrino paid off in empirical confirmations and elaborations.

The invisible items postulated by scientists do not always pay off, however (a possibility also guiding religious beliefs). In another famous case, this in mid-nineteenth-century astronomy, certain eccentricities in Mercury's orbit could not be explained within the laws of motion introduced by Kepler and Newton. Scientists postulated an unseen planet, Vulcan, to explain these irregularities. Several astronomers claimed to have seen Vulcan in its orbit at a distance of 21 million kilometers from the sun. Alas, more powerful telescopes did not reveal Vulcan, and it was finally dismissed as a fiction. Mercury's eccentricities were later explained by Einstein's theories of relativity as byproducts of the sun's gravitational field, later refined and made intelligible by quantum mechanics, neither theory requiring poor lost Vulcan.

These two standard stories are exemplars of faith surrounded and buttressed by hard science. But scientific faith is sometimes blind, as when Carl Sagan again and again professed his belief in extraterrestrial life without a scintilla of evidence to support this belief (thus fulfilling—without meaning to—Mark Twain's definition of religion as "belief without benefit of evidence"). On other occasions scientific faith is an implication of mathematics (and therefore sound). Reflect again on the fact that the standard model of physics has been jettisoned, replaced by a new set of theories that require dimensions of reality outside the three-dimensional model of space that depicts human experience. Here an unseen and unseeable existence is accepted when its only reliable indication is a mathematical representation occasioned by the need to make three-dimensional space coherent. That evidence is not empirical but good enough for even the highest standards of falsifiability. It rests on a well-founded faith in mathematics.

Then also, science has its own blocks of thick concepts providing a background that makes scientific inquiry possible. Concepts like time, space, and measurement are open variables revisable and held provisionally constant as theories change, and other concepts, like contiguity, are unexamined artifacts of the way our culture depicts the basics of experience. One does not *know* these concepts as one knows Newton's laws of motion. One takes them as constants while scientific inquiry proceeds. The very notion of a critical test for theories or laws is often contestable and influenced by non-scientific cultural understandings of causal relations. Science, like other practices and discourses, rests on tacit concepts in order to use explicit and reliable terms in its inquiries.

The one thing we must remember is that the thick stuff of indirect languages, terms and propositions that are not transparent, is always very much a part of even the most lucid and precise scientific practices. Let's return briefly, for example, to a central concept in scientific explanations, causality. If we determine that one event causes another, this means that we establish that the cause is antecedent to the effect, is a sufficient condition for the effect, and if a covering law describes the causal relationship in terms of "whenever A, then B," we have a powerful though naïve form of explanation. We have explained B as the result of A, generalized by a conjunction of A and the covering law, thus presenting a happy conjoining of explanation and prediction. But the naïvete of this account dominates its explanatory powers. So much must be assumed as background for this type of explanation to go through. There is first the need to demarcate correlation from causality.

Again, in one of the oldest textbook examples of the need for this demarcation, we do not say that sunspots cause business cycles even with a perfect correlation (whenever sunspots, then business cycles of a certain sort follow) because the two events are not contiguous, meaning there is no forcing mechanism between the two. Absent contiguity there is no causality. But, reasonable as this is, whether events are contiguous is largely a matter of how we understand experience, with little in the way of proof for these understandings. (In a sun culture, contiguity between sun activity and human events might be taken for granted.) Then there is the robust set of other background concepts that inform and drive even the most direct and linear explanations: assumptions of time, space, the nature of matter, and so on. One form of sea change in scientific inquiry occurs when background concepts are summoned and revised, since these changes often are followed by profound effects on the nature of science.

Religion obviously and explicitly relies on faith inasmuch as it negotiates the unknown and perhaps unknowable. For science the unknown is a target variable to be decomposed and spread across the knowable as a set of testable statements. Put another way, the unknown in science is an issue, a problem, a challenge to be transmuted into the known. But for religion the rich mystery of life indicates that there will always be areas that resist human efforts to make experience completely understandable. Faith is a natural affiliation of any acceptance of the unknown as an agreeable companion. The lesson here is not to credit or discredit the reliance on faith in spiritual approaches to the unknown, but instead to ask whether religious conjectures are more like Pauli's neutrino or the nonexistent planet Vulcan.

Somewhere along this line of conjecture the prospect of God or higher forms of life appears in the discussions. What is the evidence or mathematical demonstration of this type of existence? Aquinas tried to prove God's existence in part on empirical grounds from the limited and contingent nature of human existence. The critical tactic in many of these proofs is that the conditional or imperfect must be connected to the unconditional or perfect if these terms are to make sense. Like the unmoved mover in Aristotle's ontology, tracking a set of contingent events seems to require a first and stable and pristine noncontingent cause.

One of the explanations for this line of thought may be the unnerving quality of infinite regresses for all forms of explanation. A line of causes, conditionals, imperfections suggests either an unending sequence of these events (which in the literal sense is unthinkable) or some halting point that makes sense of the line: a first cause, an unconditional event, perfection. Of course the additional puzzle is raised by the fact that we can ask the obvious questions: what occurs before the first cause, what conditions the unconditional event, and is there a continuum leading us beyond perfection? (Or the postmodern inquiry: are there rival and equally plausible criteria for perfection?) We may be hardwired in our neurological powers to resist infinite regresses even as they suggest deeper mysteries, requiring that our concepts complete themselves in fulfilled and closed (and comfortable) versions of what they start out to be. Both science and religion seem to welcome agreeable halting devices for infinite regresses, even if we cannot provide an account of what occurs before the starting point (prior to the Big Bang in physics, for example, when all known natural laws have no referential powers). The difference is that religion is quicker, too quick according to critics, to serve up the complete explanation that makes the world comfortable for us. By contrast, incomplete patterns are household items in science. Good science provides counterintuitive and uncomfortable conclusions, which are less likely in religious discourse.

Finally, however, and from an outsider's point of view, science and religion are in the same holding patterns of uncertainty. A psychic once reminded me that a spider on the wall of a room has no concept of the room. What if we are the spiders on the wall in the vast room of the universe? The limitation introduced by Gödel (and refined by Turing), that a consistent system is always incomplete, with the implication that the system will contain statements not provable with its rules and axioms but which can be proved within another system external to the first, is a modern and more severe expression of an ancient awareness. The human desire for coherent wholes, defined by consistency and completeness in Gödel's theorems, may be futile yet still demand an external realm of truth only partially accessible to the human intellect. The power of limits to indicate realms beyond these limits may be one reason that Gödel and Einstein were Platonists, each believing in a larger reality beyond our powers of understanding. This is the stuff of religious belief, and a path to faith. It also suggests the limits that govern both science and religion.

To compound matters, if I can never be sure if I am working with a complete explanatory sequence for experience, if the variables are incorrigible and remain inconclusive, and I have no or little access to a fuller dimension of experience that might tell me if my sequence is complete — if I am the spider on the wall of the room of the universe — then agnosticism is the required attitude on the epistemic and ontological issues at stake in both science and religion. Maybe we can call this a general theory of limits, an intellectual humility that leavens the solemn arrogance found in both science and religion as each seeks the underlying laws and grammars of reality. It should also remind us that both discourses, now comfortably seen as "Overlapping Magisteria," rely on faith and unexamined thick oblique languages, and are needed as complements of each other if we are to negotiate our way through the permanent mysteries of human existence.

RELIGION AND ATHEISM REDUX

All of this is standard, hardly controversial, and little more than casual asides enlivened by anecdotes. But it does suggest that the current hostility to religion (as one formal expression of the metaphysical) is puzzling and usually overdone. Even though religion presents a range of benign and malignant versions throughout history; is one of our oldest and most venerable practices in its best incarnations; is maintained all over the world even in the most hostile conditions; and has roughly the same mixed record of violence, comfort, redemption, and reform found in even the most advanced secular systems, it is now more fashionable than ever to use the powers of the natural and social sciences to denigrate religion as superstitious and pernicious nonsense. The tacit and oblique expressions characterizing narratives are often regarded in these critical literatures as deficient expressions when offered in religious talk as explanations, or even just renditions, of experience.

Religion has come upon especially hard times among Western intellectuals. Richard Dawkins in *The God Delusion* and Daniel Dennett in *Breaking the Spell*, for example, move effortlessly from a thorough denigration of religion to a plea for its eradication. Dawkins, the author of the celebrated *The Selfish Gene* and many other popular works on evolution, maintains that "faith is one of the world's great evils." Dennett calls atheists the "brights," and regards their lifestyles as superior to those lamentable many who are religious. Sam Harris has many unkind things to say about religion in his popular book *The End of Faith: Religion, Terror, and the Future of Reason.* Harris provides helpful insights into spirituality and consciousness but maintains that organized religion is the source of much of the world's hatreds and violence, quoting as critical evidence the very real and disturbing passages in the Qur'an that urge violence against infidels. (Of course, other religions fare no better on these casual tests. Judaic/Christian cultures, for example, have their own long record of slaughtering infidels and even those suffering from akrasia [yes, weakness of will].) These strident laments about religion are usually wrapped into demands to cleanse the global human community of religion, to initiate a moral and intellectual hosing that will rid the world of the retrograde beliefs that define religious sensibilities.

This much can be conceded. Many of the past and current attacks on religion are well deserved. On many occasions religious practices (there is no doubt or argument about this) are hideous and destructive, toxic toward nonbelievers and disheartening for members. Religion can also be populated with retrograde beliefs, at least as measured by the canons of science. For example, Mike Huckabee's smug acknowledgment in the run-up to the U.S. presidential primaries of 2008 that he doesn't believe in evolution, when there is evidence for it all over the earth, is simple and unforgivable ignorance. (Is it God's intervention, for example, that causes the flu virus to adapt to vaccines as it rapidly evolves through natural selection almost yearly into drug-resistant strains?) Biologists dispute the forms and logic of evolution, whether linear or "lumpy" (affected by exogenous events, like massive meteor hits, or just plain uneven in its movements), but all educated persons underwrite the rudiments of Darwin's theories and evidence.

On balance, however, religion has roughly the same mixed record of violence, error, redemption, and reform found in even the most advanced secular systems. Some scientific practices have been both wrong and/or barbaric: bloodletting, lobotomies (in their early primitive form), a myriad of harmful, even deadly medicines (recently Vioxx), what causes and prevents cancer, understandings and explanations of intelligent quotients (the size and shape of the skull used in nineteenth-century "science"), theories and convictions about autism, the entire practice of astronomy under models of the solar system and universe in the Ptolemaic system (unless one is inclined to keep drawing epicycles in the traditions of science before Copernicus and Galileo), the steady state theory of the universe, and then the multiple corrections, dismissals, localizations of basic scientific theory: on the structure of the atom, black hole theory, the introduction of dark matter to explain the quantity of observable mass in the universe, the basic relationship between time and space, as well as matter and energy localized to the Newtonian paradigm, not generalizable to the full scope of reality.

Scientists can also be as dumb and unethical as religious adherents, or anyone else. Witness the intellectual peregrinations of James Watson, who, with Francis Crick, discovered and presented the double-helix structure of DNA in 1953, for which the two scientists were rightly awarded the Nobel Prize in medicine in 1962. Among their shameless actions was the exploitations of the research conducted by a female scientist, Rosalind Franklin, an intellectual aggression that included using her groundbreaking work in crystallography and X-rays of DNA to set up their discovery, and then denying her credit; as well as the recent public musings of Watson that Africans are less intelligent than Westerners and that "stupidity should be cured"—the last a recommendation that, if connected to real therapy, many believe should be first applied to Watson, though many others (including me) sympathetic to a great scientist's spontaneous utterances favor a benign neglect of such casual remarks. Then fold in Crick's reported conjectures that human life may have been a product of experimental seeding on earth by aliens (an interesting conjecture, by the way, but without any of the evidentiary possibilities required in good science) and religion begins to look at least intelligible by contrast.

It also doesn't help the brief for science that so many of the recent attacks on religion lack a reliable grasp of research methods in history and social science, to the point that Huckabee and religious hucksters in general often escape clean. Harris's harsh statements, for example, like the screeds of other critics (though more prominently and piously), get basic causal relations wrong. He conveniently misses the fact that neither beliefs nor texts in themselves typically cause behavior. At least since Gunnar Myrdal's classic work *An American Dilemma*, studies have pointed out again and again that mapping from abstract concepts to behavior is not a clean and linear exercise. People can and do subscribe to many things that do not consistently translate into actions, even when the texts that they use in their thoughts are linear and transparent. (Maybe Shakespeare understood this in making so many of his characters walking, talking contradictions.) When the texts are obscure or contradictory we might expect less consistency between ideas and actions (since a truly obscure text may not yield a satisfactory account of consistency in actions). Religious texts are notoriously difficult to interpret, often yielding readings that are both reasonable and mutually contradictory. To assume that any passage in any text is a reliable antecedent variable that can account consistently for action is more than silly. It's unintelligible. In my study of Santería, I was invited to a sacred drum ceremony in which members of the religion were to touch holy water that had been poured on the floor and then bring the water to their foreheads. In spite of the hostile theological and practical gulfs between leaders in Catholicism and Santería, over half the participants touched their forehead and then made the sign of the cross. Syncretism was alive and well among the rank and file even though antagonism was sharp and real between the sets of principals leading and defining the two religions.

This observation is clarifying: both texts and beliefs are messy, ill defined, and implicated in behavior only in the context of complex triggering conditions. And that most, maybe all religious texts offer contradictory and incomplete maxims. If we concede the violence, for example, in the history of Christianity, Christ's promise to bring the sword to human experience is born out. But then the Sermon on the Mount is abandoned, where the command is "Resist not evil," a maxim that Tolstoy adopted in his transformation into a complete and implacable pacifist. Similarly, a critic targets the wrong item when quoting the Qur'an to explain Islamic violence. One might as well cite the U.S. Constitution as a text to explain the political behaviors of the American public. It just doesn't work that way. One explanation here might be the ease with which *ceteris paribus* clauses can be invoked through the assignment of exceptions and defeats for moral rules and principles that hold true, but only in certain domains of validity.

Look at the logic of human rights, for example, as a template to understand moral and political actions. Human rights are the most recent and inclusive species of rights and are widely thought to come with all the moral and political powers of rights languages. Yet perhaps because we live in a time when rights are the privileged vocabularies in negotiating issues and constructing institutions, at least in the West, it is easy to miss limits on the powers of rights to do any of the things expected in their use. In the simplest sense, rights can conflict with each other, as a right to move across geographical territory clashes with a right to property that authorizes closing off areas from free travel; a right to disseminate information is sometimes countered and shaped by rights to privacy in some circumstances and security needs in others; a right to free speech is constrained by rights to be protected against libel and defamation and hate; rights to freedom can oppose rights to equality; and, in general, we allow these and other such conflicts to be adjudicated by understandings of the greater public good. Rights may also be limited by domains of validity. Like all terms, rights flourish in a set of conditions within which they are intelligible (have a coherent sense and reference), outside of which they are not. These are limits of scope, not those resulting from conflicts among rights, all of which are valid. Both types of limits qualify and restrict even the most powerful moral languages.

But limits fixed by scope can be especially difficult both to see and to fix. One of the more demanding issues in all inquiry is determining when a dominant vocabulary is no longer able to describe and explain the actions occasioning its own formation. The point is that one has to move to what I have called collateral reasoning to grasp conflicts and limitations of scope in the employment of higher-order languages in moral and religious thinking. This collateral domain is the venue where the primary text is bracketed and action is worked out on a variety of side principles typically not codified as part of the primary text. In short, you can read the Bible and the Qur'an to the point of exhaustion and never know what exactly is causing or motivating religious behavior. A different type of analysis is required that incorporates conditions that, coupled with a written or oral text, trigger action. Harris's preoccupation with primary texts is like the kidnapper sending the ransom note to the wrong address. It leads to puzzlement and frustration, not enlightenment, regarding the responses of rational actors in a practice.

Nor is religion all bad as a political force whatever explanatory metric is used. Two examples are prominent in the history of the United States. One is the abolitionist movement that helped eliminate slavery. Religious activists energized that movement. A second is the civil rights movement almost a century later, which originated in the black Baptist churches and, through the leadership of figures like Martin Luther King (a minister), helped diminish racial discrimination in laws and institutions by transforming popular understandings of personhood. In fact it is reasonable and rational to admit that religion summons individuals to acts of selflessness and sacrifice, what we call supererogatory actions. Acting for the sake of a higher force or cause can absorb individuals in a level of altruism that becomes routine in daily activities.

Of course sacrifice of the self can also produce suicide bombers (as can ideology and nationalism and autocratic controls and economic deprivation). This might be the oldest story in history: absorption of the self in a higher cause is consistent with both good and evil. And, given the extreme variance on the premise, a search into background variables might be prudent in explaining these different trajectories. What leads Augustine of Hippo, Tomás de Torquemada, Girolamo Savonarola, Thomas More, and Pope John XXIII (of the twentieth century) to occupy the common space of religious discourse in Christianity in such radically different ways? Unfortunately the social sciences and history are not helpful here. All that we know from the variance within the framework is that religion cannot be the sufficient condition for either good or bad actions. Harris's book unreasonably and unnecessarily deepens the confusion many have with science and religion, and with politics and religion. Many of his most important statements on religion are strident, too often entirely without an evidentiary base or the support of cogent argument. In reading the book I began to believe that Harris is driven by a kind of secular faith widely recognized as an ideology (by which I mean a structured explanation of experience impervious to falsification). This unwitting but real conceptual flirtation with ideology is odd because the main line of text in the book attributes most of the world's troubles to the faith found in organized religions, with the well-known liability that faith-driven beliefs are usually not falsifiable, at least in standard ways. These critiques of religion attempt to subsume the acknowledged limitations of the human species, drawn up from incomplete understandings of the world, a mistrust of differences, the disproportionate effects on actions of strong emotions from, one supposes, the limbic system (our reptilian brains), etc., — all of the fault lines of our natures folded into religion. Not to belabor the point, but assigning the causes of all or most wrongs in human experience to religion is unconvincing, and often just theatrics.

The catechism lesson that the reader must take on faith extends to the division of labor over violence, where the main burden also is assigned to religion. Essentially Harris is suggesting that even if rational and secular societies begin murdering each other industriously and on a grand scale (someone should tell him they have done so, twice in the twentieth century), it should not reflect on secularism. Perhaps it should be pointed out that the modern proliferation of chemical, biological, and nuclear weapons was begun in earnest by the most secular and scientific societies, beginning in World Wars I and II. Also, while Harris claims religion is the greatest threat to eradicate humanity, the evidence is less conclusive. Remember that the only use of atomic weapons in war, and on two cities with enormous destruction of innocent human life, was carried out by the United States for purely secular reasons of strategic military calculations. Only the secular/modern powers ever came close to ending life on earth, and are the only countries (Russia and the United States, in particular) that still might or can. Mutually Assured Destruction was nothing less than a "good reason to kill peaceful people indiscriminately," and it had and has nothing whatsoever to do with religion. If the current state of the world is what reveals the need to end faith and replace it with a rational secularism, would weaker nerves on either side of the Cold War, and the atomic genocide that would surely have followed, have provided the need to end secularism and rationalism? Not to many of the critics of religion, who seem ignorant of vast studies in game theory that demonstrate again and again that the uncertainty of securing primary goods in competitive conditions is one of the main causes of conflict, not beliefs per se. (Intro to Political Theory 101: read Hobbes's *Leviathan* followed by studies of n-person Prisoners' Dilemma games.) Tracking the dilemmas, the paradoxes, and contradictions, the documented *failures* of rationality might provide a deeper understanding of how disputes and conflicts occur.

The ascription of religious predicates to all evil is ad hoc categorizing. In terms now of a logical maxim we have all presumably memorized, to say that religion is a source of evil (which is true) is not equivalent to saying that whenever there is evil it must be religiously inspired, despite the claims of atheism from those secular perpetrators of the evil practices in twentieth-century dictatorships. The fact is that the anti-religious movements of the past century have killed the most people and most recently, leading us to this question: How is ending religion (which these twentieth-century tyrants did attempt) supposed to end "armed conflict in our world"? Harris's book would have been more usefully written in tenth-century Europe, when religion really did guide most wars and massacres. The current assertions are just bad arguments. Also, an ideology is *not* a religion since it contains no concept of divinity. The materialism of the Marxist and Nazi movements/regimes emptied experience of all spirit, and tended to be overtly anti-religious and atheistically inclined.

THE RELIGIOUS VERSUS THE SECULAR

But there are also natural limits to the assaults on religion that extend beyond the simple errors of using beliefs or texts as causes, of flawed rules of evidence, inference, and argument, of excluding the redeeming features and including only the pernicious sides of religion. Even if religion and science are separate and independent domains, the most natural question driving both types of inquiry into the boundaries and content of the real world, into the possibility of a material limit or spiritual plane to existence, into human experiences in general, first and always, is — on what basis can we study these subjects? For science it is an easy call, a no-brainer (maybe literally). The methods of the natural sciences, in particular when exhibiting the requirement that all statements be subject to falsification tests, are typically taken as the gold standard for respectable research. Anything else is deficient in proportion to its deviation from these methods, especially those inquiries that rely on large doses of intuition, mystical insights, in general the desiderata of languages that approach experience with crucial obscurities in place. For science, transparency is critical for establishing even provisional truths. An existence outside conventional boundaries, a domain inaccessible to the technological and lucid and skeptical state of mind, is understandably deemed to be not worth studying since no scientific methods or theories can negotiate the prospect.

For the religious state of mind it is exactly the resistance of external realms to conventional, or pedestrian, methodologies that makes the subject so challenging and intriguing—and an opportunity to forge different methods of inquiry from the thick belt of indirect assumptions found in both the wide vistas of experience and the more limited and precise terrains of conventional science. It is an appealing and provocative research opportunity, especially in a civilization driven in large part through its sometimes latent, sometimes manifest opposition to the conviction that materialism and technology can answer all the important questions about life. The truth is that even in Madonna's material world, people do ask about some of the central questions in religious thought, like the meaning of death, and typically these questions extend (as they must) to the possibility of escaping the limits of natural laws, say, surviving death in some way. Not to press the point too severely, but even in the most modern and scientific cultures the prospect of transcending the laws of nature exhibited in scientific practices, in particular in finding a life after death, is tantalizing. These thoughts and possibilities deserve serious consideration, though not just because they suggest comforting answers. The issue is not whether we should study the objects of religious modes of thought, and the evidence for and against some of the central convictions of religious thinking, but rather—how do we study these matters in a serious way given the evident hostility of science, the prime form of knowledge-gathering inquiry in the world, to the thought that a spiritual and non-empirical dimension of reality exists? And how do we approach a possibility so important to making sense out of life when inquiries into its validity may be influenced and corrupted by its desirability?

The gravitas of religious beliefs is unassailable. The uncomfortable fact for strict materialists is that religion is the discourse of choice for discussing the more profound takes on metaphysics, like the possibility of a life after death, and also is a sourcebook for the oldest conjectures on an external reality outside human experience. In some of these domains, religion joins science in exercises that rely on evidence, and is subject to the same falsification tests that address and mark off scientific practices. In other areas religion relies on metaphysical claims that are not falsifiable (as, by the way, does science, though in different ways). In terms of practical reasoning religious beliefs seem to ascend to appellate levels of debate with rocket speed, and even to transcendent levels of thought outside the conventional boundaries of secular societies.

In this respect religion is in the family of natural law and human-rights concepts that allow judgments, moral and legal, from a point of view outside the social practices that might be at issue. Absent this external perspective, in place since Antigone (in Greek mythology) opposed Creon, the king of Thebes, by invoking a higher law to oppose the king's command, we are lost in the labyrinths of evil that meet the terms of positive law and conventional morality—as with that great secular evil of the twentieth century, Nazi Germany. We need transcendence to judge whole bodies of law, even societies, as morally flawed. It is an odd conceit to think that the transcendent principles characterizing religion are the source of all evil when they have historically been among our main normative weapons against evil.

The more critical issue today is whether religion can find a venue in democratic institutions. If religion and science can occasionally be members of the same conceptual family, secular politics is not likely to be an impossible stretch for the religious state of mind. In fact, religion has been a part of democratic politics, from classical to contemporary political practices, and with a similar mix of the compatible and incompatible found with religion and science. Mike Huckabee is a familiar figure in politics, home cooking in more unfortunate ways than one.

There is a warning label in place, however, exactly at the defining juncture of religion and politics. True religion takes its cues from a reality outside the conventional boundaries of human experience. Whatever else this resource does (and whether such a reality exists or not is irrelevant), the space available for compromise, for the give-and-take of good politics, is considerably narrowed. If God commands you to do something, it is reasonable to be implacable in the face of opposition. This state of mind, what I have called reasonable intransigence, is not confined to religion. Ideologues, true believers in general, cut to the chase with remarkable speed and are resistant to dissent. Absolute truth is intolerant of error, or rival truths. It's a matter of conscience.

The unhappy fact for the West is that revealed truth is not a good fit with democratic practices, which routinely thrive on dissent as the sourcebook for truth (the last standing opinion, in the formulation offered by John Stuart Mill). All effective and true democratic systems are recursive, meaning that claims are introduced to a public space defined by its ongoing critical powers. This is an arrangement represented by H.L.A. Hart's depiction of complex systems of law as consisting of primary rules that impose duties or obligations, and secondary rules that address the primary rules (in *The Concept of Law*). In a true recursive system revisions in the primary rules will affect the secondary rules, and vice versa, in a continuing reciprocal activity. Why is this necessary? Because the secular state of mind seeks truth through the critical scrutiny of rival claims (hence the importance of free speech). Religious beliefs, nourished by revealed truth, are outside this defining feature of the democratic process. In this important sense science nourishes democracy. Religion does not.

The perverse observation is that the more effective religious ministers in politics are those who shed the skin of true belief, using religion as a prop to secure political power. It is a melancholy conclusion to hope that the politically religious are more political than religious, hypocritical than sincere. But it's just eminently rational to hope that religious politicians are less than they seem, more hustler than minister, ready to revise and even abandon their religious convictions for the sake of the greater political good. In a strange sense religion is a more compatible entry in politics if the sharp critiques of the atheists — that most religious leaders are false prophets who do not believe their own convictions — are true rather than false. Such is the paradox of secular democratic politics in an age of religious revival.

The issue in this setting is how to avoid Coleridge's dour observation that "Truths, of all others the most awful and mysterious, yet being at the same time of universal interest, are too often considered as so true that they lose all the powers of truth, and lie bed-ridden in the dormitories of the soul, side by side with the most despised and exploded errors." This risk of static and fossilized truth should make both religious and scientific temperaments thoughtful about the particular institutional arrangements — imposed consensus, partitions (the walls between church and state championed by Jefferson and Black), exemptions, *modus vivendi*—that will mediate the core differences between the religious and the secular in viable democracies.

Given the global history that is unfolding today, these issues may signal the controlling inquires of the next several generations.

BOUNDED KNOWLEDGE

The ebb and flow of materialism and spiritualism across history lays out a landscape of deep possibilities for these matters, including that tired but vital inquiry, "What is the meaning of life?" In materialism, and its constituent view that God does not exist, the full range of reality is a spiritual void. All of reality is a set of events governed by laws and principles framed within the world, not in any way transcendent to it. In the spiritual take on experience the world is a mosaic of the seen and unseen, of dimension to experience that exceeds the parameters of materialism. The spiritual perspective need not rest on the existence of God, but on the possibility that human experience is a limited theater within a vast universe to which we have only partial access. Both views—materialism and spiritualism—are luminescent, rich with laws and principles of the natural world. But they attend to vastly different senses of experience and its options.

The hubris of human thinking is remarkable—and unassailable as a fact of life—throughout ancient and modern times. Since the earliest Egyptian civilizations, the classical philosophers and Ionian scientists of ancient Greece, and, really, just about every culture in the history of the world, some of the best Enlightenment thinkers have sought and sometimes claimed to have achieved a complete knowledge of the world (such as the philosophes of eighteenth-century France) and a complete and consistent mathematics (David Hilbert's pre-Gödel program). Plato developed a hierarchy of knowledge, from sense experience through mathematical forms to the highest form, the Form of the Good, which, as the last entry in the scale of thought and being, was presented as at once the superior, transcendent, and highest resource for knowing. It is no trivial matter that Augustine saw the Platonic forms as ideas in the mind of God, and that Christianity itself has regarded both morality and knowledge as arranged on a scale ascending to perfection. In classical economics, unbounded rationality based on complete information in conditions of certainty was the ideal model for knowing. This drive to complete and redeeming knowledge is reflected in Stephen Hawkings's last sentence in *A Brief History of Time* (ironic or not, and bracketed from the many qualifications attached to it by diehard materialists): that when we have a complete theory of the universe we will at last "know the mind of God."

The problem for these traditions is that almost no one in the secular parts of the West has any reason to believe in unbounded knowledge any longer. The last century has modified all versions of hubris. The Enlightenment was a prominent casualty in the violent events of the last century, and the location and scope of the human intellect has been reduced to very modest levels in the modern age. Comfortable as it may or may not be, we are the direct descendents of the transformation in status brought about by the Copernican and Darwinian revolutions in thought. The geocentric account of the universe had the earth at its center, the venue for God's favorite children. But the historic shift to a heliocentric view of the (now) solar system was an incontrovertible displacement. Then, with the expansion of information about the universe we have discovered that the earth is a very small and minor planet in a galaxy that is itself on the periphery of the star system.

Then there is the human genome project, the mapping of the roughly 3.2 billion base pairs of human genes. The project may be the most important research in history. At the announcement in the White House of the first draft of this map, President Clinton (in a page from the religious community) said that "today we are learning the language in which God created life." He may have been right, along with British prime minister Tony Blair's more humble statement, that "for most of us, today's developments are too awesome to comprehend." The irony is that a project that has provided "the sequence of all the letters in the human book of life" without providing the meaning of the book's text also reveals that humans have only about 25,000 genes (instead of the 100,000 predicted), that many of these genes are shared with other forms of life, that a vast majority of the human genome consists of nonsense repetitive sequences, and that we really don't have many more genes than roundworms or fruit flies. We are, in short, a close evolutionary product of the biological life that we seem to want very much to distance ourselves from. But on the universe's phylogenetic scale, we're not much above the life endowments found across the earth, hardly a superior life form.

These deficiencies—moral, intellectual—are real limitations on our ability to master the main dimensions of reality, to understand and reuse the full range of moral and intellectual possibilities in real worlds.

Call the sum of these limitations (a thought introduced in chapter 1) the bounded knowledge principle. It excludes all peremptory, or absolute, beliefs. Atheism, for example, is unintelligible on current states of knowing. To know, to be convinced that God does not exist, requires a position of exquisite and precious certainty that modern scientific theory and models of knowledge in general, guided by our modest cognitive powers, cannot attain. (Interestingly enough, at earlier times in history when science was more limited and faith was more influential, atheism could be seriously entertained because we were insensitive to cognitive limits.) But so too is theism illicit on the bounded knowledge principle. One cannot know that God exists, though faith has a better play here than in atheism. (Faith that God does not exist seems a bit incongruous.) Still, the true believer in either direction is incoherent. Karen Armstrong once advised that we ask the atheist exactly which god s/he doesn't believe exists (there being so many versions of deity).

The same limits can be assigned to materialism, spiritualism—any of the dominant and basic conceptions of reality that have threaded their way through human history. These conceptions must remain as no more than rough maps in an inventory of alternative maps, little more than guides through certain restricted domains of experience (though often quite helpful as study guides). They cannot represent reality. It is not just that we have gotten things wrong in the past *even in science* (the gold standard for explanations)—the geocentric account of what we later learned was the solar system, a fixed Lamarckian-like design in a nature now understood as driven by natural selection and adaptation—but that as a species we must get things wrong. We're just not smart enough. Remember that the spider on the wall has (so far as we know) no conception of the room. And we may be the spiders in a vast room of the universe, which is a complex and largely inaccessible place to the human. Stated simply, we do not as a species know very much, at least with certainty, about the environment we occupy. The Gnostic Gospels suggest that God resides within us, and this may be true. But since no one of us is the God that might inhabit both the soul and the universe, it would be prudent to be modest and judicial in our inquiries into the possibility of a life that extends beyond death.

In some important ways, however, our hubris makes sense, though a strange sense by any standards. Here is a remarkable thing: Our intellects seem to reach for something else, something outside the conventional boundaries of human communities, no matter how the boundaries are drawn. We think about what we think, sometimes without end. Recursive inquiries (processes that are self-reflective) are presented and negotiated in a wide range of intellectual traditions. The child's repetitive "why?" signals the beginnings of a philosophical inquiry that invites recursive examinations to move outside linguistic or system boundaries. The pedigree stretches back to classical philosophy and perhaps earlier. An awareness of exit routes to levels of discourse outside a present, any present, way of thinking and talking may be as old as language itself. All self-reflection seems, at least eventually, to inspire movements to external interpretations of words and things as we interrogate meanings and explanations.

One is reminded again of the limitation introduced by Gödel (and refined by Turing), that a formal system is always incomplete, with the implication that the system will contain statements not provable with its rules and axioms but that can be proved within another system external to the first and is a modern and more severe expression of an ancient awareness. The human desire for coherent wholes, defined by consistency and completeness in Gödel's theorems, may be futile yet still demand an ascent to positions that are located beyond particular and perhaps all modes of thought, an external realm of truth only partially accessible to the human intellect. (The power of limits to indicate realms beyond revealed limits may be one reason that Gödel was effectively a Platonist—and at the end a declared, not a closet version.) We have minds or brains that are not limited to the modes of thought we develop even in our best moments. We seem to be able to think, or contemplate, thoughts that escape the limits of thought.

SCIENCE AND RELIGION: GOOD AND BAD FITS

Here's one approach to the existence of God based on the bounded knowledge principle. All known forms of life are locatable somewhere on a phylogenetic scale. One of the curiosities of this ordering of life forms is that entries at one level typically do not know entries at higher levels. I don't mean that lower entries cannot recognize higher forms of life, just that they cannot *know* them. When I enter the rich biological areas marked off as the backyards of my homes, either in New York or Miami, I see and to some degree know many of the life forms that populate these spaces. I see the lizards that dart back and forth on my back patio in Miami, the birds that swoop down (sometimes near the top of my head), the squirrels that run harmlessly along the power lines above the jasmine plants that tower over the stone fence separating my property from that of my neighbor's home. I see, know, and in my own way love that life I perceive in these areas of foliage. But this life cannot see, know, or love me. These creatures "see" a figure of some sort mediated by the sensory frames found in the various forms of life, and register "me" in the neurological settings found in these different life forms. But that life does not know me in any of the ways that I comprehend these creatures.

Of course, you might say, the world is very much a human world in terms of knowledge and being. We name the items in our worlds. These life forms do not name us (so far as we know). But that is precisely the point. Our conceptual range extends to the life forms below us on the phylogenetic scale, much as other life forms might know and negotiate the creatures on or below them on this scale. And of course we cannot be expected to know life forms on higher places on the scale since the limits we are aware of—the restrictions on knowing above one's place on the phylogenetic scale—may also, and quite likely do, apply to us. So there is no reason to think that we are the highest entries on the scale of life. There may be higher forms of life that we see but cannot know as higher life forms, in the same way that the creatures in my backyard see but do not comprehend me in terms of my essence or identity.

The knowing skeptic will ask where these odd life forms are on the planet earth. That possibility has been explored in imaginative varieties of fiction. In *The Hitchhiker's Guide to the Galaxy* the highest forms of life on earth are the white mice, who have been conducting experiments on us with those laboratory mazes, rather than (as we have thought) the reverse. Dolphins are next in intelligence, while humans come in third. When the earth is destroyed the white mice and dolphins get off the planet in time, though the white mice are furious because they lose decades of data on humans collected in those lab experiments. One supposes that other recognizable forms of life, like white mice and dolphins, can be more intelligent than humans, but a more intriguing conjecture is that higher life forms are here but unrecognizable. The one thing we know with reasonable and pragmatic certainty about humans, our species of life, is that we can be vicious and violent, murderous, especially to that type of life which seems different. If there are higher indigenous life forms here on earth with radically different takes on experience, or visitors from other areas of the universe, their masks must be absolutely foolproof for survival purposes. James Baldwin once wrote that the black man in early twentieth-century America had to have an invisible and absolutely impenetrable crafted persona in place—a carefully constructed psychic armor—in order to survive. So much would be expected of higher life forms on the planet earth.

I know: the expected statement at this point is the civilized concession that these conjectures are, well, imaginative forays. Of course they are. But we can entertain them because the dismissal mechanisms that address them are flawed, limited. We know only in terms of our modest neurological powers (this can't be doubted), and negotiate experience with verities that are inevitably limited to our cultures and locations in history. The hardest thing to do in human experience may be to see something that is utterly new. Why? Because we come to experience with the intellectual and cultural frames that form us, which we have used to make experience intelligible, manageable. Something radically different—an economy driven by unprecedented causal variables, a political event that does not fall within the familiar, a social scene that is entirely original—is typically drawn into the familiar mental instruments we employ to negotiate our way through our worlds. The inevitable consequence of this concession is that the new and unseen are understood erroneously or not at all. This may put into relief the critical importance of original, creative intellectuals and practitioners in all cultures who can see and present the new in innovative ways. One implication of this observation is that the artless scientific temperament that speaks with an authority presented as timeless misses the true nature of science. Yes, if the speed of light is an absolute limit on travel, and travel is the projection of a physical object across space, then the size of the universe and the distance among its contents make space travel impossible in any feasible sense. If matter and energy are sealed off from one another, and if the earth is the center of the universe, then . . . We must remember that all scientific principles and laws are provisional, with the implication that even basic limits and possibilities are to some degree human artifacts drawn from whatever is the current state of scientific assumptions and explanations. Are there higher forms of life in the domains of human experience? No one can know, in present time, whether that conjecture is or will ever be truth-functional in any practical way. But it cannot be denied outright.

There have always been efforts to bring scientific testing to religious claims and beliefs. The Byrd experiment, for example, was a classic instance of causal modeling with statistical measures of significance designed to test whether intercessory prayer is effective. In the experiment patients in a coronary care unit were divided into a prayer (or target) group and a control group. A set of individuals, drawn from born-again Christians who were active in a church, then prayed for individuals in the prayer group. No one in the experiment prayed for anyone in the control group. The experiment was double-blind, with the most important shield that the individuals being prayed for did not know they were the recipients of prayer, thus canceling the placebo effect. The organizers of the experiment claimed a significant difference in the healing rates between the two groups, with the individuals who were prayed for experiencing medical improvements not found in the control group.

The problem with all such assignments of scientific tests to religious beliefs and practices is that the variables and the conditions are difficult to shape in terms that meet rigorous standards of testing. The obvious issue in this experiment is controlling the extraneous variables. For example, it was and is impossible to control for the possibility that those in the prayer group were praying for themselves with more intensity than those in the control group, that others outside of the experiment (family, friends, perhaps medical personnel) were praying more for the target group than the control groups, and so on. Then there are problems in defining the independent variable. What is a prayer? Does it require for its authenticity a certain state of mind in the praying individual? Since the act of prayer is by definition a private act, how can we be sure that the members of the prayer group were in fact praying? Then, ideally, a good experiment would require that an augmentation or reduction in the independent variable be tracked in its effects on the dependent variable. But what is more prayer, or less prayer? Increased repetitions? Greater sincerity? Finally, it is possible in religious communities to set the *ceteris paribus* clauses in such a way that the efficacy of the independent variable is impossible to test, much less measure. Consider the well-known maxim: All prayers are answered by God—but sometimes the answer is no. Put that in place and it is impossible to falsify the efficacy of prayer.

In some important sense both Einstein and Gödel were trying to present in their theories and mathematics a reality that could not be seen nor understood except incompletely. We might depict this reality imperfectly with our instruments of thought, especially mathematics (which Einstein thought was the language of the universe), but it is visually inaccessible. The salient issue here is whether this essentially

one of the interviews she provided a sense of God that accords with the explorations surveyed here.

"I don't understand what the prime mover is. Whatever the prime mover is, the prime mover's insides do not work like a clock. There is serendipity involved. I would rather be lucky than good, because luck always counts. And I don't know what luck is. It isn't just random movement in the linear universe, because I think the random movement is more important than linear movement. Randomness is not a residual. Linearity is a residual."

Park leans back in her chair, her hair framed against the window at her back. The bright sunlight from outside places her face in shadow if one looks directly at her.

"I was brought up a Catholic. I remember listening to the nuns and they always said 'God is everywhere.' I remember sitting in Saturday religious instruction, which I hated, thinking about God being inside of tree trunks. At the same time being in the bark and being in the air. And being puzzled over that for a long time. The prime mover is not the God I thought about when I was sitting listening to the nuns. It is more like an Indian great spirit—it is not even a force or an energy. It is amorphous, and beyond my comprehension. I don't rely on it. I don't plan my life around it. But I assume it is there. Fundamentally it is good. It has something to do with life and it is good. It is not destructive. Even when misery and destruction happen, these are temporary. It is like a unity that is out there even in misery. Misery allows you to appreciate the goodness. Having been close to death helped me to appreciate life. Having been completely, spiritually void, and remembering what that was like, makes my life richer now that I am not. Because there was always something missing, there was always something that I was struggling with and I don't struggle anymore. I don't struggle. Most of the time I am remarkably happy. I don't worry about tomorrow and I don't try to control because I know I can't. Not only that but it is pointless. Control to what end? There isn't any end."

This recognition of God as outside the parameters of human knowledge is both agnostic, deferential to human limits, and tolerant of transcendent realities. It is not based on science, which is all right since science is only one way among many to arrive at truths about experience, including a reality of the afterlife that may be as real as the postulates and insights of our best inquiries. The issue for spiritual communities can be restated this way: Will the postulate of life after death be more like the non-existing planet Vulcan, or more like the neutrino that Pauli asserted an existence for before any evidence was extant for its existence? Time and a more robust version of science may answer that question. Right now the afterlife postulate helps render human life intelligible in terms of our own conscious and tacit sensibilities — for those who raise questions about life's meaning and scope.

sanity and a visitor, no. 2

"The blood sample," Frank says.

"The night lab technician, very young and very green, could not get it to respond to the usual tests. Left a note for the day crew to check out the anomalies and see if his test procedures were correct. Only thing is the sample was missing when the morning staff arrived. The lab is a chaotic area, understaffed with not the best record keeping. Was not the first time that a blood sample had been lost or misplaced. But it was gone, along with its donor."

"And the drug sample?" Frank asks.

"Still in the lab. And still not identified. The last I heard the chemists had defined it as a compound, an artificial derivative of unknown origins."

"My god. I feel a chill going through my body," Ellen says.

"Yes, I did too on the drive back to Manhattan. So did every prisoner and guard at Rikers who heard the story. Gary Cooper told me that everyone was spooked, convinced that they had been visited by someone from a different world."

"I can imagine. And then fear that he might return while they were still incarcerated," Ellen says.

"Then there were the feelings I had. Remember Paul, this was a long time before we met. I recalled again those feelings recently when I saw *Hannah and Her Sisters*. The description of the eligible bachelor at the end of the movie? He's brilliant, single, attractive, well educated, wealthy. The only drawback is that—he's in prison. Well, here was someone I was drawn to serving three to five. Not your ideal situation."

"But the sentence reduction. Did it go through?" Frank asks.

"Better than either one of us had a right to expect. The DA indicted and convicted the bad guy. Gary Cooper was cut back to two years. With time already served and a good record, he was paroled six months after we met."

"Now the love story," Paul says. He is obviously in a glum mood.

"Before we met, sweet. Long before we met. Keep that in mind."

"Just don't get too graphic."

Janet laughs and hits Paul on the arm. "Like your stories, you mean." It is obviously a private reference that everyone in the group lets pass. "And, Paul, dear, with two daughters we are definitely bound for all eternity. Yes?"

Paul nods and touches her arm.

"Anyway, as we say in the legal business, Gary and I started to see one another. It was nice, good, in spite of the fact that he was twenty years older than me. Casual lunches. Then weekends together. He made great efforts to get his life back together. His wife was long gone, married to someone else even before he got out of prison. Daughters — still loving, but grown, with their own lives to lead. I felt like shaking them. You know, do you realize the risk and sacrifice your father made to get you through school? But that would have sounded odd, even funny. I just tried to help Gary resume his life, a life of some sort. Banking was obviously out. But he was smart, well educated. He got into computers, eventually opened his own business selling second-hand hardware and software. Did quite well after some hard times. I think he's quite well off now, married the last I heard and living in upstate New York.

"The interesting thing, the memorable thing about Gary was his psychic experiences the first months after getting out of prison. The spooky event, the vanishing, somehow stayed with him, clung to his person like the invisible stamp on my hand. We threw all of his personal effects out. But we could not jettison the eerie feelings and thoughts of the still unexplained — to this day — disappearance of a whole living human being. Then Gary started seeing the alien — this is what we came to call the vanished person — from time to time. Across the street at a busy intersection. On a bus going the other way on Madison Avenue. In Rockefeller Center on the other side of the skating rink. Deep in Central Park, in the trees back of Tavern on the Green. Always at a point where Gary could not reach him, catch up to him. But when he saw him, always on every occasion, the alien would look at Gary, some brief moment of recognition would pass between them, bang, and then the alien would be gone."

"Holy shit." Paul is obviously intrigued with the story.

"It gets better. Gary had to see his parole officer at regular intervals. These visits always so depressed him, they were so demoralizing, that he would usually get in my car afterward and drive out of the city north into the country, usually to the green areas that adjoin the Palisades Parkway. In that area past the State Thruway toward Bear Mountain he would park the car and jog for an hour or so in the woods — on one of the rare flat terrains in that area — to relieve the tension built up by the friendly parole officer. On one of these jogs — listen to this — he comes upon a vacant house. The house is in good repair, even sparsely furnished he can see from looking in a window, and spacious. The front door is open, lock broken. Gary goes inside. It is very quiet, peaceful. No one lives there, this is obvious. He settles down in a corner, on the wood floor, leans back against the wall. Peace. He feels at one with the world. Then, after a spell of meditation that completely relaxes him, he gets up, brushes off, walks to the kitchen in back and looks out a window. Dense, lush forest scene. Sunlight and shade. Pine cones on grass leading to stately trees. Maybe part of one of the state parks. In the distance, standing quite still under a tree about a hundred yards away, is the alien. Look passes between him and Gary, maybe understanding at some level, then alien turns, walks away, blends into the forest. Disappears."

"I don't like this story." Paul shakes his head, hands on ears as if ready to shut off the flow of the sentences.

"The sighting somehow does not unnerve Gary. He returns to my car, drives home still relaxed, musing now about what he is experiencing. Naturally he goes back to the house after the next meeting with his parole officer. This time the weather is not as bright. Still balmy, but overcast, with black clouds just over the tree tops. The door is still unlocked, the house empty. Gary goes in and immediately feels that tranquility he felt on the first visit. This time he settles in one of the ancient chairs in the living room. Closes his eyes and sees many comforting visions move across what we used to call 'the mind's eye.' Then he looks around the house. No sound of any sort now, not even birds outside. The house, get this, has changed its physical configuration while his eyes have been shut. Nothing dramatic, but the inventory and arrangement of the furniture, even the physical layout of the house, are different. He is in a different house in some respects, though also mainly the same house. The interesting thing is that this does not scare the shit out of him as it should. He is still calm, at peace. No sounds, his spatial environment has shifted in some of its particulars, yet he simply sits there meditating. Then he gets up for the stroll over to the window in back — it is still there — and looks into the tree line. Yes, the alien is there. But this time—and here Gary was never successful in explaining this to me, what he saw at this point—the alien did not seem altogether separate from the environment. He was standing there in some embedded relationship with the surrounding scene. Gary told me it was not so much that he was wooden as that the whole biological setting seemed animated somehow, filled with life. Then, literally from one moment to the next Gary told me, the alien was not identifiable any longer. The greens and browns of grass, trees, did not contain a discernible human individual. The alien did not so much disappear as blend with, collapse into the surroundings.

"So Gary leaves, notices along the jogging route he takes that sounds have returned to his world, and drives back home. Now he begins to visit the house even without the negative incentives of the parole-officer visit. Roughly once a week he trudges up into the woods and meditates in an abandoned house whose physical structure seems variable, not fixed. He also refuses to take me with him on these excursions. Interesting man, Gary, with a peculiar and solitary curiosity.

"Nothing happens for several visits. House is in some stable equilibrium, alien nowhere on premises or out back. Then one day the physical world comes alive again. It is an overcast afternoon, rain imminent. Gary is looking out back, this time with kitchen door open, just standing there looking at lovely natural surroundings. A shrub near the house, a small lilac tree obviously planted by someone and at some geographical remove from the other shrubbery in the back yard, catches his attention. He stares at it and is quickly aware that it is—here I use his word—inhabited. Some spiritual presence is in the lilac tree. It is trying to enter his consciousness. He can feel its power and is properly terrified at last. He feels that if this spirit, this incubus, gains access to his thoughts it will control him, perhaps forever. He retreats to the kitchen, sits down in epic battle with some hostile force. With great concentration and will he expels the presence. He leans back in the chair and at that moment a soft rain begins falling. He shuts the kitchen door. The session is over, but now he knows that the powers connected to the house are not entirely benign. Or if they are, he is not in the mood to accommodate them in his consciousness or anywhere else.

"Still he goes back. Crime and prison, or maybe just the adventures of rehab, have made Gary reckless. On one visit, his last it turns out, he is sitting in the chair in the living room softly humming a melody that has come into his head. Origin of melody unknown. He has never heard it before. A light goes on in front of him. Only it is in his head as well as in the world. The scene that the light illuminates is not in Gary's world, however. Four figures—he does not know if they are human, yet they seem to be graceful animals of some sort and they are in human form—are reclining on a marble floor. The one to which he is drawn appears to be a young woman, flawless skin and long dark hair. She is filling a pitcher with water to serve the others. They are definitely not contemporary figures, he immediately thinks. The other three seem to be a father and two small children. All of the movements in the scene are exceedingly slow, slow motion in a cinema portrayal. Gary keeps looking at this scene, feeling nothing unusual about the experience he is having, and then sees that the man is himself only much younger. He is with his own wife and children at some earlier stage of his life, but not clearly with precise identifying features since the four individuals may not be quite human.

"Then the young woman turns, is facing Gary, looking at him without seeing him, and Gary can see—what was his phrase here?—an alignment of vectors. The scene suddenly opens to a vista more barren than an empty marble hall, illuminated with brilliant sunshine, and Gary believes that he sees, understands, some fusion of geometry and biology. The woman's body is a triangular form—representing reproductive forces, love, sex—and the austere background is the natural world. As the scene fades, lights dim, go up, I don't know, movie's over, Gary thinks he has absorbed some natural symmetry. His life, all lives, are endless, time is an illusion. He is transformed, redeemed, made whole again. It is night outside, though the vision seemed to last less than a minute. He leaves the house. The moon is three-quarters full, the grass a dark green in moonlight and shadow. He knows the alien is there and doesn't care. The universe is welcoming Gary. He kneels and plants three kisses on grass wet from an earlier rain. Soul free and properly located in reality, Gary returns to his apartment in my car and begins to remake his life having remade his soul."

No one in the group knows what to say, how to begin the discussion.

"Here are some thoughts for this assemblage to meditate on," Janet continues. "First, what was the house?"

"A church," Paul offers.

"Good," Janet responds.

"A halfway house," Mark suggests.

"Better."

"A safe house," David says.

Janet laughs. "Protection. Yes, possible. But I like the idea of a transitional place between realities that a halfway house suggests."

"Janet." Frank shakes his head. "What is your point in telling us this story? What lessons do you come away with that you want to share with us?"

"Frank. I love you in spite of your ponderous manner." Janet reaches over for Paul's hand. "And I love you for tolerating my past. Again."

"We'll survive Gary Cooper," Paul says.

"All right. No exercises, no pop quizzes, no identity questions. The question is, was Gary sane?"

Silence.

"How could he have been sane?" David finally asks. "He was hallucinating without drugs."

More silence.

"But we can say that only if we regard Gary's experiences as illusions of some sort." Paul stares straight ahead. "If they were real, in some sense that I cannot explain, then he was sane."

"Would he be considered legally sane?" The question is from Lupe. It is directed at Janet.

Janet smiles and says nothing.

"Was he able to function successfully in other parts of his life?" Ellen asks.

"Yes," Janet answers. "Better than before the visions, if that's what you want to call them. The experiences in the house, whatever they were, replenished his spirit. He was made whole again, trust me on this, as a consequence of these experiences. But one could also argue that he functioned successfully in the experiences, whatever they were."

Again, no one speaks.

"Look," Janet says. "Since this is not a mystery novel with a hidden ending, or agenda, I will tell you that of course Gary was legally sane in the direct sense of being legally competent to manage his affairs. True, he arrived at idiosyncratic beliefs about the real, but precisely because of these newly forged beliefs Gary was able to overcome his recent past."

"What are his visions now?" Ellen asks.

"The last time I talked to him was ten years ago. He said then that the signals were getting weaker, whatever that cryptic phrase means. Good thing I didn't have to get him to testify on some case of mine, I'll concede that. But he's doing fine, so far as I know."

"Yes, I can see the point," Ellen concedes. "Gary was able to secure his prudential interests because he acquired beliefs that go against conventional reality."

"Now you have it," Janet says, "though after being with Gary I am not sure any longer what the parameters of conventional reality really are."

"I have exceeded my parameters," Mark says, stretching his arms. "It's two o'clock in the morning I have just noticed, and my signals are getting weaker."

"Mine too," Janet says. "Paul, we have to go."

"Oh, stay and have another cognac," Frank says.

"No, no. It's really late."

"Shank of the evening," Frank continues.

"You always say that," David observes.

"It's always true."

The guests start moving and stretching. Several people get up. David stomps his right foot on the floor. To Ellen's querulous look he says that his whole right leg is asleep. Across the room Lupe yawns loudly.

"I adored the dinner. The whole evening." Lupe holds Ellen with both arms.

"Frank, you wily conniver." David insists on an embrace. "You have done it again. A great conversation."

Frank stretches in spite of himself. He retreats to a bedroom.

"I feel a cloud growing inside my forehead," Lupe says. "Something is inside of it. Growing stronger."

"Lupe, stop it. You are breaking the rules."

"Sorry."

Frank returns with a few light jackets over his arms. "Take. Identify. Those of you who are sensitive to balmy weather."

The guests who brought jackets put them on. The temperature outside the house has dropped slightly since the dinner party began. The night sky remains clear. A warm mist will cover the area by early morning. It is early in the month of June, however, and the sunlight will burn off the mist by mid-morning. A warm and bright Saturday afternoon is predicted. Golf and tennis weather. Boating perhaps, or nature hikes. Each of the guests has contemplated the following day in leisure terms. Frank is thinking of doing some writing, though he vows to himself to stay on his sun porch while working.

"Breakfast for anyone who stays," Frank offers.

"What will it consist of?" Paul asks.

"Ellen, here, take Paul's and Janet's jackets back to the bed." Frank helps his two guests take off their jackets and hands them to his wife while surveying the others. "Anyone else?"

"Paul, please. I am so tired." Janet makes a face.

"Just one cognac. Promise."

The other guests decline Frank's invitation with the good grace that the evening has anticipated. Goodbyes are said all around. Hugs. Some handshakes even. After everyone else departs Frank and Ellen move back into the living room.

"Wait," Paul says. "Let us help you clean up."

"No, not necessary," Ellen objects.

"We insist," Janet says, and the four remaining friends move into the kitchen and start to repair the effects of a dinner party. Dishes are cleared and placed on the counter. Paul rinses each item before placing it in the dishwasher. Finally the small group retires to the living room, Frank Perry carrying the cognac bottle and four clean glasses. They all sit down and try to sink deep into their chairs.

The full dinner party is still strong in their memories as a soothing presence. The group of friends has explored reality with all the powers of language at their disposal. The verbal exchanges have been encouraging, insightful on occasion. To some at the dinner party the ideas were as colorful as flares against a night sky, though others refused to be drawn into the psychic possibilities explored in the discussions. But now the original conversation has fractured in the usual ways, scattered with those who have returned to their homes. Random comments are being made in the separate cars, in the kitchens and bedrooms of those who have left. The guests who have departed are tracking the narratives to private destinations, personal understandings of human experience. Soon their thoughts will return to less abstract concerns. They will negotiate the different, more immediate paths of daily life.

Here, in the Perry household, is what remains of the group of close friends. Four individuals have decided to continue the conversation, to talk into the night and dawn, the conversation more restricted but still shielded for a time from the ordinary and compelling dimensions of conventional life.

The dinner party has taken place entirely within the boundaries of the Perrys' house. Did the physical location of the gathering affect the conversation? Choose your answer carefully. All the possibilities require an interpretation and an exploration. But the physical parameters of the narrative are indisputable. None of the participants entered the wooded area behind the house and walked on the sloping lawn to see the dinner party from the outside, from one of those external points where the whole conversation might be surveyed, absorbed, understood.

survival after death: how to think and talk about the unknowable

In the Stanisław Lem novel *Solaris* a space probe from earth is orbiting the distant planet Solaris in a remote solar system. The crew is trying to communicate with the alien life form they sense and seem to see enveloping the planet as a kind of ocean, an odd watery membrane that they have come to believe is a single organism on or absorbing this planet. They are unsuccessful in their communication efforts. After years of research conducted from their space station they have no more than various observations entered as data in an objective typology. Nothing about the interior mental life of the alien organism has been discovered, nor even accessed. The alien life form seems to have a consciousness utterly different from human consciousness. When the crew becomes more aggressive in their research attempts to communicate, the alien organism begins to influence their own thoughts and perceptions. It opens their personalities in conjured images of obscure or repressed memories, often presented to them in physical form. Nothing about the alien life form is discovered in return. Neither the structure nor the composition of the organism, any semblance of its consciousness—all remain distant and elusive even as the alien life form is creating replicas of deceased relatives and partners of the crew, summoning terrible events from their past lives for them to relive.

Consciousness is the last great mystery of human experience, in part because it is an exemplar of self-reflection: consciousness is the resource that studies itself. Lem's novel reminds us that other life in the universe and its conditions of existence may have a consciousness radically different from human life and its formative and sustaining conditions on earth. This possibility also calls into question the nature of an objective universe. We know that the reality we experience as human beings is an artifact of our neurological capacities. Put bluntly, the world we see and experience is the way it is because we are the way we are. Now, what if our consciousness is local, not universal? Then other forms of conscious life, with perhaps radically different intelligences, may have constructed different universes, with different covering laws and descriptions of the natural world, and different powers to influence reality. Thoughts, and the way forms of life think, may be the foundations for the structure and content of what might turn out to be a universe of multiplicity rather than uniformity. There may be different universes correlated with different forms of conscious life and their formative conditions.

MATERIALISM AND ITS LIMITS

Marx offered one broad and powerful and coldly deliberative approach to questions of consciousness and false and genuine realities. In what is reputed to be the most frequently quoted of all Marx's statements (and, I would argue, the most misunderstood), the role of religion in human affairs is depicted this way: "Religion . . . is the opium of the people." The full quote is worth reading: "Religious suffering is, at one and the same time, the expression of real suffering and a protest against real suffering. Religion is the sigh of the oppressed creature, the heart of a heartless world, and the soul of soulless conditions. It is the opium of the people." In the text that immediately precedes the selection depicting religion as an opiate, Marx acknowledges even more explicitly the appropriateness of religion in an inverted world of suffering:

Religion is, indeed, the self-consciousness and self-esteem of man who has either not yet won through to himself, or has already lost himself again. But man is no abstract being squatting outside the world. Man is the world of man—state, society. This state and this society produce religion, which is an inverted consciousness of the world, because they are an inverted world. Religion is the general theory of this world, its encyclopedic compendium, its logic in popular form, its spiritual point d'honneur, its enthusiasm, its moral sanction, its solemn complement, and its universal basis of consolation and justification. It is the fantastic realization of the human essence since the human essence has not acquired any true reality. The struggle against religion is, therefore, indirectly the struggle against that world whose spiritual aroma is religion.

Marx continues to talk—after the "opiate" portrayal—about the necessary eradication of religion, not through education or persuasion, but by changing the conditions that produce religious beliefs: "The abolition of religion as the illusory happiness of the people is the demand for their real happiness. To call on them to give up their illusions about their condition is to call on them to give up a condition that requires illusions. The criticism of religion is, therefore, in embryo, the criticism of that vale of tears of which religion is the halo."

The central holdings in Marx's program are self-evident by now. Materialism for Marx is decisive in rendering the full scope of reality. Consciousness is a derivative of the physical world. In particular, the material ordering of the political economy in a human community controls states of consciousness; and a satisfaction of needs in an equal distribution of material goods is required for authentic consciousness in the human species (not the "inverted" or false consciousness and "illusory" happiness of capitalism). The issues on which Marx is most effectively disputed are not focused on his presentation and critique of capitalism, in part because they are otiose—all economic systems today are hybrids with the two salient terms of the twentieth century, capitalism and socialism, possessing little referential power—and in part because Marx underestimated the recursive powers of capitalism in reinventing itself and the revisionist efforts of the state in redefining its scope in late twentieth-century political economies. The issues are rather these: Does materialism express the full scope of the real? Are we in the condition of true reality when we occupy without illusion a material setting? And do material goods complete the happiness metric of the human race?

Pure materialism does expunge all spiritual presence from the world. It is the intuitive energy base for atheism. God has no place in a purely material depiction of the real. Pantheism, the thesis that God is the material world, animates nature into a sacred domain, hardly the stuff of inert physical material. The critical mark of modern science complements the depiction of reality as inert in emptying the universe of all spiritual dimensions, presenting the natural world as physical events governed by laws that our independent mental powers can discover and state. The dualism between thoughts and the physical stuff of a material reality seems unassailable. The resistance of the physical world to thoughts, the revelation in childhood development that thinking something does not in itself make the something happen, is critical in the development of the human psyche. Our mental powers seem to be separate from a material or physical world even as they are influenced by that world's organization. But it is far from clear what exactly a stable and definitive material base of the world is. Nor, on a reasonable extension of this line of argument, can it be true in human experience that material goods dominate or absorb the mental or spiritual. James Baldwin once wrote that he had discovered that money, finally, was exactly like sex: when you didn't have it you thought of nothing else; when you had it you thought of other things. Materialism may be the currency of experience that allows thoughts to scan elsewhere once a material base is in place. But—again—this reality may be entirely subjective, local to human consciousness. Other forms of life may have a consciousness woven into the material stuff of the world. Can minds fuse with, be identical to, what we know as the physical universe? If they can, then materialism in human terms is limited and subjective in the strong sense, and perhaps mistaken on the scales of the universe.

Then there is this. A full account of reality is unlikely to be continuous with the conventions and laws of any version of ordinary human experience. The findings of relativity theory and quantum mechanics—stated now not as limitations on our abilities to know reality but rather as glimpses of what this reality may portend for us—indicate dimensions of the real that are inexplicable on the terms of the best scientific explanations and laws in classical physics. Relativity theory demonstrates the counterintuitive discoveries that time varies with observers, the scale of objects, and velocity, and that matter can be converted to energy (with, as we have witnessed, the creation of destructive instruments in the twentieth century).

Quantum mechanics yields even more radical disjunctions. The internal mathematics of quantum theory is not problematic. The theory works almost algorithmically in grinding out predictions and explanations of the movements of micro particles. The issue has always been with the internal grammar, the *logic* of the world depicted in quantum theory. This world collapses many of the traditional and venerable distinctions between observer and observed. On standard accounts of quantum mechanics the term *observable* is a synonym for a physical state of the system. The physical state is not an independent and objective state to be observed, but a function in some way of the observation. In ordinary terms, there is no there *there* since the position of an electron or photon is not fixed until it is observed. Also, whatever the *there* is, it is not governed by the laws of classical physics. Causality (if it is causality) seems to occur without contiguity, since particles can affect one another over vast distances with no discernible connections among them. Also an eerie duality obtains among entities, most dramatically represented by the complementarity principle, which famously depicts light simultaneously as both wave and particle. This possibility is hardly among the expectations driving the ordinary reality in which human experience mainly occurs. The theories and implications of the new physics invite, no, demand, new ways of thinking about traditional polarities, among them, as addressed here, life and death.

The one conclusion that we can render about the reality suggested by the new physics is that it is radically unlike the comfortable worlds of traditional human experiences. The one implication we can accept is that we cannot use the traditional laws of classical physics to deny the existence of a life after death since these laws do not extend to the full ranges of reality, and an afterlife might comport with a reality outside life in the finite terms in which we experience it. The one speculation we can embrace is that a universe so vastly outside human experience might conserve life in all forms in venues we cannot see or understand from a temporal perspective. Relativity theory and quantum mechanics deprive us of the particular certainty needed to refute this possibility.

ACKNOWLEDGING DIFFERENCES

There are thirteen spiritual camps in the United States populated by people who believe that persons live on after they die, and that we can see the dead and communicate with them. From an Associated Press story published on August 25, 2007: "Oh yeah, they're all over the place," says Judy Ulch, a jovial sixty-year-old who claims not only to see dead people but also receive messages from them. "Sometimes I see them so close, I see the stubble on their face," Ulch says. She passes the messages on to their loved ones, who pay $40 per half hour for her services. Fifteen-minute mini-readings are available on Mondays for $20. Seniors can get a $35 reading for half an hour on Wednesdays, while the price for workshops varies from $20 to $40. Wonewoc Spiritualist Camp in Wisconsin, where Ulch conducts her business as a seer, is a typical spiritual camp. People come to the camp every summer to explore possibilities and get readings. These camps are run by members of Spiritualism, a religion that began and flourished in the nineteenth century. Though Spiritualism has declined in recent times, it still has 250,000 followers. The religion is a variant on Christianity that rejects heaven and hell but maintains beliefs that life is eternal.

The stories told and heard are quintessential stories. For example (from one of my interviews): "I have an acquaintance who talks with a dead friend. This friend knows that he's dead, my acquaintance knows that he's dead. Yet the friend shows up from time to time for a casual conversation. Nothing mysterious happens, no special insights are provided about the other side, just a talk between friends sitting usually on a park bench. My acquaintance, who actually is a bit of a skeptic, believes that his friend is simply checking up on things, finding out how his circle of friends is faring in his absence." One could suppose that this is one of those reports that signify the conventional religious belief that the human community consists of both the living and the dead. Or it might just indicate the hallucinatory powers of even ordinary experience. These commonplace and mysterious reports (among others) prompt many types of thoughts about an afterlife.

How do we talk about and to individuals with these beliefs? Or, to refine and redirect the question: If we can't know with certainty that external realms of being do or do not exist, what are the means that we can use to explore the parameters of the real?

Imagine that two individuals, equal in knowledge and power, are at a table talking to one another, trying to interpret, to settle on the truth of beliefs in the existence of God and life after death. Suppose that the two individuals are charged with reaching a joint or shared agreement on the rules of evidence needed to negotiate these matters, with the focal point of their discussion the claims of those who say they talk with God. Say also that one of these two individuals is a member of a secular community that regards all texts as constructed by humans, all evidence as generated by human effort or produced from the workings of natural laws that depict a material universe (like Kepler's laws of planetary motion). The other individual is a member of a religious community that accepts certain texts as sacred, meaning originating in a supernatural domain, and evidence as at least occasionally generated by forces outside of nature as conventionally understood in secular communities. Suppose also that the "evidence" in question is seen as dubious or inconclusive by the secular individual, and true and conclusive by the religious individual.

Both individuals are united, however, in seeking out the truth expressed by the material in front of them, and are sincere in trying to establish a consensus between them on what exactly that truth is.

One can assume that the two individuals will approach the contested evidence with at least some overlapping characteristics. Each presumably has a conscience (secular in the one case, religious in the other) and is prepared to employ recursive or dialectic methods to interpret the material, meaning in the broadest sense that they will examine and reexamine claims, tacking them to more basic rules and principles in order to reach mutually agreeable conclusions. In this exercise both will see in some, perhaps different, ways the disparities in theoretical orientations that separate them but will be prepared to craft a language game that can house both sets of beliefs in a way that meets the needs of their respective communities. This will likely require the sympathetic acceptance of the definition of the other's beliefs as religious or secular. It will also involve a difficult provisional bracketing of truth in this encounter and a willingness to acknowledge textual readings of evidence that are granted standing, or provisional validity, just in order to negotiate the larger truths at issue in claims to talk with God. Put succinctly, the two individuals may each have to accept some small part of the other's approach to evidence as a condition for starting the discussion.

If the two begin talking to one another about the justifications they have for their own beliefs, and in general the uses of evidence to support beliefs, and if each is good at philosophy (meaning knowledgeable about and sensitive to prominent arguments on justification and evidence), then some curious strategies will be disclosed that limit the possibilities of reaching a common belief, or a reasonable agreement resting on a shared truth that can reconcile their differences. These strategies begin forming with a look at how evidence is defined and handled in each of the rival communities. The first sentence in Paul Giannelli's standard text, *Understanding Evidence*, is "Lee Harvey Oswald either shot President Kennedy or he did not." He goes on to say that the question for trial lawyers is whether the prosecution "could have proved Oswald's guilt at a trial." Then he discusses evidence law in terms of relevance, competence, reliability, and other rules that govern the content of evidence, rules governing witnesses, and so on, convincing even the casual reader that evidence in law is quite different from evidence in other practices.

For example, the probative value of evidence (that which makes something more or less likely to be true) is weighed against a variety of considerations, including the prejudicial effects on one side or the other in a trial (the sexual history of a rape victim, for example). The rules of evidence themselves vary within sectors of law, as the evidence admitted in a grand jury is different from that allowed in a trial. Background matters are relevant, as items of influence that bear on a trial but are not evidence. (The attire of a defendant at trial, for example, is usually scripted by defense attorneys eager to present the defendant as a law-abiding citizen. Domicile may be important. When the jury in the O.J. Simpson trial visited the defendant's home, his defense attorneys cleaned up the residence before the visit, removing all the pornographic videos and so forth and placing elegant reading material and works of art throughout the residence.)

Sometimes evidence is measured by strong admissibility tests influenced by background concepts. The admissibility of information in a legal trial, for example, is differentially fixed by how we define a trial. If we accept, in scanning the rules of evidence in American courts, Justice Brennan's definition of a trial as an adversarial contest between the state and a defendant with the state having disproportionate resources, then the admissibility of evidence will be (and has been) sharply restricted by the methods of its acquisition. On this understanding of a trial, information has to be acquired on high constitutional standards or it is not admitted ("fruit of the poisonous tree"), even if relevant for deciding on guilt or innocence. But if a trial is seen as primarily a search for truth, then even illegally acquired information might be admitted if it bears on findings of guilt or innocence (while perhaps punishing the state for its constitutional transgressions).

On occasion the criteria for validity are dramatically different across practices. Pope John Paul II accepted as authentic the first of the two miracles by Mother Teresa required in establishing her as a saint. An Indian woman afflicted with an abdominal tumor was supposedly cured by a locket with Mother Teresa's photo on it. A commission of doctors examining the case confirmed the remission of the cancer, announcing in doing so that they could provide no explanation for the cure. The pope took this as evidence for a supernatural intervention overseen by Mother Teresa. But of course physicians are quick to acknowledge the spontaneous healing that occurs as part of the healing powers of the body. The main character (an alien?) in the film K-Pax extends that acknowledgment when he says (to his doctor) that all life in the universe has the power to heal itself. These healing powers sometimes extend to spontaneous cures of illnesses diagnosed as fatal (and there are many false positives in diagnosing such illnesses). It is not an exaggeration to say that in the case of the Indian woman allegedly cured of cancer by Mother Teresa's indirect ministrations, the doctors could still attest to the fact that the cancer had been eliminated, holding to the view that the cure was a form of natural healing, while religious authorities could see the cure as evidence for a miracle. Cases like this, and the multiple criteria and admissibility tests for evidence, suggest that the phrase, "a single body of evidence," is unclear in most practices even in a uniform culture, and certainly murky in the extreme in a multicultural world with diverse and reasonable standards for evidence across disparate practices.

As an example of variable background concepts within a practice, and as a case study of cultural influence, consider how circumstantial evidence in a local bribery case was regarded differently between court levels in one state in the United States. On March 9, 2000, in Miami, Florida, according to court records, a police officer stopped a female motorist for speeding. She was clearly drunk (and admitted as much). He drove her to a deserted area and had sexual intercourse with her, saying afterward that "she was lucky he did not give her a ticket." But he did not say that the sex was a quid pro quo for not arresting her. The Third Circuit Court of Appeals acquitted the officer of bribery, saying that there had to be a "spoken understanding" to prove a gift was exchanged for a favor. But the Florida Supreme Court ruled that explicit talk about bribery by public officials, a spoken agreement, was not necessary to reach a conviction, and that the circumstantial evidence was enough to convict the officer. In this case two courts within the same political culture and lodged within the same practice assigned different significance to the events on the basis of subtle background understandings of causal chains in ordinary experience.

If we track these tests for evidence in the domains of the rational, we will soon concede that there are multiple frames within which statements are determined to be true and become evidence through tests of relevance and admissibility. On this easy admission we will first dismiss (as good philosophers) explanations for intractable disagreements based on the perceptual errors documented in the famous and overcooked Bruner-Postman experiments, because there a "correct" standard was in place to demonstrate that the subjects perceived what was not there. Disagreements based on false perception have easy remedies. Instead, second, a harder and more intractable condition follows: there are several competing ways to define and accept evidence, and the possibility of a correct standard for reconciling these ways is remote. The immediate gain is a restatement and fresh understanding of the well-known proposition that "reasonable people can disagree, even when confronted with a single body of evidence." There may be no single body of evidence generalizable across different frames, and the disagreement among reasonable people may be a function of the variability across practices of veridical criteria and admissibility for evidence. Worse (perhaps), evidence may be infinitely and subtly variable even inside practices with slight modifications in background concepts, with the singular result that any range of evidence is insufficiently stable to claim standing as "a single body of evidence." The most important implication of these findings is that the heterogeneity of evidence provides a menu of opportunities to build and tear down a case for life after death.

The moral lesson in the thought experiment is self-evident. In any interesting community with multiple ways of life and different social practices, evidence will be deeply mired in a variety of different and rival contexts. Even what are called "epistemic peers" in the same practice or institution can track back to rival definitions of the settings in which they are located, and in doing so see the evidence in front of them in radically different ways. Practical reasoning is always contextual, and reasons for action (this is indisputable) can be artifacts of the conditions in which the rational agent thinks things through. The first question one must ask of any assignment of practical reason is—what is the situational location of the rational actor? The professions in Western cultures are probably clearest in delineating a variety of forms in practical reasoning. A physician, an attorney, accountant, dentist, detective, teacher—experience is filled with individuals trained to think in certain ways by virtue of their professional requirements. Practices follow suit. Chefs, race car drivers, deep sea divers, thieves, mechanics—all manner of skills leads to practical thinking formed by the rules and purposes defining the practice at issue. If we include the practices of science and religion we can assume that different rules of evidence, inference, and argument adorn these different practices. The key to understanding the supernatural in human experience then requires an assessment of the generalizing powers of science and religion as they compete with and complement each other in making eschatology intelligible within a pluralist society that yet recognizes—in certain sectors—the existence of sacred evidence.

NEGOTIATING THE UNKNOWABLE

In one of his early routines, the comedian David Brenner reflected on the treachery of mosquitoes. After regaling and dismaying his audience with funny stories about the absolutely repugnant habits of mosquitoes, he pointed out that the male mosquito does not bite, that it is the female of the species who is after our blood. Then he reported that the high whine that signals a mosquito is close is the male signature trait. The female is silent. So, Brenner observed, if you are in bed at night in the dark and you don't hear anything—watch out.

This kind of eerie inverted logic seemed to be visible in the Bush administration early on when FBI director Robert Mueller reported that the main danger to Americans within the country is the possible presence of al-Qaeda cells that we know nothing about. Homeland Security Secretary Tom Ridge used to say that we have to worry about what we do not know. The Bush administration and the U.N. inspectors in prewar Iraq were preoccupied with weapons of mass destruction for which we had little or no evidence and later found did not exist. At one point in that fruitless prewar search the inspectors suggested that the absence of evidence was a kind of proof that the weapons did exist.

Defense Secretary Donald Rumsfeld described three types of terrorist threats recognized by the Pentagon. One is the known threat. The second is the unknown threat that analysts know about (we know that we don't know it). The third, easily the most intriguing, is the "unknown unknown" (this is not a stutter). Let Rumsfeld's words carry us here: "I think this construct is just powerful. The unknown unknowns, we don't even know we don't know them." Rumsfeld was widely mocked for these statements, but the strange thing is that the typology makes sense. We can know things. We can also know that, and perhaps what, we don't know. And, yes, at other times there probably are realities that are outside our zones of awareness (the unknowns we don't know that we don't know). The ancient epistemological questions, how do we know *what* we know, how do we know *that* we know, are inverted to an extreme: how can we know those domains that are not entries in the set of the known unknowns? These distinctions carry easily across all political divisions and cultural orientations. But the issue is how we get working knowledge that leads us to make rational decisions on vital matters, war or peace, for example, or anything else, from the extreme senses of the unknown that Rumsfeld contemplated. This is the area of conjecture, the construction of inferences from defective or presumptive evidence.

Many practices substitute maxims for conjectures in negotiating the unknown, those pithy sayings that give us shortcuts to rational decisions. For example, a maxim in medicine—when you hear hoof beats, look for horses, not zebras—urges doctors to suppose the probable or conventional in diagnosing illnesses. The maxim assumes normal patterns of disease. But the world has long been filled with the unexpected, almost the unthinkable. Hoof beats might signal the approach of the grim reaper. What do we use when great risk or importance is attached to all the alternatives and the outcomes are unknown, even invisible? The notable secrecy of the Bush administration always made it hard to see what decision rules were in play when the stakes were high. But the anecdotal accounts suggest that President Bush's highest conjectures were too often grounded in worst-case scenarios coupled to the belief that marvelous successes can be achieved if enough force is applied. Bracket probabilities and actual data, suspend formal decision rules, and imagine the greatest disasters that can occur. Then develop radical and coercive security measures to protect against them without any real inquiry into the little we might know about the targeted situation.

Microeconomics has offered a better training manual for rational decisions. Traditional rational models are refined instruments that guide us in navigating the domains of what we know. Conditions are broken up into certainty, risk, and uncertainty, with decision rules controlled by the conditions. These instructions on the rational have guided any number of business and political leaders. But the guidebook depends on a particular and narrowly defined typology of information framed in terms of its contribution to the connections between alternatives of choice and their outcomes. Conditions of certainty obtain when this base provides a probability of 1 between an alternative and an outcome. In conditions of risk the probability is between 0 and 1, and in conditions of uncertainty there is not enough information to establish any objective probabilities between alternatives and outcomes. The proper decision rules to be used in each of these conditions follow the effects of the available information: maximize utility in conditions of certainty; in conditions of risk use Bayesian decision rules that require multiplying the probabilities of an outcome by its expected value to yield a utility integer that permits a rank ordering of alternatives. In conditions of uncertainty one uses more theatrical decision rules: dominance, maximax, or maximin. The latter two rules—where one chooses the alternative with the best best (this is also not a stutter) payoff in maximax strategies, or the alternative with the best worst outcome in maximin—follow psychological considerations like risk-averse or risk-inclined mindsets and the types of goods at issue. In these arrangements rationality is a four-step procedure: the rational actor correctly discerns the conditions of choice, selects the decision rule appropriate for these conditions, rank orders the alternatives with the use of the rule, and then chooses the highest ranked alternative.

These are the rudiments. It gets more enchanting when one folds information into knowledge sets. The first issue in this transformation is whether one can increase levels of information to move across the typology to the gold standard of certainty. Here is where theories of bounded rationality begin to make a sidebar appearance. Herbert Simon's famous "satisficing" model relies on cognitive and cost limitations in the acquisition of knowledge. These two considerations are quite different from one another. The first is testimony to the real limits on our neurological powers and attends to the approaches in information and computer technology that try to augment these powers. It also presupposes that there may be inaccessible areas of knowledge. The second is a practical judgment call. On occasion we can divide alternatives into satisfactory and unsatisfactory sets without ordering the alternatives, and then select any entry in the approved set, without losses so severe that one slides the cost tolerance measure up several notches. Here the presupposition is that there are areas of knowledge that are cognitively available but not worth the costs of incorporation into the decision matrix.

The second issue is twofold: what makes information count as knowledge, and when is it rational to require or seek or have complete knowledge. This *epistemology* question is exceedingly complex. Generally what counts as knowledge is a function of particular theories and cultures, with an acknowledgment: that the rationality frames within all sets of knowledge are local. There is nothing new in this observation since a multicultural world has disabused even the true believers of the idea that the rational can track a permanent and universal knowledge. Such knowledge doesn't exist, at least not now. The dream of classical and early modern thought that complete knowledge is possible, that we can survey an infinite domain, at least aspire to see what God sees, is gone.

Even the aspiration has been inverted for special occasions. Rawls's use of contrived ignorance with the by-now legendary Veil of Ignorance in the Original Position of choice is aimed at establishing a condition of fairness elusive in states of full information. One is rational in this framework if one does *not* know certain vital things about oneself. In all these exercises knowledge is a variable and open item, meaning we can manipulate it for certain purposes, recognize when we are in a deficit state of knowing, and use levels and types of knowledge to arrange various forms of reason and rationality.

The powers of high positive and negative outcomes to trump probabilities are also part of the legacy of decision theory. In a straightforward way the values of the goods at issue will influence the selection of maximax and maximin decision rules in conditions of uncertainty. I might be risk inclined to gamble recklessly to win at penny-ante poker, but risk averse when it comes to high-stakes poker. Or, the choice of maximax and maximin decision rules will be influenced by the levels and types of payoffs at issue. Peremptory values attached to outcomes also influence choices in conditions of risk, where on occasion the values of outcomes can subordinate probabilities. In Pascal's Dilemma, the prospects of union for eternity with God versus eternal damnation in Hell dominate the probabilities of the alternatives. No matter how low a probability, if the negative payoff is off-the-charts high, dominating all other possibilities with the costs it presents, one can be rational in choosing another alternative. Also, a consummately high payoff with low probabilities might be selected over a high-probability event with a modest payoff, *ceteris paribus* clauses in place. Note, however—and this is the point to this standard rehearsal of the two decision rules—that the use of God in Pascal's Dilemma is only theatrical.

Think of it. Any exceedingly high positive or negative outcome will make the point. The earlier list of practice reasoning can be elaborated: prize fighters, daredevil motorcyclists, stunt doubles in early moviemaking, high-wire freelance walkers, balloonists trying to circumnavigate the globe—the world is rich with individuals who rationally risk life and limb for generous payoffs while neglecting or simply accepting fine calculations of probabilities. In more mundane terms, university students will often (not always) calculate the overriding negative payoffs of being caught cheating no matter how low the probabilities, and proceed in honest fashion through an exam for no good ethical reasons. But these well-known scenarios have nothing to do with Pascal's, or anyone else's, metaphysics. They just remind us of the symbiotic intertwining of likelihoods and payoff values in human experience.

The issue of life after death seems to be located in a different framework. The center of these inquiries is how to handle realms of being that are in principle inaccessible, at least into their entirety, to the human intellect and resistant to our efforts to bring them in human realms of knowledge. How can we understand an unbounded reality that is forever beyond our full grasp? What are the rules of evidence, inference, and argument, the forms of inquiry that can survey transcendent prospects, the unknown and even unknowable? Do alternative devices, like heuristics and narratives, fare better in negotiating the issues in these areas of inquiry? And, in terms of the topic here, how can we judge whether we survive in any fashion outside the boundaries of conventional human reality? This is material for an extended inquiry, but the starting answers are likely in the subfields of abductive logic as they yield hypotheses instead of conclusions, conjectures instead of decisions, maps instead of truths.

A DIFFERENT LOGIC

The storyboard version of science instructs us that we must bracket the intensity of an account and move deliberatively from evidence to conclusions, allowing a tracking pattern of data to lead us to the theories and laws that render the evidentiary foundation understandable, intelligible. When individuals impose prearranged (and usually self-serving) patterns on a factual base, the reasoning is widely regarded as flawed. The critics of the second Bush administration, for example, maintained that the decision process for going to war in Iraq was compromised by allowing a reality and an outcome to be imposed on data in such a way that evidence was buried or controlled to secure the "right" results. The evidence should govern us, it is often said; we should not govern (manipulate) the evidence. In those critical moments in science where hypotheses are maintained or dismissed, test-independence is crucial. Desirable outcomes cannot define, control, or influence the tests. This is standard schoolboy science, and eminently reasonable in a variety of conditions.

The only problem with this simple version of science is that even the most objective tests are subject to judgments about what counts as evidence and licit inference rules. Even the most rigorous forms of thought routinely argue back and forth between concepts and evidence—not by cooking the books in manipulating evidence but by reinterpreting it, and by recalculating its influence on our judgments given the imperfections of evidence in so many critical areas of inquiry. The issue in the domains of the supernatural is handling incompleteness when the resources that would complete the knowledge set are permanently inaccessible and insulated from conventional truth tests, and, in a theatrical sense, inferring wholes from parts when the nature of the whole (its scope and logic) is fugitive. The broad family of logical rules that must do this includes those that are inclined to infer backwards, from indicators or symptoms to the underlying principles that can explain surface patterns.

A version of this reverse form of identity assignments was used by Justice William O. Douglas in *Griswold v. Connecticut* (1965). Douglas listed phrases and rights in the Bill of Rights that, if accepted by the reader, require (on Douglas's argument) the recognition of a principle of privacy yet unmentioned in the Constitution. The intellectual strategy is to survey a set of indicators and then assign to the text an overarching principle or theory or explanation that renders the collection intelligible, that must be present implicitly in the text to provide coherence. In medical diagnosis, for example, a physician will use her clinical training and experience, and a variety of maxims that represent the prudential wisdom of medical practice (the "if you hear hoof beats, look for horses not zebras" maxim) at least occasionally to infer from symptoms the presence or absence of a pathology. In these cases a diagnosis, not a principle, is asserted from a mapping of symptoms back to a condition of the patient. In both cases a set of indicators is made intelligible with the reverse assignment. Any inquiry into exogenous dimensions of the real, especially when approaching what is presented as the supernatural, seems to be best depicted as a form of abductive logic in the *active* exercise of compositional skills influenced by a pragmatism that is proportionately sharpened as the issues are complicated.

Abductive logic, in imposing or arranging frames to make data intelligible, must be exquisitely sensitive to the holistic possibilities offered in background conditions. For example, one can use abduction as a riff on a logical fallacy, affirming the consequent:

If a, then b
  b
  It is possible and maybe likely that a is present in certain conditions

Here one looks at a variable, b, and then maps back to an antecedent variable, a, which in the deduction is a sufficient condition for b. Yes, there can be b without a (a is not a necessary condition for b) but the almost intimate (sufficient) relationship that a has with b might warrant a search for a in certain third-variable triggering experiences whenever b occurs. In a real-world scenario, for example, a street drug contaminated with a highly toxic substance can cause a fatal liver disease, but a fatal liver disease can occur on a number of other causes. Still, if physicians are inspecting a rash of fatal liver diseases, and there is a sudden increase in an illicit drug trade in a given region, it is reasonable for them to explore the possibility of an antecedent cause called a contaminated drug. It is in this way that abductive reasoning invites patterns of experience, a holistic perspective that can modify causal and deductive inferences with reasoned judgments. There is in fact a reverse form of diagnosis in medicine in which an undiagnosed disease is treated in serial fashion with different medicines. When the disease responds to a particular medicine the physicians will deduce in backward fashion the identification and presence of the disease from the effectiveness of a therapy that works when used to treat the disease. The providential direction of diagnosis followed by treatment is reversed. Instead, treatment is used first to diagnose a disease, and then the diagnostic medicine doubles as an immediate therapy when the treatment-inspired diagnosis is successful.

There is nothing startling here. Good explanations track in both directions in causal relations. Sometimes we have events or practices that we regard as dependent variables, and we look for antecedent variables that cause or are correlated with these variables. At other times we have a state of affairs that might serve as independent variables bringing about certain effects, and we track the effects of these independent variables on events in hypothetical terms from previous experience. The difference is that abductive logic characteristically seeks the more synoptic patterns in experience within which discrete relations among variables become coherent in some larger sense. Abduction is, or can be, concerned to identify or impose wholes on experience, in the example weaving a mosaic of multiple causes and effects interacting in recursive (*self-reflective*) systems.

The nearest cohort of this logic in scientific inquiry is coherence theory, an approach that does not attempt to produce explanations corresponding to reality but rather generates maps that arrange items in a pattern that makes the data coherent. Like a map, coherence explanations are not true or false in any complete or correspondence sense but rather useful or not in a variety of selective ways in helping one navigate experience (as when a map presents topological contours or the road systems of cities, for example). These are renditions that make relevant parts of the world intelligible, manageable. When pursued as rational thinking this logic can be used to fold the desiderata of the supernatural into the arrangements that yield a satisfactory intellectual order. If we think of the most demanding gestalt approach to experience, rational inquiry on this account tracks, retrieves, and imposes the patterns that make sense of indicators, in this way indemnifying an appropriate ordering of experience. It is a view of thinking, of broad rationality, that presents our judgments as a vessel pulled by multiple smaller vessels, each of which contributes to the forward movement of the act of thought—sense experience, calculative and theoretical reason, evidence, inference rules, formal tests, intuition—all contributing to a holistic view of experience that is not bound to the serial and particular canons of science *simpliciter*.

CONJECTURES: MATERIAL AND SPIRITUAL REALITIES

How should this form of logic work in evaluating the claims and reports, the information presented as evidence for a life after death, and the models or frames that depict experience in one way or another along these lines?

In the bluntest and crudest sense there are two dominant frames for depicting the boundaries of the real in human experience. One is the materialism celebrated by Marx and adopted by the now-fashionable atheists discussed earlier. The other is a mélange of views, some holding to beliefs in an external world that promises an existence after death. The evidence for the materialist denial of a transcendent reality is empty, a consequence of trying to prove a negative, in this case a negative that requires a certainty unattainable on the premises of the arguments. Or, put another way, the nonexistence of God or higher realities can only be established with a privileged access to transcendent realms whose existence is prohibited by the starting belief. Conversely, the evidence for what we can call the metaphysical view is scant, unreliable, uncertain—hardly the base for establishing the reality of conjectures so ambitious that there is life after death.

The one clear observation in scanning this array of views and evidence is that the full scope of human experience includes both material and supernatural dimensions, with a rich variety of inflections on these polar extremes. And from a survey of evidence none of these beliefs underwriting the natural or the supernatural, on the extremes or those arrayed on a continuum between the extremes, can be truth functional in any hard sense (meaning we cannot imagine, especially at the extremes, a decisive test to falsify any of the salient convictions). Claims about these dimensions of the real typically are retained or dismissed in a process conditioned by the conceptual arrangements in which they are located. The first observation to make on this mix is an obvious gambit. We have to recognize that the conceptual patterns within which such beliefs are located are crucial, not the truth or falsity of any single belief isolated from context. This point, by the way, applies generally to ordinary experience. We don't and can't say that going to the store, filling in tax forms, visiting a friend, what used to be called making love—none of these experiences are true or false in any important way. They simply are. Nor, to make another obvious point, would these experiences survive transformations to test their truth or falsity, like taking them into laboratory conditions for formal testing. Their meaning and significance derive from their location in ordinary life.

The second observation is an acknowledgment that even the most fundamental beliefs in human experience are fallible, that they change, and sometimes dramatically, over time and theory and geography. It is interesting that the hard takes on materialism, when folded into science, change more radically than metaphysical beliefs. The history of science is guided by an activity that is fashionably called paradigm replacements, in which even definitions and relationships of basic terms, and the scope of the universe and the inventory of items composing it, change in fundamental ways. The object lesson here is that science may be the least reliable perspective on a transcendent or fixed reality since scientific practices are a constant (and properly so) moving collection of methods and conclusions that yield different accounts of the "real." Only if—and this is an enchanting possibility—a set of variable research methods matches and interacts with a mutable external reality can science be a viable candidate to render metaphysical dimensions coherent. Religion also undergoes change (as does every institution, organization, state, individual, discourse, etc.). But the instruments of change differ from science. No new explanation of the natural or social world typically dominates religious doctrine. Arguments that trump traditional views are the decisive agents of change. Martin Luther railed against the corruption of the established Christian church (correctly so) but revolutionized the religion in the Reformation by successfully maintaining, against the Aristotelian and Thomist traditions, that a good soul does not result simply from good acts but that acts are good because the state of the soul is good within the individual actor. The high standing of current state-of-mind considerations in law (e.g., premeditation), morality (intentionality), and sports (the intentional foul in basketball) indirectly derive from the power of Luther's arguments.

If we accept the facts of intellectual pluralism and routine change in our understandings of the real, then it follows that no perspective can be anything other than partial, and no doctrine can be more than provisional. Imagine a setting populated by multiple points of view, no single one of which can dominate the others, and the ordering among them changes with shifts in theory and argument. Say also that the observer's perspectives must always be aimed at a reality that does not include the one looking through the lens, applying the theory, examining the evidence—indicating that no theory can be complete since the one observing or explaining the experience will be excluded from the vistas of the theory brought to bear on what is observed. Here is the dilemma presented in Frommer's guidebook on Paris inviting visitors to view the city from the top level of the Eiffel Tower with a limiting note in place: "On a clear day, you can see the entire city, but you face an epistemological problem: What is a view of Paris worth that doesn't take in the Eiffel Tower?" So while the sky view is in some sense best, it is incomplete in a radical way. The view from the streets, while not as good, may be more complete in sections. Both views are incomplete. The melancholy truth is that the human perspective *must* be a mosaic, able to survey and rely on different maps depending on what one is seeking in experience.

Part of this mosaic is the cold fact that rules of evidence, inference, and argument vary across types of inquiry, practices, professions, and not just on the objective accuracy and reliability of evidence. Conventional thinking seems at times to rely on a single model of reasoning. Yet issues in critical thinking often turn on what counts as evidence, and inference from evidence, and licit and illicit arguments, and sometimes even requires a ranking not, for example, of data/evidence but of the models in terms of which the evidence is identified and accepted. The diversity here is even more profound. As noted: the attorney and physician

and scientist and religious disciple, for example, have radically different ways of reasoning, of critical thinking. But the best critical thinking
may not be just a sophisticated tracking along the intricacies of problem
solving within practices, which is at best a form of noncreative science.
It must extend to the intellectual resources employed in identifying and
using a set of reasoning models, only some of which include problem
solving. Critical thinking wedded to a conventional way of thinking
things through may be at odds with the robust range of possibilities
throughout history and across the globe currently.

Some of these maps may lead us to realms not evident in experience.
Reflect again: privacy is not in the text of the U.S. Constitution. Yet from
a survey of the items explicitly present in the text of the Bill of Rights,
Justice Douglas reasonably inferred that a principle of privacy could
be drawn from the text. It exists as a presupposition, indicated though
unmentioned. In Douglas's reasoning a denial of privacy would render
much of the Bill of Rights incoherent. This reasoning, when assigned
to the mosaic of human experience, permits beliefs in entities not explicitly present in experience, unseen, invisible, but inferable from explicit items and required to make the explicit coherent. Or, we may be
required to accept the existence of something that is not directly present, not palpable or visible, as a condition for an experience to be intelligible. When joined to the obvious fact that we have limited access to
transcendent experiences, the existence of unknown dimensions of life
may be one implication from experience that renders large parts of it understandable. It is a melancholy recognition. To think fully may require
a belief in what we cannot see, and a capacity to acknowledge what we
cannot comprehend. The issue is whether we can craft rules that allow
us to infer, to map from the visible to the invisible, the known to the unknown, and perhaps unknowable, in ways that meet tests of good thinking while conceding our fallible natures.

The conclusions we can draw from a thinking that surveys frames for
making experience understandable, which looks to compose or recognize patterns that make experiences coherent rather than engage exclusively in a quest for serial and discrete truths, is that this way of thinking
can comfortably accept the possibilities of a life after death. No one, no
set of reported events, can close the deal on behalf of a hard no-quali-
fications take on the supernatural. But it is obvious from the perspectives of maps rather than truth-functional statements that an external
reality is suggested, implied by so many accounts of both ordinary and

extraordinary experiences. Near-death experiences, reincarnation reports, visitations, clairvoyance, telepathy, precognitions, even (and perhaps the least likely) psychokinesis—the human map has always been filled with experiences that defy the tenets of an inert and physical universe emptied of external realms. Put another way, if we were presenting human experience to aliens in another world, we would be obligated for accuracy's sake to include the natural and the supernatural, the capacities of our thoughts to slide along dimensions of a reality that cannot be either contained by the parameters of human consciousness nor known in its own venues by the powers of the human intellect.

RECOGNITIONS

To return to an earlier and very brief thought experiment on limits: The spider on the wall of the room may sense without knowing it the presence of the room. What the spider cannot do is dismiss the powers of the room, its governing laws, to affect and mediate its life. We may legitimately contemplate an afterlife, as dream, hope, expectation, destiny without definitive proof but with an arrangement of those traditional maps that guide us through human experience. No one anywhere can dismiss these maps by producing a definitive proof that physical life exhausts the span of life. Tropes exist, but no such proof exists. We are left with those maps of the supernatural forged by human experience.

The belief that the human community consists of both the living and the dead is common enough in many religions, for example, Christianity, and a recognition issue often occurs. In Luke 24:13–35, one finds the story of two men walking to Emmanaus, a village "about seven miles from Jerusalem." On their journey they are joined by a stranger, a man who asks them what it is they are discussing. In response they ask him "if he is the only stranger in Jerusalem who does not know the things that have taken place there in these days. He asks them, 'What things?'" The two men then proceed to describe the crucifixion of Christ and his burial. The stranger joins them in a deeply informed discussion of the events and the failed and fulfilled prophecies. "As they came near the village to which they were going, he walked ahead as if he were going on. But they urged him strongly, saying 'Stay with us, because it is almost evening and the day is nearly over.' So he went in and sat with them. When he was at the table with them, he took bread, and broke and gave it to them. Then their eyes were opened and they recognized him; and he vanished from their sight."

In the immediate months following the tragedy of 9/11, memorial services in New York City reminded the nation of our losses. A friend of mine was riding the subway on a morning when the city's firefighters were being honored in an elaborate ceremony. Across from her was a firefighter, seated alone, dressed in formal regalia, white starched uniform replete with hat and jacket. She assumed he was going to the ceremony. When their eyes met each other she mouthed the words, "Thank you." He nodded silently and handed her a laminated card and a piece of paper. The card was for a memorial service honoring a particular firefighter. She saw that it included an engraved photo of the dead firefighter along with photos of his family. The subway came to a stop at the next station. When she studied the photos she looked up in surprise. The firefighter was leaving the car with a group of people. She looked back down at the card. The photograph displayed a firefighter, the one who had died, identical to the one who had been sitting across from her. She thought, in a state of shock, I have seen the dead firefighter to be honored in the service.

The eulogy under the photos he had given her, the paragraph "Death is nothing at all," was written by Henry Scott Holland (1847–1918), Regis Professor of Divinity at the University of Oxford. He was also a Canon of Christ Church, Oxford, and, later, of St. Paul's Cathedral. The paragraph is quoted in full below. It is one of the most frequently used texts in the liturgy of funeral services.

Death is nothing at all. It does not count. I have only slipped away into the next room. Nothing has happened. Everything remains exactly as it was. I am I, and you are you, and the old life that we lived so fondly together is untouched, unchanged. Whatever we were to each other, that we still are. Call me by my old familiar name, speak to me in the easy way which you always used. Put no difference in your tone, wear no forced air of solemnity or sorrow. Laugh as we always laughed, at the little jokes we enjoyed together. Pray, smile, think of me, pray for me. Let my name be ever the household word it always was, let it be spoken without effect, without the trace of a shadow on it. Life means all that it ever meant. It is the same as it ever was; there is unbroken continuity. Why should I be out of mind because I am out of sight? I am waiting for you, for an interval, somewhere very near, just round the corner. All is well.

What can we make of such events and the emotional responses we have to such texts? And how can we bring these matters into our understandings of human experience?

This eulogy provides one answer to the skeptic's question. If individuals live on after death, where do they go? Perhaps nowhere. They're still here.

closures

This scene is set. Do not think for one moment that you can change a line.
Frank Perry is sitting on the bed waiting for his wife to finish her ministrations in the bathroom. He picks up his watch from the night table with his right hand. He passes his left hand over the closed right hand. When he opens the hand holding the watch it is empty.

Ellen enters the bedroom holding a small white towel.

"No more tricks, Frank. We've seen enough for one evening."

She lies back in the bed and pulls the spread up to her waist. Frank turns off the light and joins her under the bed covers. They lie quietly together for a moment. They have slept together for their entire married life, the last twenty years in a king-size bed that allows them space for thrashing out bad dreams alone and for voluntary intimacy in some shared area of the bed, usually on Frank's side of things. They are each reflecting on the evening dinner party.

Frank speaks his thoughts first, in a voice so quiet that he could be talking to himself.

"I always come away from these sessions with some enlightenment, principally with a renewed appreciation for how one's creations can take on a life of their own."

"That's because you insist on a plan. If you would just let things happen, you wouldn't have to worry about enlightenment."

"A libertarian dinner party."

"Or an existentialist happening. Where meaning flows out of the events, rather than being imposed by the host."

"Imposed?"

"Well. Formed in advance and used as a guide to measure the success of the evening."

"I plead innocent to the charge. If anyone had a tabula rasa in place tonight it was me. Every idea, every thought I had was formed inductively, from the experience of the conversation. From listening to our friends tell stories about themselves as if the events were happening to someone else, as if they were spectators outside of their own lives."

A noise downstairs.

Frank moves his head up higher on one of the pillows.

"Good God. Has one of the guests returned? Ellen, do you think?"

"Maybe it really is Banquo's ghost."

They both laugh quietly.

"Ellen, no, not permitted. Too scary. Bring back Descartes."

"Frank, what exactly were Descartes' thoughts on mind and body?"

"That we are dualistic, binary creatures of infinite variety, mental selves in bodies. A soul for Descartes. In property dualism a mind in the body. A ghost within, if you accept Ryle's arguments."

"Do you believe in the ghost within?"

Frank turns and looks directly at her.

"Of course. Which also might mean that I believe in a life of the psyche after the body dies."

In the silence that follows Frank Perry begins again.

"Paul Lorca."

Ellen turns on her side to face her husband in the dark.

"Your saying the name just then reminds me of Duke Ellington. The old jazz quartet that became big in the 1950s? Ellington had a player, a saxophonist I think, who went off on this amazing improvisation one night in a concert. Fortunately it was recorded. At the end of this long exploration Ellington kept saying his name again and again."

"That was Paul Gonsalves."

"Oh."

Frank turns on his side, using his elbow to prop his body up a bit. He reaches over and rubs Ellen's hair.

"But who knows after tonight. Maybe that person was really Paul Lorca."

"It is a musical name."

"Paul Lorca. Paul Lorca."

More laughter.

"Frank, you are closer to Paul than any of us."

"Yes. And I share this with you. Paul thinks that he is shielded by magical forces. Once, when he was a young man just starting the courtship of Janet that led to their marriage, he was driving home on an icy country road at a high rate of speed and his car went into a slide. Just before he reached the ditch on the right side of the road and the inevitable flip of the car he hit the brakes and the car seemed to bounce off an invisible barrier. It started sliding back to the other side of the road toward a grassy knoll when at the last second he pumped the brakes again and the car veered off another invisible buffer to go caroming down the center of the road until he could bring it to a stop. When he exited the vehicle he slipped down immediately on the road, so slick was the surface. He knew there was no way that the dynamics of the physical universe could have permitted his automobile to move back and forth the way it did. He is convinced that there was some intervention. That he was spared for a purpose."

"Frank. How could you know all this?"

Frank Perry looks at his wife.

"He told me the story."

"Ah."

"He also told me something else, same evening. Let this be the last entry of the night."

"Please."

"He told me that in his work on counterfactual realities—the work in pure theory that Paul cannot resist—he came to believe in the reality of the fragmented self, the self distributed across possible worlds."

"So much for the integrated self of psychotherapy."

"But he dreams so vividly that he has lately started to believe in alternative realities, rival conditions where the true incarnate self has a fixed identity. Unfortunately the fixed identity of the self is not in this world that we know and love."

"That sounds awfully theatrical, even for Paul."

"Except when you bring it home to his experiences. Did you listen to him tonight? The man believes in the migration of the self, but he still doesn't comprehend real anomalies. Where things don't fit at the most basic levels. How the soul is located in affective reality, not in the physical world."

"Frank. You are not God. Stop pontificating."

"No, I'm not. But you asked. And I am trying to be helpful."

Frank Perry looks up at the dark ceiling of their bedroom. Ellen touches his face.

"How did you make the watch disappear? As many times as I've seen you do that I still don't know where the item goes."

"A parlor trick. It doesn't go anywhere. Here."

Frank reaches over and takes the watch from her hair.

"I miss the magic shows you used to give, back when we were starting out. When we were young."

"I know a better trick. When we go to sleep every object in this room will cease to be."

"My husband, Bishop Berkeley."

Ellen moves over so that her body is touching her husband's body along its entire length. She drapes one of her arms around him.

"Sleep. Forgetting. That would be helpful."

"Agreed. The benign shift in consciousness. The dinner party in the past. The noises outside ignored. Let them—eat cake."

"They need bread."

"We all need something."

"I need sleep. I can't stay awake another second."

The Perrys move their arms around each other so that they are physically joined. They each begin sliding along the thin line between sleep and wakefulness as they slowly continue talking to each other, their last words pleasantly slurred.

A visitor gazing at them would see two intertwined bodies, a configuration of physical stuff with diminishing powers to perceive, to talk, to think about the realities they inhabit. The objects in the room will soon be unmediated by human perceptions, and so will have neither form nor content. At dawn the Perrys will each be in a dreamless sleep where language has no life and the events of the evening have begun slipping toward the domains of memory.

notes

Each note refers to text found on the page(s) indicated on the left.

CHAPTER ONE: LIFE BEYOND LIFE

18   Robert Bolt, *A Man for All Seasons* (New York: Vintage Books, 1962), 87. Richard Rich, alas, the most despicable of all the characters seeking More's conviction and death, lived the longest (and, reportedly, the most comfortable) life of the lot. See also Peter Ackroyd's *The Life of Thomas More* (New York: Anchor Books, 1988) for a history that delineates many of the scenes and the languages depicted in fictional terms by Bolt in his play.

18   Paley's inquiry is reported in "Success Was Not Enough," *New York Times*, November 4, 1990.

19   Plato, *Apology*, in *Euthyphro, Apology, Crito, Phaedo*, trans. Benjamin Jowett (Amherst, N.Y.: Prometheus Books, 1988).

19–20   M. J. Stephey, "What Happens When We Die?" *Time*, September 18, 2008. See also Sam Parnia, *What Happens When We Die: A Groundbreaking Study into the Nature of Life and Death* (Carlsbad, Calif.: Hay House, 2007).

21   Michael Ondaatje, *Anil's Ghost* (New York: Knopf, 2000).

22   The phrase "the life of the world to come" is found in the Nicene Creed and was used by Carol Zaleski as the title for her study of the narratives of near-death experiences and Christian beliefs in the afterlife. See *The Life of the World to Come: Near-Death Experiences and Christian Hope* (Oxford: Oxford University Press, 1996).

24   Leo Tolstoy, *War and Peace*, trans. Richard Pevear and Larissa Volokhonsky (New York: Random House, 2007), 916.

24–26   Ernest Hemingway, "The Snows of Kilimanjaro," in *The Short Stories of Ernest Hemingway* (New York: Charles Scribner's Sons, 1953). The hyena crossing is mentioned on 63, the hyena slipping lightly along the edge of death on 64, Harry musing that death went "in pairs, on bicycles" on 71, the two bicycle policemen image on 74, death sitting on Harry's chest at bottom of 74, the weight going from his chest on 75, the scene with Compton arriving in the plane on 75–76, the quote on the flight on 76, the last scene on 76–77. See also Alex A. Vardamis and Justine E. Owens, "Ernest Hemingway and the Near-Death Experience," *Journal of Medical Humanities* 20, no. 3 (1999): 216, for the connection between Compton and Denys Finch Hatton, and for other insights into the story.

26 Or, the projection of images of the self to others that we all do in ordinary life, depicted in the phrase "To prepare a face to meet the faces
that you meet," in T. S. Eliot's *The Wasteland* (New York: Harcourt,
Brace & Company, 1958), 4.

27 William Wharton, *Ever After* (New York: Newmarket Press, 1995).

28–31 The relevant dialogues are collected in Plato, *The Last Days of Socrates*,
trans. Hugh Tredennick (Middlesex: Penguin Classics, 1975). See *The
Apology* for the account of the trial, the *Crito* for the ideas on obligation, the *Phaedo* for the discussion of Simmias's example of the musical instrument, 163–170 for the theory of opposites and arguments for
the immortality of the soul, 170–179 for the description of judgments
and Hades, and 181–183 for the death scene.

31 Jean-Paul Sartre, "The Wall" in *The Wall*, trans. Lloyd Alexander (London: Hesperus Press, 1939).

32 See Stephen Jay Gould, *The Structure of Evolutionary Theory* (Cambridge,
Mass.: Belknap Press, Harvard University Press, 2002).

33 Karl Popper, *Conjectures and Refutations: The Growth of Scientific Knowledge*
(London: Routledge, 1963).

34 Bertolt Brecht, "The Life of Galileo," in *Collected Plays:Five*, trans. John Willett, ed. John Willett and Ralph Manheim (Boston: Little, Brown, 1994).

35 The paragraph relating the story of Foscarini is from the preface to my
book *Bounded Divinities: Sacred Discourses in Pluralist Discourses* (New York:
Palgrave Macmillan, 2006).

37 See the excellent treatment of these matters by Rebecca Goldstein, *Incompleteness: The Proof and Paradox of Kurt Gödel* (New York: Norton, 2005).

CHAPTER TWO: PAST LIVES AND REINCARNATIONS

47 Giuseppe Di Lampedusa, *The Leopard*, trans. Archibald Colguhoun
(New York: Avon Books, 1960), 260.

48 The biblical parable of Lazarus is in John, chapter 11.

48 Thom Gunn, "Lazarus Not Raised," *Trinity Magazine* (1952).

49 The encounter between Raskolnikov and Sonia comes from Dostoyevsky's *Crime and Punishment* (New York: Bantam Books, 1981),
302–306. "The Grand Inquisitor" is from Dostoevsky's *The Brothers Karamazov*, trans. Constance Garnett (New York: Bantam Books,
1981), 297–319.

49–50 Shakespeare, *Henry IV, Part I*, act 3, scene 1.

50 Shakespeare, *The Winter's Tale*, act 5, scene 3. Hermione dies offstage
earlier in the play, an uncharacteristic bit of stagecraft for Shakespeare. Though he allowed reports of death to be declared on stage
(e.g., *Macbeth*, act 5, scene 5: "The queen, my lord, is dead"), he loved
visible, "played" stage deaths for his major characters. The statue

shows Hermione as having aged exactly the sixteen years since her "death," which, if a true statue, would require us to grant magical powers to the sculptor.

50   Shakespeare, *Pericles*, act 3, scene 2.

51–57   Brian Weiss, *Many Lives, Many Masters* (New York: Simon & Schuster, 1988). Dr. Weiss is presently chairman emeritus of psychiatry at the Mount Sinai Medical Center in Miami and maintains a private practice in the city. He also holds seminars and conducts workshops on past-life therapy.

57–71   Ian Stevenson, *Twenty Cases Suggestive of Reincarnation* (Charlottesville: University Press of Virginia, 1974). Dr. Stevenson, after a long and brilliant career, died on February 8, 2007, at the age of eighty-eight.

58–59   Stevenson, *Twenty Cases Suggestive of Reincarnation*, discusses Prakash on 19–34 and Corliss Chotkin on 259–269.

64–71   See "General Discussion" in Stevenson, *Twenty Cases Suggestive of Reincarnation*, 331–339.

CHAPTER THREE: TRANSITIONS: FROM LIFE TO NEAR DEATH

Much of the text in this chapter is drawn from very prominent secondary and tertiary sources and used in robust and diffuse ways throughout the text, providing little opportunity to assign sources to page numbers (the usual practice employed in this book). The sources critical for understanding the narratives of Sunny von Bülow and Terri Schiavo are found in numerous newspaper accounts of the events and websites, especially www.crimelibrary.com, Mark Gribben, "The Claus von Bulow Case," True TV Crime Library, www.trutv.com/library/crime, and wikipedia.org/wiki/Sunny_von_Bülow; Dominick Dunne, "Fatal Charm: The Social Web of Claus von Bülow," *Vanity Fair* (August 1985); Alan Dershowitz, *Reversal of Fortune: Inside the Von Bulow Case* (New York: Random House 1986); Wikipedia; and any and everything else I could find. The same types of omnibus and uneven resources provide the Terri Schiavo story, including the numerous newspaper accounts and websites summarizing the events, especially the helpful presentation in the Wikipedia site, "The Whole Terri Schiavo Story" by Diana Lynne; and, again, everything I could retrieve from any other source. I have also read and used in different ways two books by the adversaries: (her husband) Michael Schiavo and Michael Hirsh, *Terri: The Truth* (New York: Dutton, 2006), and (her parents) Mary and Robert Schindler et al., *A Life That Matters: The Legacy of Terri Schiavo—A Lesson for Us All* (New York: Knopf, 2006). And I have profited from a panel discussion, "Terri Schiavo in Perspective: Ethics, Politics and

Medicine," held at the University of Miami Miller School of Medicine on the medical, legal, and political intricacies of the Schiavo experience, on February 29, 2008. The discussion was led by three of the principals in the case plus an award-winning documentarian and author—Michael Hirsh, the coauthor of *Terri: The Truth*; Jon Eisenberg, an attorney who represented Michael Schiavo and the author of *The Right vs. the Right to Die: Lessons from the Terri Schiavo Case and How to Stop It from Happening Again* (New York: HarperOne, 2006); Robert Walker, a physician and director of medical ethics at the University of South Florida; and Jay Wolfson, a physician and lawyer on the medical faculty at the University of South Florida who served for a time under gubernatorial appointment as Ms. Schiavo's guardian. Then there are resources on the Schiavo case on the University of Miami Ethics Programs website, http://www6.miami.edu/ethics/index.html, in particular scholarly, peer-reviewed articles and books that are listed under the "Selected Schiavo/PVS/PEG Bibliography" (PEG is an acronym for the feeding tube, percutaneous endoscopic gastrostomy, inserted into PVS patients to provide artificial nutrition and hydration). The material on zombies I have drawn from numerous sources, including Gino Del Guercio, "The Secrets of Haiti's Living Dead," *Harvard Magazine*, (January/February 1986); Wade Davis, *Passage of Darkness: The Ethnobiology of the Haitian Zombie* (Chapel Hill: University of North Carolina Press, 1988); David Chalmers, "Self-Ascription without Qualia: A Case-Study," consc.net/papers/goldman.html (accessed December 1, 2008); a compilation, "Zombies on the Web," consc.net/zombies .html (accessed December 1, 2008); Jakki Rowlett, "You Think I Therefore Am: The Ethnobiology and Ethics of the Haitian Zombie"; Daniel C. Dennett, "The Unimagined Preposterousness of Zombies," *Journal of Consciousness Studies* 2, no. 4 (1995); and the summary of the medical study in *Lancet*, "Zombies May Not Be What They're Reputed to Be," pslgroup.com/dg/3d806.htm (accessed December 1, 2008). Also note the brief references to other tangential works, like Malcolm Gladwell, *Blink: The Power of Thinking without Thinking* (New York: Little, Brown, 2005).

81–82   *Cruzan v. Director, Missouri Dept. of Health*, 497 U.S. 261 (301) (1990).

84   One indication that some parts of Haiti regard zombies as possible realities is the declaration in the Haitian Penal Code, Article 249, outlawing the practice of zombie creation: "It shall also be qualified as attempted murder the employment which may be made against any person of substances which, without causing actual death, produce a lethargic coma more or less prolonged. If, after the person had been

buried, the act shall be considered murder no matter what result follows." Then, in other parts of the text, instruction can be found for creating zombies: "The methods of creating and controlling zombies vary among bokors. Some bokors use blood and hair from their victims in conjunction with voodoo dolls to zombify their victims. Other methods of zombification involve a specially prepared concoction of mystical herbs, in addition to human and animal parts (sometimes called 'coup padre'). Ingestion, injection, or even a blow dart may be used to administer the potion variety. When these substances come into contact with the victim's skin, bloodstream, or mucous membranes, the victim is rendered immobile within minutes, succumbing to a comatose-like state resembling death. The victim retains full awareness as he is taken to the hospital, then perhaps to the morgue and finally buried in a grave. The bokor then performs an ancient voodoo rite; taking possession of the victim's soul, and replacing it with the loa that he or she controls. The victim's 'trapped' soul is usually placed within a small clay jar or some other unremarkable container. The container is wrapped in a fragment of the victim's clothing, a piece of jewelry, or some other personal possession owned by the victim in life, and then hidden in a place of secrecy known only to the bokor. The bokor raises the victim after a day or two and administers a hallucinogenic concoction, called the 'zombie's cucumber,' that revives the victim. Once the zombie has been revived, it has no power of speech, its past human personality is entirely absent, and the memory is gone. Zombies are thus easy to control and are used by bokors as slaves for farm labor and construction work. One case in 1918 involved a voodoo priest named Ti Joseph who ran a gang of laborers for the American Sugar Corporation, took the money they received, and fed the workers only unsalted porridge. Indeed, giving a zombie salt is supposed to restore its personality, and send it back to its grave and out of the bokor's influence." This is an inexplicable level of detail if a culture truly holds that zombies are not real.

85   Gino Del Guercio, "The Secrets of Haiti's Living Dead," *Harvard Magazine* (January/February 1986).

85   Wade Davis, *The Serpent and the Rainbow: A Harvard Scientist's Astonishing Journey into the Secret Societies of Haitian Voodoo, Zombies, and Magic* (London: Fontana Press, 1987).

87   VBS.TV, "Colombian Devil's Breath," http://www.vbs.tv/video.php?id =1119242704.

87–88   Richard Littlewood and Chavannes Douyon, "Clinical Findings in Three Cases of Zombification," *Lancet* 350 (1997): 1095–96.

88–89   See the title essay that presents the coping mechanisms of an autistic woman, "An Anthropologist on Mars," in Oliver Sacks, *An Anthropologist on Mars* (New York: Vintage Books, 1995).

91   J.R.R. Tolkien, *The Two Towers: Being the Second Part of The Lord of the Rings* (Boston: Houghton Mifflin, 2005).

92   Hemingway uses the phrase "the little death" eleven times in *For Whom the Bell Tolls* (New York: Scribner, 1943). See *American Popular Culture*, "Appreciate the Mushrooms Completely: Hemingway's Mixed Message," http://www.americanpopularculture.com/archive/bestsellers/hemingway_message.htm (accessed December 10, 2008).

92   Jean-Paul Sartre, *No Exit and Three Other Plays* (New York: Vintage Books, 1989).

96   Gilbert Ryle, *The Concept of Mind* (Chicago: University of Chicago Press, 1949).

96   Daniel Dennett, *Consciousness Explained* (Boston: Little, Brown, 1991), 452.

96–97   The Michaela Roser experience (along with other episodes of near death) is recounted in the National Geographic Explorer blog, "Close calls and brushes with death," on August 31, 2008.

98–99   The cases of Bede and Montaigne are drawn from Stephanie Wienrich and Josefine Speyer, *The Natural Death Handbook* (London: Rider Books, 2003), chap. 3, "Near-Death Experiences."

99–100   The case of the six-year-old boy is taken from Richard J. Bonenfant, "A Child's Encounter with the Devil: An Unusual Near-Death Experience with Both Blissful and Frightening Elements," *Journal of Near-Death Studies* 20, no. 2 (2001).

CHAPTER FOUR: A CATALOG OF VIVID
NEAR-DEATH EXPERIENCES

107   Jody A. Long, "Soulmates and Consciousness: New Understanding from *Near-Death Experience Research*," Near Death Experience Research Foundation, available at http://www.near-death.com/experiences/experts101.html (accessed October 2, 2008); Wikipedia, "Parapsychology," available at http://en.wikipedia.org/wiki/Parapsychology (accessed October 2, 2008); Joseph C. Segen, *Dictionary of Modern Medicine* (New York: Taylor and Francis, 1992), 483.

108   Division of Perceptual Studies, "Types of Experiences We Study," available at http://www.healthsystem.virginia.edu/internet/personalitystudies/case_types.cfm#NDE (accessed October 2, 2008).

108–109   Ernest Hemingway, *A Farewell to Arms* (New York: Charles Scribner's Sons, 1929), 54; Alex A. Vardamis and Justin E. Owens, "Hemingway and the Near-Death Experience," *Journal of Medical Humanities* 20, no. 3 (1999).

109 Katherine Anne Porter, *Pale Horse, Pale Rider* (New York: Harcourt, Brace, 1939), 251–256. See also Steve Straight, "A Wave among Waves: Katherine Anne Porter's Near-Death Experience," *Anabiosis — The Journal for Near-Death Studies* 4, no. 2 (Fall 1984).

109–110 Robert Roy Britt, "Near-Death Experience: Find Out If You're a Candidate," *Live Science*, April 11, 2006, available at www.livescience.com/health/060411_near_death.html (accessed December 1, 2008).

110 Horn's NDE was reported in almost all newspapers. For example, see "Horn hoped the attack was just a bad nightmare," September 16, 2004, available at http://www.msnbc.msn.com/id/6019154/ (accessed December 1, 2008).

110 Clinton described his NDE in the interview with Diane Sawyer on ABC's *PrimetimeLive*, "How Clinton Recovered from Surgery," October 28, 2004, available at abcnews.go.com/Primetime/story?id=207370&page=1 (accessed October 2, 2004).

110–111 Bob Woodruff's story is recounted in numerous places, for example, Nancy Chandross, "Bob Woodruff: Turning Personal Injury into Public Inquiry" (ABCNews.com on the web, February 26, 2007). A summary of the events can also be found in "Bob Woodruff," Wikipedia.

111–113 The Thai cases are drawn from "Eleven Thai Near-Death Experiences," available at http://www.innerworlds.50megs.com/bkknde.htm (accessed December 10, 2008).

114 Susan Blackmore, "Near-Death Experiences: In or Out of the Body?"

114–115 The extended quote defining spiritual emergencies is an adumbrated version of a quote in Sharon G. Mijares and Gurucharan Singh Khalsa, eds., *The Psychospiritual Clinician's Handbook* (New York: Routledge, 2005), 238, and is also bandied about in the Spiritual Emergence Network, available at http://www.spiritualemergence.org.au/pages/what_is.html (accessed January 2, 2009).

114–115 See also (of course) Stanislav Grof, *Spiritual Emergency* (New York: Tarcher, 1989), and David Lukoff, "Visionary Spiritual Experiences, Special Section: Spirituality/Medicine Interface Project," *Southern Medical Journal* June 1 (2007), available at http://goliath.ecnext.com/coms2/summary_0199–6700957_ITM (accessed October 2, 2008).

114 *Skeptical Inquirer* 16 (1991): 34–45, available at http://www.susanblackmore.co.uk/si91nde.html (accessed October 2, 2008).

115 Wikipedia, "Near death experience," available at http://en.wikipedia.org/wiki/ (accessed October 2, 2008).

115 Kenneth Ring, *A Scientific Investigation of the Near-Death Experience* (New York: William Morrow, 1982), and Ring, *Heading toward Omega: In Search of the Meaning of the Near-Death Experience* (New York: Harper Perennial, 1985).

115–116   Bruce Greyson, "Brief Report: Near-Death Experiences in a Psychiatric Outpatient Clinic Population," *Psychiatric Services* 54, no. 12 (2003): 1649–1651, available at psychservices.psychiatryonline.org /cgi/reprint/54/12/1649 (accessed October 2, 2008).

116   S. Renee Mitchell, "To End Rape, End Silence!" *Oregonian*, April 16, 2007, available at http://blog.oregonlive.com/reneemitchell/2007/04/ to_end_rape_end_silence.html (accessed October 2, 2008).

118–119   Bruce Greyson presents both theories in "Near Death Experiences as Evidence for Survival of Bodily Death," presented at "Survival of Bodily Death," an Esalen Invitational Conference, February 11–16, 2000. For William James, see his *Human Immortality: Two Supposed Objections to the Doctrine* (New York: Houghton, Mifflin, 1898), and (especially) *The Varieties of Religious Experience* (New York: Longmans, Green, 1916).

119   See the informal reports of after-effects from the NDE on "Posting: Spiritual and Psychological After-Effects," *The Mystic Board Forum Index: Paranormal Phenomena*, May 5, 2006, available at www.mysticboard. com/ paranormal_ phenomena /8541-near-death_experience-1.html (accessed October 2, 2008).

119   On the psychological antecedents of NDEs, Bruce Greyson, "Findings: Dissociation in People Who Have Near-Death Experiences: Out of Their Bodies or Out of Their Minds?," *Lancet* 355 (2000): 460–463, available at http://linkinghub.elsevier.com/retrieve /pii/ S0140673600820139 (October 2, 2008). Also, for another take on the relationships (if any) between mental disorders and NDEs, see Greyson, "Brief Report: Near-Death Experiences in a Psychiatric Outpatient Clinic Population," *Psychiatric Services* 54, no. 12 (2003): 1649–1651, available at http://psychservices.psychiatryonline.org/cgi/ reprint/54/12/1649 (accessed October 2, 2008).

119   Wikipedia, "Autoscopy," available at http://en.wikipedia.org/wiki/ (accessed October 2, 2008).

119–120   Greyson has reported the Al Sullivan case in a variety of venues, for example (in brief form) in his presentation to the Esalen Institute, "Near Death Experiences as Evidence for Survival of Bodily Death" (see above).

120   Raymond Moody, *Life after Life: The Investigation of a Phenomenon — Survival of Bodily Death* (San Francisco: HarperSanFrancisco, 2001).

120–121   Moody, *Life after Life.*

122–123   Michael Sabom, *Light and Death* (Grand Rapids, Mich.: Zondervan, 1998). I have drawn the quotes from the web page "People Have NDEs While Brain Dead," http://www.near-death.com/experiences/ evidence01.html (accessed August 16, 2009). But see also chap. 3,

"Death: Defining the Final Frontier," in Sabom, *Light and Death*; a summary of the pros and cons on the validity of the Reynolds case in *Wikipedia*, "Pam Reynolds' NDE"; and the critical discussion of the case by Keith Augustine in "Hallucinatory Near-Experiences," Library: Modern Documents, http://www.infifdels.org/library/modern / keith_augustine/hnde.html (accessed August 13, 2009).

123   The perceptual powers in NDEs are widely documented, e.g., in "People See Verified Events While Out-Of-Body," available at http://www .near-death.com/experiences /evidence02.html (accessed October 2, 2008).

123–126   "Interview with Dr. Bruce Greyson by Lese Dunton," *New Sun*, available at www.newsun.com/greyson.html (accessed October 2, 2008).

123–124   The implications of these and other cases are found in the summaries of research conclusions provided by Kevin Williams in "The NDE and Out-of-Body," available at http://www.near-death.com/experiences/ research11.html (accessed October 2, 2008).

124   For a popular discussion of the possible roles of stress in NDEs, see Cherry Norton, "Near Death Experiences, Triggered by Stress, Not Delusion or Mental Illness, Says Survey," *Independent*, February 4, 2000, available at http://www.independent.co.uk/ news/science/ neardeath-experiences-triggered-by-stress-not-delusion-or-mental -illness-says-survey-726387.html (accessed October 2, 2008).

124–125   Laura Darlene Lansberry, "First Person Report: A Skeptic's Near-Death Experience," *Skeptical Inquirer* (Summer 1994), available at http://find-articles.com/p/articles/mi_m2843/is_/ai_16139352 (accessed October 2, 2008).

126   Barbara Rommer, *Blessing in Disguise: Another Side of the Near Death Experience* (Woodbury, Minn.: Llewellyn, 2000).

127   "Does Ketamine Produce NDEs?," available at http://www.mind spring.com/~scottr/nde/_ketamine.html (accessed October 2, 2008). More scientific skepticism is summarized by Laura Blue, "The Science of Out-of-Body Experiences," *Time*, August 23, 2007, available at http://www.time.com/time/health/article/0,8599,1655632,00.html (accessed October 2, 2008). Also see Rebecca Sato, "Beyond Virtual Reality: Neuroscientist Discovers How to Induce Out-of-Body Experiences," *Daily Galaxy*, August 27, 2007, available at http://frontier sciences.spaces.live.com/ ?_c11_BlogPart_BlogPart=blogview&_c=Blog Part&partqs=cat%3DSundhed%2B0g%2Bvelv%25c3%25a6re.

130   R. D. Laing, *The Divided Self: An Existential Study in Sanity and Madness* (Harmondsworth: Penguin, 1960).

131   The mathematical needs in string theory for alternative realities (or

extra-dimensional universes) are described lucidly by Lisa Randall in her accessible book, *Warped Passage* (New York: Harper, 2006), especially chap. 5.

CHAPTER FIVE: SCIENCE, RELIGION, AND THE
LANGUAGES OF FAITH

139   Jerome Bruner, *Actual Minds, Possible Worlds* (Cambridge, Mass.: Harvard University Press, 1985); Bruner, *Making Stories: Law, Literature, Life* (Cambridge, Mass.: Harvard University Press, 2003).

139   Stephen Jay Gould, "Non-Overlapping Magisteria," *Natural History* 106, 2 (March 1997): 16–22.

140   Ronald Dworkin, *Law's Empire* (Cambridge, Mass.: Harvard University Press, 1986).

141   *Carl Sagan's Cosmic Connection: An Extraterrestrial Perspective*, ed. Jerome Agel (New York: Cambridge University Press, 2000).

141   And the actual quote is even harsher: "There are those who scoff at the school boy, calling him frivolous and shallow. Yet it was the school boy who said Faith is believing what you know ain't so." Mark Twain, *Following the Equator and Anti-Imperialist Essays* (Oxford: Oxford University Press, 1996). The quote is from a vignette in "Pudd'nhead Wilson's New Calendar," chap. 12, p. 132.

142   On causality, see Hubert Blalock, *Causal Inferences in Nonexperimental Research* (Chapel Hill: University of North Carolina Press, 1964), and Blalock, ed., *Causal Models in the Social Sciences* (Piscataway, N.J.: Aldine Transaction, 1985) — see especially Herbert Simon's paper in the book that discusses the primordial assumption that correlation does not causality make — "Spurious Correlation: A Causal Interpretation."

143   For instance, Aristotle, *Physics* (Whitefish, Mont.: Kessinger, 2007).

144   Rebecca Goldstein, *Incompleteness: The Proof and Paradox of Kurt Gödel* (New York: W.W. Norton, 2005).

145   Richard Dawkins, *The God Delusion* (Boston: Mariner Books, 2008); Daniel C. Dennett, *Breaking the Spell: Religion as a Natural Phenomenon* (New York: Penguin, 2007); Richard Dawkins, *The Selfish Gene* (New York: Oxford University Press, 2006); Richard Dawkins, "Is Science a Religion?" *Humanist* (January/February 1997); Daniel C. Dennett, "The Bright Stuff," *New York Times*, July 12, 2003; Sam Harris, *The End of Faith: Religion, Terror, and the Future of Reason* (New York: W.W. Norton, 2005).

146   Youtube.com, "Mike Huckabee Responds to Evolution Debate," available at http://www.youtube.com/watch?v=n-BFEhkIujA.

146   James Watson, *The Double Helix: A Personal Account of the Discovery of the Structure of DNA* (New York: Touchstone, 2001).

146–147   Brenda Maddox, *Rosalind Franklin: The Dark Lady of DNA* (New York: Harper Perennial, 2003).

147   S. Bhattacharya, "Stupidity should be cured, says DNA discoverer," *New Scientist*, February 28, 2003.

147   Comments on Crick's conjecture as a type of Panspermia—a spare theory which holds that life on earth originated in outer space, usually buttressed with the proposition that the instrument of propagation was alien colonization—are in "Panspermia," Wikipedia.

147   Gunnar Myrdal, *An American Dilemma: The Negro Problem and Modern Democracy* (Piscataway, N.J.: Transaction Books, 1996).

147   Fred M. Frohock, "The Free Exercise of Religion: Lukumí and Animal Sacrifice," Institute for Cuban and Cuban-American Studies Occasional Paper Series, University of Miami (November 2001).

148   See Frohock, "Human Rights and Research on Inchoate Life: An Emerging Set of Limits for Rights Vocabularies?" *Human Rights Quarterly* 30 (2008): 959–983.

149   Frohock, *Public Reason* (Ithaca, N.Y.: Cornell University Press, 1999).

153   Frohock, *Bounded Divinities* (New York: Palgrave Macmillan, 2006).

154   H.L.A. Hart, *The Concept of Law* (New York: Oxford University Press, 1997).

154   *Samuel Taylor Coleridge*, vol. 1, ed. J. R. de J. Jackson (New York: Routledge, 1996), 431–432.

155   Carol Zaleski, "Ancient Christian Magic," *Christian Century*, October 25, 2000.

155   Plato, *The Republic* (New York: Penguin, 1955).

155–156   Stephen Hawking, *A Brief History of Time* (New York: Bantam, 1998), 193.

156   Steve Paulson, "The Believer," Salon.com, August 7, 2006.

156   Robin Cook, "Decoding Health Insurance," *New York Times*, May 22, 2005.

157   Karen Armstrong, *A History of God* (New York: Ballantine Books, 1994).

158   Goldstein, *Incompleteness: The Proof and Paradox of Kurt Gödel*.

160–161   Randolph C. Byrd, "Positive Therapeutic Effects of Intercessory Prayer in a Coronary Care Unit Population," *Southern Medical Journal* 81, no. 7 (July 1988).

162   Isak Dinesen, *Out of Africa* (New York: Vintage, 1989), 75.

163   Frohock, *Healing Powers* (Chicago: University of Chicago Press, 1992), 202.

CHAPTER SIX: SURVIVAL AFTER DEATH: HOW TO
THINK AND TALK ABOUT THE UNKNOWABLE

174   Stanislaw Lem, *Solaris* (New York: Harcourt, 1970).

175–176   Karl Marx, "Introduction to a Contribution to the Critique of Hegel's

Philosophy of Right," *Deutsch-Französische Jahrbücher*, February 1844, available at www.marxists.org/archive/marx/works/1843/critique-hpr/intro.htm#n1 (accessed October 2, 2008).

177 James Baldwin, *Nobody Knows My Name* (New York: Dial Press, 1961), 222.

177–178 The two-slit experiments, for example, which demonstrate effects without (at least apparent) contiguity are described accurately in "Double-Slit Experiment," http://en.wikipedia.org/wike/double-slit_experiment. For the purists, just browse in the excellent set of references that follows the article, including of course the wonderful work by Richard Feynman, especially *The Feynman Lectures on Physics*, vols. 1–3 (Upper Saddle River, N.J.: Addison-Wesley Longman, 1970). See also Werner Heisenberg, *Physics and Philosophy* (London: George Allen & Unwin, 1959), and, for some of the implications of the new physics, Bernard d'Espagnat, *On Physics and Philosophy* (Princeton, N.J.: Princeton University Press, 2006).

178 See "The Nobel Prize and After: A Talk with Frank Wilczek," *Edge* 272 (January 15, 2009).

178 "Wis. Camp Caters to Those Who See the Dead," August 29, 2007, available at http://www.msnbc.msn.com/id/20377308/ (accessed October 2, 2008).

179–184 This section is a riff on a philosophical discussion that begins with the issue of how two rational actors relying on the sane evidentiary base can disagree with each other when both meet tests of sincerity, honesty, familiarity with arguments, and evidence for and against conclusions drawn from the evidence (and so on). The quote on 204 is from one of the seminal papers in this discussion: Richard Feldman, "Reasonable Disagreements," presented at (among other places) the University of Miami, January 2004; and, for earlier variations on the basic arguments, Feldman, "Evidentialism" (written with Earl Conee) in *Essential Knowledge*, ed. Steven Luper (New York: Longman, 2004). Whether this species of disagreement should or should not affect the standing of the beliefs held by either intellectual adversary is explored in a paper presented to the University of Miami's Department of Philosophy on March 6, 2009, "The Semantic Significance of Disagreement." The author, Gurpreet Rattan, scans literatures that adopt skeptical and dogmatic approaches to this problem and introduces his own dialectical resolution. I am suggesting here that the storyline may present a false problem.

180 Paul C. Giannelli, *Understanding Evidence* (New York: LexisNexis, 2005).

182 This is what Andrew Mason labels "the imperfection conception," in his *Explaining Political Disagreement* (Cambridge: Cambridge University

Press, 1993), 2. The Bruner-Postman experiments have provided variations on seeing-as experiences, including the frequent-flyer mileage earned by Thomas Kuhn with his critical use of the anomalous playing card experiments in *The Structure of Scientific Revolutions* (Chicago: University of Chicago Press, 1996).

184   ABC News, "Secret FBI Report Questions Al Qaeda Capabilities," March 9, 2005, available at abcnews.go.com/WNT/Investigation/Story?id=566425&page=1 (accessed October 2, 2008).

184   Tom Ridge, "Traces of Terror: Perspectives," *New York Times*, September 6, 2002, available at query.nytimes.com/gst/fullpage.html?res=9C04E0DE123EF935A3575AC0A9649C8B63 (accessed October 2, 2008).

184   Jeffrey Goldberg, "A Reporter at Large: The Unknown," *New Yorker*, February 10, 2003, available at www.jeffreygoldberg.net/articles/tny/a_reporter_at_large_the_unknow.php.

186   Herbert Simon, *Models of Bounded Rationality*, 2 vols. (Cambridge, Mass.: MIT Press, 1982).

187   John Rawls, *A Theory of Justice* (Cambridge, Mass.: Harvard University Press, 1999).

189   *Griswold v. Connecticut*, 381 U.S. 479 (1965).

189–190   Modern explorations of abductive logic originate with Charles Peirce, in *Pragmatism as a Principle and Method of Right Thinking*, which are his 1903 Harvard lectures on pragmatism, edited and introduced with a commentary by Patricia Ann Turrisi (Albany: State University of New York Press, 1997). The most productive contemporary treatment of abduction (and many other matters) in the social sciences and historiography is John R. Hall, *Cultures of Inquiry: From Epistemology to Discourse in Sociohistorical Research* (Cambridge: Cambridge University Press, 1999). See also the discussion of abduction in Eugene Charniak and Drew McDermott, *Introduction to Artificial Intelligence* (Reading, Mass.: Addison-Wesley, 1985), and the iconic works: Karl Popper on discovery, not falsification, in *The Logic of Scientific Discovery*, 2nd ed. (New York: Harper & Row, 1976); Hillary Putnam, "Peirce the Logician," *Historia Mathematica* 9/3 (1982): 290–301; and W.V.O. Quine, "Peirce's Logic," in *Peirce and Contemporary Thought: Philosophical Inquiries*, ed. by K. L. Ketner (New York: Fordham University Press, 1995), 23–31. I am grateful to Gavan Duffy and Everita Silina for reminding me of abductive logic and some of the relevant literatures that expound it, and to Ms. Silina for sharing with me the fallacy-of-the-consequent riff she uses in her dissertation (and that I have borrowed and tweaked here for my own honorable uses).

191   This thought—of a vessel as a metaphor for thought—was suggested in different ways by E. Sosa in his excellent colloquium at the

University of Miami on March 27, 2009, "Intuitions: Their Nature and Probative Value."

191   One of the best discussions of the influences of subjective considerations on "critical tests" in determining whether hypotheses should be retained or falsified might still be Anthony O'Hear's *Karl Popper* (New York: Routledge, 1992). The distinction between synthetic and analytic and the truth tests that follow this distinction are influenced by the larger conceptual systems in which statements are located. See the classic article by W.V.O. Quine, "Two Dogmas of Empiricism," *Philosophical Review* 60 (1951): 20–43.

193   Darwin Porter, *Frommer's Paris* (Hoboken, N.J.: Wiley, 2003).

bibliography

ARTICLES

"'Appreciate the Mushrooms Completely': Hemingway's Mixed Message." Available at http://www. americanpopularculture.com/archive/bestsellers/heming-way_message.htm. Accessed December 10, 2008.

"Are NDEs Hallucinations?" Available at http://www.near-death.com/experiences /Isd04.html.

Augustine, Keith. "Hallucinatory Near-Experiences." Available at http://www .infidels.org/library/modern/keith_augustine/hnde.html. Accessed August 13, 2009.

"Autoscopy." Wikipedia. Accessed October 2, 2008.

"Beyond Virtual Reality: Neuroscientist Discovers How to Induce 'Out-of-Body Experiences.'" August 27, 2007. Available at http://frontiersciences.spaces .live.com/?_c11_BlogPart_BlogPart=blogview&_c=BlogPart&partqs=cat%3DS undhed%2B0g%2Bvelv%25c3%25a6re. Accessed October 2, 2008.

Bhattacharya, S. "Stupidity Should Be Cured, Says DNA Discoverer." New Scientist, February 28, 2003. http://www.newscientist.com/article/dn 3451-stupidity -should-be-cured-says-dna-discoverer.html. Accessed October 2, 2008.

Bianchi, Antonio. "Comments on 'The Ketamine Model of the Near-Death Experience: A Central Role for the N-Methyl-D-Aspartate Receptor.'" Journal of Near-Death Studies 16, no. 1 (Fall 1997): 71–78.

Blackmore, Susan. "Near-Death Experiences: In or Out of the Body?" Skeptical Inquirer 16, (1991): 34–45. Available at http://www.susanblackmore.co.uk/ sig1nde.html. Accessed October 2, 2008.

Blanke, Olaf, Theodor Landis, Laurent Spinelli, and Margitta Seeck. "Out-of-Body Experience and Autoscopy of Neurological Origin." Brain 127, no. 2 (2004): 243–258.

Blue, Laura. "The Science of Out-of-Body Experiences." Time, August 23, 2007. Available at http://www.time.com/time/health/article/0,8599,1655632,00.html. Accessed October 2, 2008.

"Bob Woodruff." Wikipedia.

Bonenfant, Richard J. "A Child's Encounter with the Devil: An Unusual Near-Death Experience with Both Blissful and Frightening Elements." Journal of Near-Death Studies 20, no. 2 (2001).

Britt, Robert Roy. "Near-Death Experience: Find Out If You're a Candidate." Live

Science, April 11, 2006. Available at http://www.livescience.com/health/060411_near_death.html. Accessed December 1, 2008.

Britton, Willoughby B., and Richard R. Bootzin. "Near-Death Experiences and the Temporal Lobe." *Psychological Science* 15, no. 4 (2004): 254–258.

Buckley, Christopher. "Success Was Not Enough." Book review of *In All His Glory: The Life of William S. Paley* by Sally Bedell Smith. *New York Times*, November 4, 1990.

Byrd, Randolph C. "Positive Therapeutic Effects of Intercessory Prayer in a Coronary Care Unit Population." *Southern Medical Journal* 81, no. 7 (July 1988).

Calabrese, Joseph D., II "Reflexivity and Transformation Symbolism in the Navajo Peyote Meeting." *Ethos* 22, no. 4 (December 1994): 494–527.

Chalmers, David. "Self-Ascription without Qualia: A Case-Study." Available at http://consc.net/papers/goldman.html. Accessed December 1, 2008.

———. "Zombies on the Web." Available at http://consc.net/zombies.html. Accessed December 1, 2008.

Chandross, Nancy. "Bob Woodruff: Turning Personal Injury Into Public Inquiry." ABC News on the web, New York, February 26, 2007.

Cherry, Christopher. "Self, Near-Death and Death." *International Journal for Philosophy of Religion* 16 (1984): 3–11.

Clark, Stephen R. L. "Waking-up: A Neglected Model for the Afterlife." *Inquiry* 26, no. 2 (1983): 209–230.

"Colombian Devil's Breath." VBS.TV. Available at http://www.vbs.tv/video.php?id=1119242704. Accessed October 2, 2008.

Cook, Emily Williams, Bruce Greyson, and Ian Stevenson. "Do Any Near-Death Experiences Provide Evidence for the Survival of Human Personality after Death? Relevant Features and Illustrative Case Reports." *Journal of Scientific Exploration* 12, no. 3 (1998): 377–406.

Cook, Robin. "Decoding Health Insurance." *New York Times*, May 22, 2005.

Culliford, Larry. "Spiritual Care and Psychiatric Treatment: An Introduction." *Advances in Psychiatric Treatment* 8 (2002): 249–261.

Dawkins, Richard. "Is Science a Religion?" *Humanist*, January/February 1997. Available at http://www.thehumanist.org/humanist/articles/dawkins.html. Accessed October 2, 2008.

Del Guercio, Gino. "The Secrets of Haiti's Living Dead." *Harvard Magazine*, January/February 1986.

Dennett, Daniel C. "The Bright Stuff." *New York Times*, July 12, 2003.

———. "The Unimagined Preposterousness of Zombies." *Journal of Consciousness Studies* 2, no. 4 (1995).

———. "Zombies May Not Be What They're Reputed to Be." Available at http://www.pslgroup.com/dg/3d806.htm. Accessed December 1, 2008.

Dilworth, James. "Zombies." Available at http://www.themystica.com/mystica/articles/z/zombies.html. Accessed October 2, 2008.

Division of Perceptual Studies. "Types of Experiences We Study." Available at http://www.healthsystem.virginia.edu/internet/personalitystudies/case_types .cfm#NDE. Accessed October 2, 2008.

"Does Ketamine Produce NDEs?" Available at http://www.mindspring.com/ ~scottr/nde/_ketamine.html. Accessed October 2, 2008.

"Double-Slit Experiment," Wikipedia. http://en.wikipedia.org/wike/double-slit _experiment.

Dunne, Dominick. "Fatal Charm: The Social Web of Claus von Bülow." *Vanity Fair*, August 1985.

"Eleven Thai Near-Death Experiences." Available at http://www.innerworlds .50megs.com/bkknde.htm. Accessed December 10, 2008.

Feldman, Richard. "Reasonable Disagreements." Paper presented to the Department of Philosophy, University of Miami, January 2004.

Feldman, Richard, and Earl Conee. "Evidentialism." In *Essential Knowledge*, ed. Steven Luper. New York: Longman, 2004.

Frohock, Fred. "The Free Exercise of Religion: Lukumí and Animal Sacrifice." Institute for Cuban and Cuban-American Studies Occasional Paper Series, University of Miami, November 2001.

———. "Human Rights and Research on Inchoate Life: An Emerging Set of Limits for Rights Vocabularies?" *Human Rights Quarterly* 30 (2008): 959–983.

Goldberg, Jeffrey. "A Reporter at Large: The Unknown." *New Yorker*, February 10, 2003. Available at http://www.jeffreygoldberg.net/articles/tny/a_reporter_at _large_the_unknow.php. Accessed October 2, 2008.

Gottlieb, Anthony. "Atheists with Attitude." Book review of Christopher Hitchens's *God Is Not Great: How Religion Poisons Everything*, Sam Harris, *The End of Faith*, and Richard Dawkins, *The God Delusion*. *New Yorker* (February 22, 2007).

Gould, Stephen Jay. "Non-Overlapping Magisteria." *Natural History* 106 (March 1997): 16–22.

Greyson, Bruce. "Brief Report: Near-Death Experiences in a Psychiatric Outpatient Clinic Population." *Psychiatric Services* 54, no. 12 (2003): 1649–1651. Available at http://psychservices.psychiatryonline.org/cgi/reprint/54/12/1649. Accessed October 2, 2008.

Greyson, Bruce, and Mitchell B. Liester. "Auditory Hallucinations following Near-Death Experiences." *Journal of Humanistic Psychology* 44, no. 3 (Summer 2004): 320–336.

———. "Findings: Dissociation in People Who Have Near-Death Experiences: Out of Their Bodies or Out of Their Minds?" *Lancet* 355 (2000): 460–463. Available at http://linkinghub.elsevier.com/retrieve/pii/S0140673600820139. Accessed October 2, 2008.

———. "Near Death Experiences as Evidence for Survival of Bodily Death." Paper presented at Esalen Invitational Conference, "Survival of Bodily Death," February 11–16, 2000.

Gribben, Mark. "The Claus von Bulow Case." True TV Crime Library http://www
.trutv.com/library/crime/ and wikipedia.org/wiki/Sunny_von_Bülow.

Grosso, Michael. "Afterlife Research and the Shamanic Turn." *Journal of Near-Death Studies* 20, no. 1 (Fall 2001): 5–14.

Gunn, Thom. "Lazarus Not Raised." *Trinity Magazine*, 1952.

Haack, Susan. "Dry Truth and Real Knowledge: Epistemologies of Metaphor and Metaphors of Epistemology." In *Aspects of Metaphor*, ed. Jaakko Hintikka, 23–39. Dordrecht: Kluwer Publishers, 1994.

Habermas, Gary R. "Near Death Experiences and the Evidence—A Review Essay." *Christian Scholar's Review* 26, no. 1 (1996): 78–85.

Haitian Penal Code. Article 249. Available at http://zombies.monstrous.com/ becoming_a_zombie.htm. Accessed December 1, 2008.

Haraldsson, Erlendur, and Majd Abu-Izzeddin. "Development of Certainty about the Correct Deceased Person in a Case of the Reincarnation Type in Lebanon: The Case of Nazih Al-Danaf." *Journal of Scientific Exploration* 16, no. 3 (2002): 363–380.

Haussamen, Brock. "Three Fictional Deaths Compared with the Near-Death Experience." *Journal of Near-Death Studies* 19, no. 2 (Winter 2000): 91–102.

"Horn Hoped the Attack Was Just a Bad Nightmare." September 16, 2004. Available at http://www.msnbc.msn.com/id/6019154/. Accessed December 1, 2008.

"How Clinton Recovered from Surgery." *Primetime Live*, ABC News. October 28, 2004. Available at http://abcnews.go.com/Primetime/story?id=207370&page =1. Accessed October 2, 2004.

"Interview with Dr. Bruce Greyson by Lese Dunton." *New Sun*. Available at http:// glidewing.com/bridge /content/view/42/47/. Accessed October 2, 2008.

Keil, Jurgen, and Ian Stevenson. "Do Cases of the Reincarnation Type Show Similar Features over Many Years? A Study of Turkish Cases a Generation Apart." *Journal of Scientific Exploration* 13, no. 2 (1999): 189–198.

Klauber, Robert D. "Modern Physics and Subtle Realms: Not Mutually Exclusive." *Journal of Scientific Exploration* 14, no. 2 (2000): 275–279.

Lakoff, George. "The Contemporary Theory of Metaphor." In *Metaphor and Thought*, 2nd ed., ed. Andrew Ortony, 202–251. Cambridge: Cambridge University Press, 1993.

Lansberry, Laura Darlene. "First Person Report: A Skeptic's Near-Death Experience." *Skeptical Inquirer*, Summer 1994. Available at http://findarticles.com/p/ articles/mi_m2843/is_/ai_16139352. Accessed October 2, 2008.

Lee, Raymond L. M. "Death at the Crossroad: From Modern to Postmortem Consciousness." *Illness, Crisis & Loss* 12, no. 2 (April 2004): 155–170.

Littlewood, Richard, and Chavannes Douyon. "Clinical Findings in Three Cases of Zombification." *Lancet* 350 (1997): 1095–96.

Long, Jody A. "Soulmates and Consciousness: New Understanding from Near-Death Experience Research." Near Death Experience Research Foundation.

Available at http://www.near-death.com/experiences/experts101.html. Accessed October 2, 2008.

Lukoff, David. "Visionary Spiritual Experiences, Special Section: Spirituality/Medicine Interface Project." *Southern Medical Journal*, June 1, 2007. Available at http://goliath.ecnext.com/coms2/summary_0199-6700957_ITM. Accessed October 2, 2008.

Lynne, Diana. "The Whole Terri Schiavo Story." Wikipedia.

Mailer, Norman. "The Steps of the Pentagon." *Harper's*, March 1968.

———. "Superman Comes to the Supermarket." *Esquire*, November 1960.

Marx, Karl. "Introduction to 'A Contribution to the Critique of Hegel's Philosophy of Right.'" *Deutsch-Französische Jahrbücher*, February 1844. Available at http://www.marxists.org/archive/marx/works/1843/critique-hpr/intro.htm#n1. Accessed October 2, 2008.

"Mike Huckabee Responds to Evolution Debate." Available at http://www.youtube.com/watch?v=n-BFEhkIujA.

Mitchell, S. Renee. "To End Rape, End Silence!" *Oregonian*, April 16, 2007. Available at http://blog.oregonlive.com/reneemitchell/2007/04/to_end_rape_end_silence.html. Accessed October 2, 2008.

Morris, Linda L., and Kathleen Knafl. "The Nature and Meaning of the Near-Death Experience for Patients and Critical Care Nurses." *Journal of Near-Death Studies* 21, no. 3 (Spring 2003): 139–167.

Newberg, Andrew B. "Putting the Mystical Mind Together." *Zygon* 36, no. 3 (September 2001): 501–507.

"The Nobel Prize and After: A Talk with Frank Wilczek." *Edge* 272, January 15, 2009.

Norton, Cherry. "Near Death Experiences, Triggered by Stress, Not Delusion or Mental Illness, Says Survey." *Independent*, February 4, 2000. Available at http://www.independent.co.uk/news/science/neardeath-experiences-triggered-by-stress-not-delusion-or-mental-illness-says-survey-726387.html. Accessed October 2, 2008.

"Pam Reynolds' NDE," Wikipedia.

"Panspermia," Wikipedia.

"Parapsychology." Wikipedia. Available at http://en.wikipedia.org/wiki/Parapsychology. Accessed October 2, 2008.

Pasricha, Satwant K. "Cases of the Reincarnation Type in South India: Why So Few Reports?" *Journal of Scientific Exploration* 15, no. 2 (2001): 211–221.

Paulson, Steve. "The Believer." *Salon.com*, August 7, 2006. Available at http://www.salon.com/books/int/2006/08/07/collins/. Accessed October 2, 2008.

"People Have NDEs While Brain Dead." http://www.near-death.com/experiences/evidence01.html. Accessed August 16, 2009.

"People See Verified Events While Out-of-Body." Near-Death Experiences and the Afterlife. Available at http://www.near-death.com/experiences/evidence02.html. Accessed October 2, 2008.

Peters, Karl E. "Neurotheology and Evolutionary Theology: Reflections on *The Mystical Mind*." *Zygon* 36, no. 3 (September 2001): 493–500.

"Posting: Spiritual and Psychological After-Effects." *The Mystic Board Forum Index: Paranormal Phenomena*, May 5, 2006. Available at http://www.mysticboard.com/ paranormal_phenomena/8541-near-death_experience-1.html. Accessed October 2, 2008.

Putnam, Hillary. "Peirce the Logician." *Historia Mathematica* 9, no.3 (1982): 290–301.

Quine, W.V.O. "Two Dogmas of Empiricism." *Philosophical Review* 60 (1951): 20–43.

Rattan, Gurpreet. "The Semantic Significance of Disagreement." Paper presented to Department of Philosophy at the University of Miami, March 6, 2009.

Rawat, K.S. "Interview with Dr. Ian Stevenson." *Children's Past Lives Research Center*. Available at http://www.childpastlives.org/stevenson_intv.htm. Accessed October 2, 2008.

Ridge, Tom. "Traces of Terror: Perspectives." *New York Times*, September 6, 2002. Available at http://query.nytimes.com/gst/fullpage.html?res=9C04E0DE123EF 935A3575AC0A9649C8B63. Accessed October 2, 2008.

Rousseau, David. "Challenging the Paradigm Systematically: A New and Generic Approach to Classifying Anomalous Phenomena." *Journal of the Society for Psychical Research* 66, no. 2 (867) (April 2002): 65–79.

Rowlett, Jakki. "You Think I Therefore Am: The Ethnobiology and Ethics of the Haitian Zombie." Available at http://serendip.brynmawr.edu/biology/b103/ foo/web2/rowlett2.html. Accessed December 1, 2008.

Sahlman, James M., and Max C. Norton. "The Meaning and Intensity of the Near-Death Experience." *Journal of Near-Death Studies* 17, no. 2 (Winter 1998): 101–110.

Sato, Rebecca. "Beyond Virtual Reality: Neuroscientist Discovers How to Induce 'Out-of-Body Experiences.'" *Daily Galaxy*, August 27, 2007. Available at http:// frontiersciences.spaces.live.com/?_c11_BlogPart_BlogPart=blogview&_c= BlogPart&partqs=cat%3DSundhed%2Bog%2Bvelv%25c3%25a6re.

Searle, John. "Minds, Brains, and Programs." *Behavioral and Brain Sciences* 3, no. 3 (1980): 417–457.

Secrest, Meryle. "Omni Magazine Interview with Dr. Ian Stevenson." *Omni Magazine* 10, no. 4:76 (1988).

"Secret FBI Report Questions Al Qaeda Capabilities." ABC News, March 9, 2005. Available at http://abcnews.go.com/WNT/Investigation/Story?id=566425&page =1. Accessed October 2, 2008.

Shroder, Tom. "A Matter of Death & Life: Ian Stevenson's Scientific Search for Evidence of Reincarnation." *Washington Post Magazine*, August 8, 1999.

Skelton, John. "Death and Dying in Literature." *Advances in Psychiatric Treatment* 9 (2003): 211–220.

Smith, Rogers. "Religious Rhetoric and the Ethics of Political Discourse: The Case of George W. Bush," *Political Theory* 36 (2008): 272–300.

Sosa, E. "Intuitions: Their Nature and Probative Value." Colloquium at the University of Miami, March 27, 2009.

Spezio, Michael L. "Engaging d'Aquili and Newberg's *The Mystical Mind*: Understanding Biology in Religious Experience: The Biogenetic Structuralist Approach of Eugene d'Aquili and Andrew Newberg." *Zygon* 36, no. 3 (September 2001): 477–484.

Spiritual Emergency Network. Available at http://www.spiritualemergence.org.au/pages/what_is.html. Accessed January 2, 2009.

Stephey, M. J. "What Happens When We Die?" *Time*, September 18, 2008. Available at http://www.time.com/time/health/article/0,8599,1842627,00.html. Accessed December 1, 2008.

Stevenson, Ian. "Some of My Journeys in Medicine: A Lecture about Science and Reincarnation." *Children's Past Lives Research Center*. Flora Levy Lecture in the Humanities, University of Southwestern Louisiana, Lafayette, 1989. Available at http://www.childpastlives.org/stevensonlecture.htm. Accessed October 2, 2008.

———. "Unusual Play in Young Children Who Claim to Remember Previous Lives." *Journal of Scientific Exploration* 14, no. 4 (2000): 557–570.

Stevenson, Ian, and Erlendur Haraldsson. "The Similarity of Features of Reincarnation Type Cases over Many Years: A Third Study." *Journal of Scientific Exploration* 17, no. 2 (2003): 283–289.

Stevenson, Ian, and Jurgen Keil. "The Stability of Assessments of Paranormal Connections in Reincarnation-Type Cases." *Journal of Scientific Exploration* 14, no. 3 (2000): 365–382.

Straight, Steve. "A Wave among Waves: Katherine Anne Porter's Near-Death Experience." *Anabiosis—The Journal for Near-Death Studies* 4, no. 2 (Fall 1984): 107–123.

"Terri Schiavo in Perspective: Ethics, Politics and Medicine." Panel discussion presented at the University of Miami Miller School of Medicine on the medical, legal, and political intricacies of the Schiavo experience, February 29, 2008.

"The Third Culture." *Edge*, January 15, 2009. Available at http://www.edge.org/3rd_culture/wilczek09/wilczek09_index.html. Accessed January 20, 2009.

Thomson, Judith Jarvis. "A Defense of Abortion." *Philosophy and Public Affairs* 1 (Fall 1971): 47–66.

Tong, Frank. "Out-of-Body Experiences: From Penfield to Present." *Trends in Cognitive Sciences* 7, no. 3 (March 2003): 104–106.

Tucker, Jim B. "A Scale to Measure the Strength of Children's Claims of Previous Lives: Methodology and Initial Findings." *Journal of Scientific Exploration* 14, no. 4 (2000): 571–581.

Vardamis, Alex A., and Justine E. Owens. "Ernest Hemingway and the Near-Death Experience." *Journal of Medical Humanities* 20, no. 3 (1999).

Williams, Kevin. "The NDE and Out-of-Body." Available at http://www.near-death
.com/experiences/research11.html. Accessed October 2, 2008.

"Wis. Camp Caters to Those Who See the Dead." August 29, 2007. Available at
http://www.msnbc.msn.com/id/20377308/. Accessed October 2, 2008.

Wolfe, Tom. "Radical Chic: That Party at Lenny's." New York Magazine, June 8, 1970.

Wood, James. "The New Anti-atheists." Book review of Terry Eagleton, Reason,
Faith, and Revelation. New Yorker, August 31, 2009, 75–78.

Zaleski, Carol. "Ancient Christian Magic." Christian Century, October 25, 2000.
Available at http://findarticles.com/p/articles/mi_m1058/is_29_117/ai_6680
9969. Accessed October 2, 2008.

CASES

Cruzan v. Director, Missouri Dept. of Health, 497 U.S. 261 (1990). Available at http://
www.oyez.org/cases/1980-1989/1989/1989_88_1503/. Accessed October 2, 2008.

Griswold v. Connecticut, 381 U.S. 479 (1965). Available at http://www.oyez.org/
cases/1960-1969/1964/1964_496/. Accessed October 2, 2008.

BOOKS

Ackroyd, Peter. The Life of Thomas More. New York: Anchor Books, 1988.

Adams, Douglas. The Ultimate Hitchhiker's Guide to the Galaxy: Five Complete Novels and
One Story. New York: Gramercy Books, 2005.

Arcangel, Dianne. Afterlife Encounters, Charlottesville, Va.: Hampton Roads, 2005.

Aristotle. Physics. Whitefish, Mont.: Kessinger, 2007.

Armstrong, Karen. A History of God. New York: Ballantine Books, 1994.

Atwater, P.M.H. Coming Back to Life: The After-Effects of the Near-Death Experience. New
York: Dodd, Mead, 1988.

Ault, James M., Jr. Spirit and Flesh: Life in a Fundamentalist Baptist Church. New York:
Knopf, 2004.

Baldwin, James. Nobody Knows My Name. New York: Vintage, 1992.

Bede Venerablis. The History of the English Church and People. New York: Penguin,
1955.

Bernstein, Morey. The Search for Bridey Murphy. New York: Doubleday, 1989.

Blalock, Hubert. Causal Inferences in Nonexperimental Research. Chapel Hill: University
of North Carolina Press, 1964.

———. Causal Models in the Social Sciences. Piscataway, N.J.: Aldine Transaction,
1985.

Bolt, Robert. A Man for All Seasons: A Play in Two Acts. New York: Random House,
1962.

Botkin, Allan L., with R. Craig Hogan. Induced after Death Communication: A New Therapy for Healing Grief and Trauma. Charlottesville, Va.: Hampton Roads, 2005.

Brams, Steven J. Superior Beings: If They Exist, How Would We Know? New York:
Springer, 2007.

Brecht, Bertolt. *Life of Galileo; The Resistible Rise of Arturo Ui; The Caucasian Chalk Circle.* Trans. John Willett et al. Introduction by Hugh Rorrison. New York: Little, Brown, 1994.

Bruner, Jerome. *Actual Minds, Possible Worlds.* Cambridge, Mass.: Harvard University Press, 1985.

———. *Making Stories: Law, Literature, Life.* Cambridge, Mass.: Harvard University Press, 2003.

Cameron, Lynne, and Graham Low. *Researching and Applying Metaphor.* Cambridge: Cambridge University Press, 1999.

Capote, Truman. *In Cold Blood.* New York: Modern Library, 2002.

Carroll, Robert Todd. *The Skeptic's Dictionary: A Collection of Strange Beliefs, Amusing Deceptions, and Dangerous Delusions.* New York: Wiley, 2003.

Charniak, Eugene, and Drew McDermott. *Introduction to Artificial Intelligence.* Reading, Mass.: Addison-Wesley, 1985.

Chopra, Deepak. *Life after Death: The Burden of Proof.* New York: Harmony Books, 2006.

Davis, Wade. *Passage of Darkness: The Ethnobiology of the Haitian Zombie.* Chapel Hill: University of North Carolina Press, 1988.

———. *The Serpent and the Rainbow: A Harvard Scientist's Astonishing Journey into the Secret Societies of Haitian Voodoo, Zombies, and Magic.* London: Fontana Press, 1987.

Dawkins, Richard. *The God Delusion.* Boston: Mariner Books, 2008.

———. *The Selfish Gene.* New York: Oxford University Press, 2006.

Dear, Peter. *The Intelligibility of Nature: How Science Makes Sense of the World.* Chicago: University of Chicago Press, 2006.

Dennett, Daniel C. *Breaking the Spell: Religion as a Natural Phenomenon.* New York: Penguin, 2007.

———. *Consciousness Explained.* Boston: Little, Brown, 1991.

Dershowitz, Alan. *Reversal of Fortune: Inside the Von Bulow Case.* New York: Random House, 1986.

d'Espagnat, Bernard. *On Physics and Philosophy.* Princeton, N.J.: Princeton University Press, 2006.

Dinesen, Isak. *Out of Africa.* New York: Vintage, 1989.

Doctorow, E. L. *Ragtime: A Novel.* New York: Random House, 2007.

Dos Passos, John. *U.S.A.* New York: Penguin, 2001.

Dostoyevsky, Fyodor. *The Brothers Karamazov.* Translated by Constance Garnett. New York: Bantam Books, 1981.

———. *Crime and Punishment.* Translated by Constance Garnett. New York: Bantam Books, 1981.

Dworkin, Ronald. *Law's Empire.* Cambridge, Mass.: Harvard University Press, 1986.

Eadie, Betty J. *Embraced by the Light.* New York: Bantam Books, 1992.

Eisenberg, Jon. *The Right vs. the Right to Die: Lessons from the Terri Schiavo Case and How to Stop It from Happening Again.* New York: HarperOne, 2006.

Eliot, T.S. *The Wasteland*. New York: Harcourt, Brace & Company, 1958.

Feynman, Richard. *The Feynman Lectures on Physics: Volumes 1–3*. Upper Saddle River, N.J.: Addison-Wesley Longman, 1970.

Fontana, David. *Is There an Afterlife?* Berkeley, Calif.: O Books, 2005.

Foucault, Michel. *The Birth of the Clinic: An Archaeology of Medical Perception*. Translated A. M. Sheridan Smith. New York: Vintage, 1975.

Frohock, Fred. *Abortion: A Case Study in Law and Morals*. Westport, Conn.: Greenwood Press, 1983.

———. *Bounded Divinities: Sacred Discourses in Pluralist Democracies*. New York: Palgrave Macmillan, 2006.

———. *Healing Powers*. Chicago: University of Chicago Press, 1992.

———. *The Lives of Psychics: The Shared Worlds of Science and Mysticism*. Chicago: University of Chicago Press, 2000.

———. *Public Reason*. Ithaca, N.Y.: Cornell University Press, 1999.

Funk, Robert. *Language, Hermeneutic, and Word of God*. New York: Harper & Row, 1966.

Geddes, Barbara. *Paradigms and Sand Castles*. Ann Arbor: University of Michigan Press, 2006.

Gell-Mann, Murray. *The Quark and the Jaguar: Adventures in the Simple and the Complex*. New York: W. H. Freeman, 1994.

Giannelli, Paul C. *Understanding Evidence*. New York: LexisNexis, 2005.

Gladwell, Malcolm. *Blink: The Power of Thinking without Thinking*. New York: Little, Brown, 2005.

Goldstein, Rebecca. *Incompleteness: The Proof and Paradox of Kurt Gödel*. New York: W.W. Norton, 2005.

Gould, Stephen Jay. *The Structure of Evolutionary Theory*. Cambridge, Mass.: Belknap Press, Harvard University Press, 2002.

Green, Thomas F. *Voices: The Educational Formation of Conscience*. Notre Dame: University of Notre Dame Press, 1999.

Grof, Stanislav. *Spiritual Emergency*. New York: Tarcher, 1989.

Grosso, Michael. *Experiencing the Next World Now*. New York: Paraview, 2004.

Hall, John R. *Cultures of Inquiry: From Epistemology to Discourse in Sociohistorical Research*. Cambridge: Cambridge University Press, 1999.

Harris, Sam. *The End of Faith: Religion, Terror, and the Future of Reason*. New York: W.W. Norton, 2005.

Hart, H.L.A. *The Concept of Law*. New York: Oxford University Press, 1997.

Hasker, William. *The Emergent Self*. Ithaca, N.Y.: Cornell University Press, 1999.

Hawking, Stephen. *A Brief History of Time*. New York: Bantam, 1998.

Heisenberg, Werner. *Physics and Philosophy*. London: George Allen and Unwin, 1959.

Hemingway, Ernest. *A Farewell to Arms*. New York: Scribner's, 1929.

———. *For Whom the Bell Tolls*. New York: Scribner, 1943.

———. *The Short Stories of Ernest Hemingway*. New York: Scribner's, 1953.

The Holy Bible. King James Version. Oxford: Oxford University Press, 1937.

Horgan, John. *Rational Mysticism*. Boston: Houghton Mifflin, 2003.

Husserl, Edmund. *Cartesian Meditations: An Introduction to Phenomenology*. Translated by Dorion Cairns. New York: Springer, 2008.

Jackson, J.R. de J., ed. *Samuel Taylor Coleridge*. Vol. 1. New York: Routledge, 1996.

James, William. *Human Immortality: Two Supposed Objections to the Doctrine*. New York: Houghton Mifflin, 1898.

———. *The Varieties of Religious Experience*. New York: Longmans, Green, 1916.

Kapstein, Matthew T., ed. *The Presence of Light: Divine Radiance and Religious Experience*. Chicago: University of Chicago Press, 2004.

Krippner, Stanley, and Susan Marie Powers, eds. *Broken Images, Broken Selves: Dissociative Narratives in Clinical Practice*. Washington, D.C.: Brunner/Mazel, 1997.

Kuhn, Thomas. *The Structure of Scientific Revolutions*. Chicago: University of Chicago Press, 1996.

Laing, R. D. *The Divided Self: An Existential Study in Sanity and Madness*. Harmondsworth: Penguin, 1960.

Lakoff, George, and Mark Johnson. *Metaphors We Live By*. Chicago: University of Chicago Press, 1980.

Lampedusa, Giuseppe Tomasi di. *The Leopard*. Translated by Archibald Colguhoun. New York: Avon Books, 1960.

Lem, Stanisław. *Solaris*. New York: Harcourt, 1970.

Maddox, Brenda. *Rosalind Franklin: The Dark Lady of DNA*. New York: Harper Perennial, 2003.

Mailer, Norman. *Armies of the Night: History as a Novel, the Novel as History*. New York: Plume, 1995.

———. *The Executioner's Song*. New York: Vintage, 1998.

———. *The Fight*. New York: Vintage, 1997.

———. *Oswald's Tale: An American Mystery*. New York: Random House, 1996.

Mannheim, Karl. *Essays on the Sociology of Knowledge*. New York: Routledge, 1998.

Mason, Andrew. *Explaining Political Disagreement*. Cambridge: Cambridge University Press, 1993.

Mayer, Elizabeth Lloyd. *Extraordinary Knowing: Science, Skepticism, and the Inexplicable Powers of the Human Mind*. New York: Bantam Books, 2007.

McDermott, Drew. *Introduction to Artificial Intelligence*. Reading, Mass.: Addison-Wesley, 1985.

Mijares, Sharon G., and Gurucharan Singh Khalsa, eds. *The Psychospiritual Clinician's Handbook*. New York: Routledge, 2005.

Mill, John Stuart. *On Liberty*. New York: Norton, 1975.

Montaigne, Michel de. *Essays*. New York: Penguin, 1993.

Moody, Raymond. *Life after Life: The Investigation of a Phenomenon—Survival of Bodily Death*. San Francisco: HarperSanFrancisco, 2001.

Myrdal, Gunnar. *An American Dilemma: The Negro Problem and Modern Democracy.* Piscataway, N.J.: Transaction Books, 1996.

O'Hear, Anthony. *Karl Popper.* New York: Routlege, 1992.

Ondaatje, Michael. *Anil's Ghost.* New York: Knopf, 2000.

Ortony, Andrew, ed. *Metaphor and Thought.* 2nd ed. Cambridge: Cambridge University Press, 1993.

Pagels, Elaine. *Beyond Belief: The Secret Gospel of Thomas.* New York: Random House, 2003.

Pals, Daniel L. *Eight Theories of Religion.* New York: Oxford University Press, 2006.

Parnia, Sam. *What Happens When We Die: A Groundbreaking Study into the Nature of Life and Death.* Carlsbad, Calif.: Hay House, 2007.

Peirce, Charles. *Pragmatism as a Principle and Method of Right Thinking.* Harvard Lectures on Pragmatism (1903), ed. and introduced with a commentary by Patricia Ann Turrisi. Albany: State University of New York Press, 1997.

Plantinga, Alvin, ed. *The Ontological Argument.* Garden City, N.Y.: Doubleday, 1965.

Plato. *Euthyphro, Apology, Crito, Phaedo.* Trans. Benjamin Jowett. Amherst, N.Y.: Prometheus Books, 1988.

———. *The Last Days of Socrates.* Trans. Hugh Tredennick. Middlesex: England, 1975.

———. *The Republic.* New York: Penguin, 1955.

Popper, Karl. *Conjectures and Refutations: The Growth of Scientific Knowledge.* London: Routledge, 1963.

———. *The Logic of Scientific Discovery.* 2nd ed. New York: Harper & Row, 1976.

Porter, Darwin. *Frommer's Paris.* Hoboken, N.J.: Wiley, 2003.

Porter, Katherine Anne. *Pale Horse, Pale Rider.* New York: Harcourt, Brace, 1939.

Quine, W.V.O. "Peirce's Logic." In *Peirce and Contemporary Thought: Philosophical Inquiries,* ed. K. L. Ketner, 23–31. New York: Fordham University Press, 1995.

Randall, Lisa. *Warped Passages: Unraveling the Mysteries of the Universe's Hidden Dimensions.* New York: Harper Perennial, 2006.

Rawls, John. *A Theory of Justice.* Cambridge, Mass.: Harvard University Press, 1999.

Ring, Kenneth. *Heading toward Omega: In Search of the Meaning of the Near-Death Experience.* New York: Harper Perennial, 1985.

———. *Life at Death: A Scientific Investigation of the Near-Death Experience.* New York: William Morrow, 1982.

Roach, Mary. *Spook: Science Tackles the Afterlife.* New York: W.W. Norton, 2005.

Rommer, Barbara. *Blessing in Disguise: Another Side of the Near Death Experience.* Woodbury, Minn.: Llewellyn, 2000.

Ryle, Gilbert. *The Concept of Mind.* Chicago: University of Chicago Press, 1949.

Sabom, Michael. *Light and Death.* Grand Rapids, Mich.: Zondervan, 1998.

Sacks, Oliver. *An Anthropologist on Mars: Seven Paradoxical Tales.* New York: Vintage, 1995.

———. *The Man Who Mistook His Wife for a Hat: And Other Clinical Tales.* New York: Simon & Schuster, 1998.

Sagan, Carl. *Carl Sagan's Cosmic Connection: An Extraterrestrial Perspective.* Ed. Jerome Agel. New York: Cambridge University Press, 2000.

Sartre, Jean-Paul. *Being and Nothingness: An Essay on Phenomenological Ontology.* New York: Simon & Schuster, 1993.

———. *No Exit and Three Other Plays.* New York: Vintage Books, 1989.

———. *The Wall.* Trans. Lloyd Alexander. London: Hesperus Press, 1939.

Schiavo, Michael, and Michael Hirsh. *Terri: The Truth.* New York: Dutton, 2006.

Schindler, Mary, and Robert Schindler, et al. *A Life That Matters: The Legacy of Terri Schiavo – A Lesson for Us All.* New York: Knopf, 2006.

Schwartz, Gary E., with William L. Simon. *The Afterlife Experiments.* New York: Atria Books, 2003.

Segen, Joseph C. *Dictionary of Modern Medicine.* New York: Taylor and Francis, 1992.

Shakespeare, William. "Henry IV." In *William Shakespeare: The Complete Works,* ed. Stanley Wells and Gary Taylor. New York: Oxford University Press, 1986.

———. "Julius Caesar." In *William Shakespeare: The Complete Works,* ed. Stanley Wells and Gary Taylor. New York: Oxford University Press, 1986.

———. "A Midsummer Night's Dream." In *William Shakespeare: The Complete Works,* ed. Stanley Wells and Gary Taylor. New York: Oxford University Press, 1986.

———. "Pericles." In *William Shakespeare: The Complete Works,* ed. Stanley Wells and Gary Taylor. New York: Oxford University Press, 1986.

———. "The Tempest." In *William Shakespeare: The Complete Works,* ed. Stanley Wells and Gary Taylor. New York: Oxford University Press, 1986.

———. "The Winter's Tale." In *William Shakespeare: The Complete Works,* ed. Stanley Wells and Gary Taylor. New York: Oxford University Press, 1986.

Shelley, Mary Wollstonecraft. *Frankenstein.* New York: Pearson Longman, 2008.

Simon, Herbert. *Models of Bounded Rationality: Vols. 1 & 2.* Cambridge, Mass.: MIT Press, 1982.

Stevenson, Ian. *Twenty Cases Suggestive of Reincarnation.* Charlottesville: University Press of Virginia, 1974.

Storm, Howard. *My Descent into Death.* London: Clairview, 2000.

Tolkien, J.R.R. *The Two Towers: Being the Second Part of The Lord of the Rings.* Boston: Houghton Mifflin, 2005.

Tolstoy, Leo. *War and Peace.* Translated by Richard Pevear and Larissa Volokhonsky. New York: Random House, 2007.

Tucker, Jim B. *Life before Life: A Scientific Investigation of Children's Memories of Previous Lives.* New York: St. Martin's Press, 2005.

Twain, Mark. *Following the Equator and Anti-Imperialist Essays.* Oxford: Oxford University Press, 1996.

Violette, John R. *Extra-Dimensional Universe: Where the Paranormal Becomes the Normal.* Charlottesville, Va.: Hampton Roads, 2001.

Watson, James. *The Double Helix: A Personal Account of the Discovery of the Structure of DNA*. New York: Touchstone, 2001.

Weiss, Brian L. *Many Lives, Many Masters: The True Story of a Prominent Psychiatrist, His Young Patient, and the Past-Life Therapy That Changed Both Their Lives*. New York: Simon & Schuster, 1988.

Wharton, William. *Ever After*. New York: Newmarket Press, 1995.

Wienrich, Stephanie, and Josefine Speyer. *The Natural Death Handbook*. London: Rider Books, 2003.

Wolfe, Tom. *The Electric Kool-Aid Acid Test*. New York: Bantam,1999.

———. *Radical Chic and Mau-Mauing the Flak Catchers*. New York: Farrar, Straus & Giroux, 1987.

Zaleski, Carol. *The Life of the World to Come: Near-Death Experiences and Christian Hope*. Oxford: Oxford University Press, 1996.

Zman, Adam. *Consciousness: A User's Guide*. New Haven, Conn.: Yale University Press, 2002.

index

Fairies, Cottingley, 57
Fermi, Enrico, 140–142
Feynman, Richard, 36
Fiction. *See* Narratives
Films
    personification of death, 47, 72–73
    zombie, 90–92
Finch Hatton, Denys, 25
Foscarini, Paolo Antonio, 35
Foucault, Michel, *The Birth of the
    Clinic*, 129
Franklin, Rosalind, 146–147
Fugu, 86
Funeral liturgies, 196

Galileo Galilei, 34–35
"Ghost in the machine," 93, 96,
    199
Ghosts, 19
Giannelli, Paul, *Understanding
    Evidence*, 180
Gifford, Robert Swain, 68
Gnostic Gospels, 157
God
    existence, 158–160
    outside parameters of human
        knowledge, 163
    proving existence, 143, 191
    See also Atheism; Religions; Theism
Gödel, Kurt, 8, 144, 158, 161
Good Will Hunting, 36
Gould, Stephen Jay, 33, 139
Greece, ancient, views of death and
    afterlife, 28–30. *See also* Plato;
    Socrates
Greyson, Bruce, 115–116, 118, 119–120,
    123–124, 125–126
Griswold v. Connecticut, 189
Grof, Cristina, 114–115
Grof, Stanislav, 114–115
Gunn, Thom, "Lazarus Not
    Raised," 49

Haiti
    penal code, 84–85, 206–207n
    zombies, 81, 84–88
Hallucinations, near-death
    experiences seen as, 114, 118,
    121–122
Hallucinogenic drugs, 86
Hannah and Her Sisters, 165
Harris, Sam, 145, 147, 149, 150,
    151
Hart, H. L. A., 154
Harvey, Joyce, 126
Hawking, Stephen, *A Brief History of
    Time*, 155–156
Healing
    power of prayer, 160–161
    by saints, 181–182
    spiritual powers, 162–163
Healing Powers (Frohock), 162–163
Heaven, 22, 31, 112, 114. *See also* Life
    after death
Hemingway, Ernest
    A Farewell to Arms, 108–109
    on "little death," 92
    near-death experience, 19
    "The Snows of Kilimanjaro," 24–26
    The Sun Also Rises, 39
Higher forms of life, 55, 143
Hinduism, reincarnation beliefs, 22
The Hitchhiker's Guide to the Galaxy, 159
Holland, Henry Scott, 196
Horn, Roy, 110
The Horse Whisperer, 129
Hubris, 155–156, 157–158
Huckabee, Mike, 146, 147, 153
Human Consciousness Project, 20
Human genome project, 156
Human rights, 148–149
Hume, David, 101–102

Identity, 66–67, 96. *See also* Self
Ideologies, 150, 151

Immortality. *See* Life after death
International Association of Near
 Death Studies, 19
Iraq
 U.N. inspectors, 184
 U.S. war in, 188
Islam
 afterlife beliefs, 22–23
 differences from Christianity, 23
 Qur'an, 22, 145, 148
 See also Religions

James, William, 118
Jansen, Karl L. R., 127
Jesus Christ
 appearances after death, 195
 Sermon on the Mount, 148
John Paul II, Pope, 181–182
Judaism
 criticism of, 145
 resurrection of body, 21

Keller, Helen, 9
King, Martin Luther, Jr., 102, 149
Knowledge
 bounded, 155–157, 158–160, 186
 complete, 186–187
 learning, 33
 Plato on, 155
 scientific, 3
 Socrates on, 33
 unknowns, 184–188
K-Pax, 73, 181

Laing, R. D., 130
Lampedusa, Giuseppe di, *The Leopard*,
 47, 98
Law
 complex systems, 154
 evidence, 180–181, 182
 history of, 140
 right-to-die cases, 81–82, 94–95

Lazarus, 48–49
Lazarus complex, 108
Learning, 33
Lem, Stanislaw, *Solaris*, 38, 174
The Leopard (Lampedusa), 47, 98
Life after death
 beliefs, 19, 128–129
 framework for discussion, 36–37
 human need for possibility of, 7, 31
 impossibility of scientific proof or
  falsification, 34, 35, 37
 literary depictions, 24–26
 methods of inquiry, 152–153, 179–
  180, 188
 potential, 163–164
 religious beliefs, 21–23, 31
 Socrates' arguments, 30–32
 See also Death; Evidence for life
  after death; Reincarnation;
  Resurrection stories; Soul; Spirits
Life after Life, 120
Life forms, higher, 158–160
"Little death," 92
Littlewood, Richard, 87–88
The Lives of Psychics (Frohock), 9
Logic, abductive, 188, 189–190
The Lord of the Rings: The Two Towers
 (Tolkien), 91
LSD, 86, 103–106
Luther, Martin, 33–34, 193

Mailer, Norman, 4, 5
A Man for All Seasons (Bolt), 18
Marx, Karl, 175–176, 191
Materialism
 compared to metaphysical model,
  9–10, 191
 limits, 157
 methods of inquiry, 162
 pure, 176–177
 view of consciousness, 176
Maternal psychokinesis, 70–71